# CHESAPEAKE BAY

MICHAELA RIVA GAASERUD

POWER PLANT

BARNES & NOBLE
BOOKSELLERS

Hard Rock
SAVE THE PLANET

CHESAPEAKE

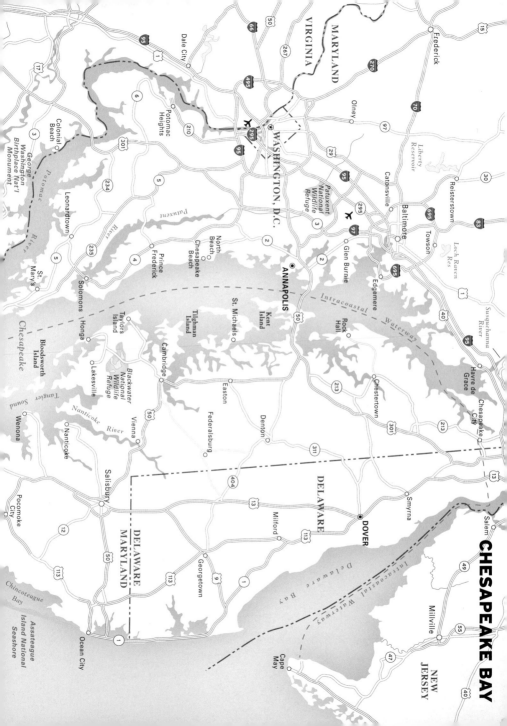

# Contents

DISCOVER

# Chesapeake Bay

**H**istoric towns, charming fishing villages, and miles of untouched beauty…a trip to the Chesapeake Bay is like stepping back in time. On the Eastern Shore, you'll find antiques dealers, woodworkers, and farmers. Just across the way in Virginia is the historic triangle, which includes the colonial cities of Williamsburg, Jamestown, and Yorktown.

But the bay has a modern side as well. Virginia Beach attracts tourists with its beachfront resorts and bustling nightlife. Annapolis, at once quaint and posh, is known as the "Sailing Capital of the World" due to its popularity as a port for both resident and international vessels. And even industrial Baltimore flaunts world-class museums, fine dining, and luxury hotels.

Above all, life in the bay revolves around water. Bayside towns are still supported by the local fishing industry and the city-dwellers who seek their weekend refuge on sailboats. Experience the life that so many have come to love. Crack into a soft shell crab on Tangier Island. Discover more than 250 species of birds at the Blackwater National Wildlife Refuge. Cruise through the St. Michaels Harbor on an authentic skipjack.

Slow down and take in the beauty of the Chesapeake Bay.

**Clockwise from top left:** the United States Naval Academy in Annapolis; Virginia Beach's *Neptune* sculpture by Paul DiPasquale; a statue at the Maryland State House; colorful Baltimore rowhouses; the weather vane at the Mariners' Museum in Newport News; Virginia Beach Fishing Pier.

# Planning Your Trip

## Where to Go

### Baltimore

The city of Baltimore, once a rough industrial port, has undergone a series of urban renewal plans over the past few decades. As a result, it has blossomed into a major tourist destination that offers many **fascinating museums, entertainment venues,** professional sporting events such as the **Preakness Stakes,** and the famous **Inner Harbor.** Side trips include **Westminster,** which hosted both Union and Confederate troops during the Civil War, and lovely **Havre de Grace,** sitting at the head of the Chesapeake Bay.

### Annapolis and Southern Maryland

The nation's sailing capital, **Annapolis,** is the top destination on the mainland banks of the Chesapeake Bay due to its waterfront location, charming historic district, and trendy boutiques and taverns. A busy recreational harbor, the city features an endless supply of blue crabs, oysters,

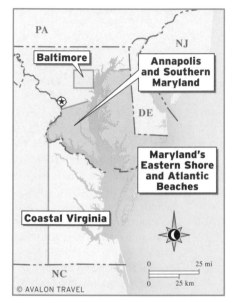

PA

NJ

Baltimore

Annapolis and Southern Maryland

DE

Maryland's Eastern Shore and Atlantic Beaches

Coastal Virginia

NC

0        25 mi
0      25 km

© AVALON TRAVEL

the Annapolis waterfront

and other delectable seafood. It is also home to the **U.S. Naval Academy.** Scenic Southern Maryland offers a slower, relaxed pace in its idyllic seaside towns such as **Solomons Island** and **Chesapeake Beach** and historic cities such as **St. Mary's City.**

## Maryland's Eastern Shore and Atlantic Beaches

Picturesque fishing towns, blue crabs, and sunsets—these are all traits of Maryland's Eastern Shore. **Chestertown, St. Michaels,** and **Tilghman Island** offer alluring charm and a window into life along the Chesapeake Bay. Maryland's Atlantic beaches are a symphony of contrasts. **Assateague Island** calms your spirits as you share the beaches with wild ponies. **Ocean**

**City** offers an exciting boardwalk and active nightlife. Three neighboring beach communities on the Delaware shore—**Bethany Beach, Rehoboth Beach,** and **Lewes**—are popular vacation spots.

## Coastal Virginia

Visiting Coastal Virginia is a great way to take a break from everyday stresses and learn about history or relax on the beach. **Colonial Williamsburg,** a living museum that vividly displays what life in colonial times was like, is one of the most popular historical attractions in the country. Just a short drive away is the resort area of **Virginia Beach** and the sleepy seaside communities on **Virginia's Eastern Shore.** The region offers port towns, battleships, and beautiful, clean beaches all within a short drive of one another.

# When to Go

If you have the luxury of choosing your time to visit, **late spring** (May and June) and **fall** (September and October) are usually the **best times** to explore the Chesapeake Bay. The weather is most pleasant, and there are fewer tourists to compete with. If you are interested in water sports, then

summer is the ideal time to visit. Beware, however, as summer also brings the **peak tourist season** and hot and humid weather. Be sure to book your accommodations far in advance if you plan to visit during the summer. The bay has cold winters and many businesses close during this time.

springtime blossoms on the Chesapeake Bay

# Chesapeake Bay Road Trip

## Annapolis
**DAY 1**
Start your journey in Maryland's capital city, **Annapolis**. This beautiful and historic waterfront city on the Chesapeake Bay is known as "the Sailing Capital of the World." Visit the **Annapolis City Dock,** the **U.S. Naval Academy,** and the **Maryland State House.** Be sure to dine on local blue crabs if you're a seafood lover.

## Maryland's Eastern Shore and Atlantic Beaches
**DAY 2**
Drive about an hour southeast over the **Chesapeake Bay Bridge** and across Kent Island to the charming Eastern Shore town

Colonial Williamsburg

of **St. Michaels.** Stroll through the historic downtown area full of restaurants and boutiques or perhaps take a cruise from the waterfront. Spend the night in St. Michaels in one of the waterfront inns.

**DAY 3**
Drive another two hours southeast to **Ocean City.** Soak in the activity on the busy boardwalk and be sure to eat some **Thrasher's French Fries.** Spend the rest of your day at the beach.

## Coastal Virginia
**DAY 4**
Continue down the scenic Eastern Shore and through the famous **Chesapeake Bay Bridge-Tunnel** for another three hours until you reach **Virginia Beach.** Visit the **Virginia Aquarium & Marine Science Center** and walk the famous boardwalk. Enjoy fresh seafood at one of the local restaurants and spend the night in a hotel right on the ocean.

## With More Time
**DAY 5**
Make the 1.25-hour drive to **Colonial Williamsburg.** Dine in **Merchants Square** and spend the night in one of several hotels run by the **Colonial Williamsburg Foundation.**

**DAY 6**
Lose yourself in U.S. history by dedicating the day to exploring Colonial Williamsburg. Visit the **museums,** shop in the authentic **colonial shops,** grab a sweet potato muffin at the **Raleigh Tavern Bakery,** talk to the costumed interpreters, and drink and dine in the local **taverns.** Spend another night in Williamsburg.

Make your departure the following morning. Airports in Richmond and Norfolk are each an hour away by car.

# Seven Days on the Eastern Shore

Virginia and Maryland share a rare commodity in the Eastern Shore. This coastal area is a 180-mile-long peninsula that sits east of the Chesapeake Bay and west of the Atlantic Ocean. It is sparsely populated in both states and contains one-third of Maryland's land area but only 8 percent of its population. A trip to the Eastern Shore is like stepping back in time. Historic towns, charming fishing villages, vast natural areas, and abundant seafood make this a prime recreation destination.

## Day 1

Begin your trip in the northern part of the region in **Chestertown,** Maryland. This historic colonial waterfront town sits on the banks of the Chester River and is a wonderful place to stroll, eat, and just relax. You can also take an educational course on the schooner *Sultana.* Stay the night in a local inn.

## Day 2

Drive south for an hour to the charming waterfront town of **St. Michaels** in Maryland. This is one of the loveliest spots on the Eastern Shore and where many Washingtonians have second homes. The town has fine restaurants, shopping, a good museum, and a lot of character. Spend the night in St. Michaels in one of the fine inns or a local bed-and-breakfast.

## Day 3

Step back in time by taking a ferry from Crisfield, Maryland, to **Tangier Island** in Virginia. Crisfield is a two-hour drive south of St. Michaels, and the ferry is a 1.25-hour ride. The isolated island sits in the middle of the Chesapeake Bay and is rapidly sinking into the bay (it should hang on while you visit). There are no cars on the island, but you can rent a golf cart.

The people are friendly, the seafood is fantastic, and there is a nice quiet beach that will make you feel miles away from civilization (which you actually are). If you don't mind the solitude, stay the night on the island, or else head back to the Eastern Shore the same day on the ferry.

## Day 4

Continue south from Crisfield (1.25 hours) to the charming village of **Onancock,** Virginia. Rent a kayak, have lunch, and take a leisure day exploring the town. Spend the night in Onancock.

## Day 5

Drive about an hour northeast to the Atlantic side of the Eastern Shore to **Chincoteague Island** in Virginia. Explore the **Chincoteague National Wildlife Refuge** and look for signs of the wild ponies that live there. Take a short hike to the **Assateague Island Lighthouse** and spend the night on the island.

## Day 6

Leave the calm of nature behind and drive 1.25 hours north to bustling **Ocean City,** Maryland. This beach town is crazy-busy in the summer and offers a wide, active boardwalk, nightlife, and many amusements. Eat some french fries on the boardwalk, ride a Ferris wheel, and then rent a beach umbrella for some downtime on the sand.

## Day 7

End your trip with a drive one hour north to the harborfront community of **Lewes,** Delaware. Enjoy a sightseeing cruise from the harbor, spend the afternoon at **Cape Henlopen State Park,** or stroll the enchanting streets of the historic town.

# Best Places to Eat Crab

the Jumbo Lump Crab Cakes from Chick & Ruth's Delly

The slogan "Maryland is for Crabs" is meant to be taken literally. People in the bay know how and where to crack a claw.

## MARYLAND

- The Jumbo Lump Crab Cakes (quarter-pound crab cakes seasoned to perfection with no filler) are the calling card of a local Annapolis favorite called **Chick & Ruth's Delly** (page 79). Just a block from the State House, this sandwich shop opened in 1965 under owners Chick and Ruth Levitt, and it has been growing ever since.

- A traditional crab house with huge notoriety in the Annapolis area is **Cantler's Riverside Inn** (page 79). It is situated on a cove right on the water and sells local steamed crabs by the dozen (in all sizes).

- **Buddy's Crabs and Ribs** (page 79) is a lively icon on Main Street in Annapolis. Steamed crabs is the entrée of choice at Buddy's, but the home-made crab cakes are also famous.

For more suggestions on where to crack a claw in Maryland, see page 80.

## VIRGINIA

- **The Crazy Crab Restaurant** (page 152) in the Reedville Marina is a small family-owned restaurant on the waterfront. The seafood can't get any fresher, as you can literally see the owner walk outside and harvest it.

- The **Crab Shack** (page 180) sits on the James River in Newport News and has great views throughout its window-lined dining room and deck. It offers fresh seafood and a casual atmosphere.

- The folks at **A. W. Schuck's** (page 188) in Norfolk believe that any meal can include seafood. They are famous for burgers topped with lump crab, and the portions are huge.

- **Four Brothers Crab House & Ice Cream Deck** (page 205) is out on Tangier Island, the "Soft Crab Capital of the World." A trip to this isolated island in the middle of the Chesapeake Bay requires a 12-mile ferry ride.

# Baltimore

# Highlights

★ **National Aquarium, Baltimore:** The gem of the Inner Harbor, the National Aquarium offers close encounters with sharks, dolphins, and many other sea creatures. Catch a show or sign up for a special slumber party; there's no shortage of awe-inspiring exhibits and activities (page 19).

★ **Historic Ships:** This unique collection on display in the Inner Harbor features four military ships and one lighthouse within easy walking distance of each other (page 21).

★ **Port Discovery Children's Museum:** One of the top children's museums in the country, this educational playground offers three floors of interactive exhibits (page 23).

★ **B&O Railroad Museum:** See the birthplace of the American railroad system and learn about its development in Baltimore. Vintage engines and cars are part of the fun (page 25).

★ **Baltimore Museum of Industry:** Baltimore is the home of many manufacturing firsts. This fascinating museum shares the history of many everyday conveniences (page 30).

★ **Fort McHenry National Monument and Historic Shrine:** This fort dating back to 1802 inspired the poem written by Francis Scott Key that became the U.S. national anthem (page 32).

★ **The Walters Art Museum:** This remarkable collection of 5,000 pieces of work spans 5,000 years and includes a mummy from 1000 BC and two imperial eggs (page 33).

★ **Carroll County Farm Museum:** Glimpse what rural life in the mid-19th century was like on a 142-acre farm (page 66).

# B altimore has been a major port city since the 1700s. The hardworking city is the birthplace of many industries: the first sugar refinery in the country (1796), the first gaslight company (1819), and the first railroad for commercial

transportation (1828). Having spent much of its history as a rough industrial seaport, Baltimore managed to keep its treasures to itself. In the 1970s, outsiders started to recognize the city's hidden charm, and the working-class town was nicknamed "Charm City." Today, after a series of successful urban renewal projects, Baltimore has blossomed into a major mid-Atlantic tourist destination. It flaunts world-class museums, state-of-the-art sports venues, fine dining, and luxury hotels—all while retaining its fierce spirit and authenticity.

## ORIENTATION

For simplicity's sake, we're going to focus on six primary sections of Baltimore. They are key areas where popular sights are located, as well as trendy neighborhoods where you can find a delightful selection of food, nightlife, and activities.

## Downtown and the Inner Harbor

Most of the beauty shots of Baltimore are taken downtown and at the Inner Harbor. The harbor has long been the center of activity in this port city and was once a thriving destination for visitors and supplies arriving by steamship. Although most people think that Baltimore sits on the Chesapeake Bay, the harbor is actually the mouth of the Patapsco River. The river flows into the bay east of the city, which is why this deepwater yet protected harbor has been popular for centuries. After the collapse of the steamship era, the port still saw industrial action, but lapsed into a state of neglect as the city fell off the radar as a vacation destination.

In the 1970s interest in the city was revived as Baltimore underwent extensive innovative redevelopment. The Inner Harbor benefited greatly from the rejuvenation and

# Baltimore

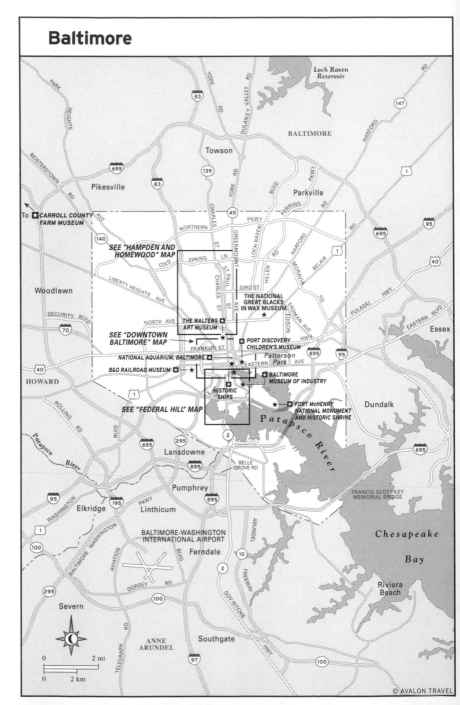

Baltimore's Inner Harbor

became home to many attractions, museums, restaurants, upscale hotels, and a beautiful waterfront promenade. The surrounding downtown area received a boost as well and offers a blend of businesses, historic buildings, and museums.

## Fell's Point and Little Italy

Fell's Point is on the harbor to the east of the Inner Harbor. It is about a five-minute drive from the Inner Harbor or can be reached by water taxi. It is one of the oldest neighborhoods in Baltimore, with many historic buildings and trendy eateries. Fell's Point was first settled by William Fell, an English Quaker, in 1726 and many of the 350 historic buildings were constructed before 1800 (200 predate the Civil War). Fell's Point thrived until the need for sailing ships declined in the early 1900s, after which the neighborhood entered a steep decline. The waterfront became a collection of rough saloons, and in the mid-1960s plans for the building of I-95 had it running right through the neighborhood. The community was able to stop the highway, and instead the neighborhood became the first National Historic District in Maryland.

Nearby Little Italy (www.littleitalymd.com)

was settled by Italian immigrants in the mid-1800s, who opened businesses and restaurants in the cozy little area between the Inner Harbor and Fell's Point. The area now boasts almost 30 restaurants and also offers visitors vibrant festivals and a bit of old-world Italy.

## Canton

East of Fell's Point on the waterfront is the historic community of Canton, which dates back to the late 19th century. Modern condos and old row houses fuse Baltimore's past and present, and lively **Canton Square** on O'Donnell Street offers bars, restaurants, and endless nightlife for the local partying crowd. The Canton waterfront includes views of navy ships as they dock nearby.

## Federal Hill

Federal Hill sits opposite the Inner Harbor on the south side of the harbor. It is named after an imposing hill that boasts a fantastic vantage point for viewing the Inner Harbor and downtown Baltimore. Federal Hill has great shopping, bars, restaurants, and entertainment as well as a thriving residential area. It is home to the famed 120-by-70-foot neon Domino Sugar sign that casts a glow over

Little Italy

the city from its 160-foot perch. The sign is a Baltimore icon and has been a fixture in the harbor since 1951.

## Mount Vernon

Mount Vernon, north of downtown Baltimore, is the cultural center of the city. Museums and halls provide endless opportunities to take in a show or listen to the symphony. The neighborhood is full of grand 19th-century architecture, and marble-clad homes originally built for wealthy sea captains surround the first monument to honor our first president.

## Hampden and Homewood

Northwest of Mount Vernon is the settlement of Hampden. This 19th-century neighborhood was originally a mill town but is now an eclectic mix of bars, restaurants, thrift stores, galleries, and boutiques. The local residents are both hardworking families and young adults, which gives the area a hip yet grounded feel. To the east of Hampden is the neighborhood of Homewood. Homewood is best known as the home of **Johns Hopkins University,** but it also has nice parks and museums.

## PLANNING YOUR TIME

You could easily spend a couple of weeks in Baltimore to really see all the city has to offer, but most people pick and choose sights of particular interest to them and explore the city in a long weekend.

People traveling with children may wish to stay at the Inner Harbor so they can visit the **National Aquarium,** the **Maryland Science Center,** and the **Port Discovery Children's Museum,** and see the **Historic Ships** in the harbor. A visit to **Fort McHenry** is another fun option to pique the little ones' interest in history.

History buffs can pick almost any location in the city as their base and from there take in the **Baltimore Civil War Museum,** the **Star-Spangled Banner Flag House and Museum,** the **Washington Monument, Fort McHenry,** and Edgar Allan Poe's grave site at **Westminster Hall Burying Ground & Catacomb.**

Others come to sample the many restaurants and bars in the busy Fell's Point area or to take in a ball game at Camden Yards. No matter what your interests, there is no shortage of exciting itineraries to create. Baltimore is easy to get around and offers many exciting

# Best of Baltimore

### DAY 1
Start in the popular **Inner Harbor,** where you can get around on foot and visit the **National Aquarium** and the **Historic Ships** collection. Choose one of the restaurants in the busy harbor area for lunch before driving or taking the water taxi to the **Fort McHenry National Monument,** where Baltimore fended off a British attack during the War of 1812 and Francis Scott Key penned "The Star-Spangled Banner." Jump back on the water taxi or drive over to **Fell's Point** for exploration of its charming waterfront streets before having dinner at the **Red Star Bar and Grill.** End your evening at the cozy **Cat's Eye Pub** for some blues, jazz, or folk music, and then turn in for the night at the **Inn at Henderson's Wharf.**

### DAY 2
Start your day with breakfast at the popular **Blue Moon Café.** After breakfast, drive or take a cab to the Mount Vernon neighborhood and visit the **Walters Art Museum,** then climb the 228 stairs of the **Washington Monument** for a great view of the city. Grab some pizza at **Joe Squared,** then continue your cultural tour at the **Baltimore Museum of Art** in Homewood. Have dinner at **Woodberry Kitchen** just west of Hampden and finish in time to take in a performance at **Centerstage** in Mount Vernon. Finish up your two-day tour with a drink and a wonderful view of the city at the classy **13th Floor** in the historic Belvedere Hotel building.

sights and activities regardless of how long you have to spend there.

If you have time for a full- or half-day excursion from Baltimore, consider putting Westminster or Havre de Grace on your list of places to visit. Westminster, 45 minutes northwest of Baltimore by car, sits in a rural part of the state and has a history of Civil War battles, spies, and ghosts. An hour car ride north on I-95 will take you to the bayside town of Havre de Grace. Its charming seaside atmosphere at the head of the Chesapeake Bay makes the town a rewarding destination for touring and outdoor recreation.

# Sights

## DOWNTOWN AND THE INNER HARBOR
### ★ National Aquarium, Baltimore
The **National Aquarium, Baltimore** (501 E. Pratt St., 410/576-3800, www.aqua.org, Mon.-Thurs. 9am-5pm, Fri.-Sat. 9am-8pm, Sun. 9am-6pm, $39.95) is perhaps the most treasured sight in Baltimore's Inner Harbor. Opening in 1981, it was the anchor venue to the redevelopment plan of the Inner Harbor. The aquarium was one of the first large aquariums in the country and remained independent until it joined with the National Aquarium in Washington DC under the blanket name "National Aquarium" in 2003.

Close to 20,000 animals live at the National Aquarium, representing more than 660 species of fish, amphibians, reptiles, birds, and mammals. See the brilliant coral-filled Blacktip Reef exhibit, which mimics Indo-Pacific reefs and offers stunning floor-to-ceiling "pop-out" viewing windows so visitors can get personal with 65 species of animals. Then watch fearsome sharks swim by in their 225,000-gallon ring-shaped tank in Shark Alley, or see divers feed brightly colored fish as you descend the winding ramp through the

# Downtown Baltimore and the Inner Harbor

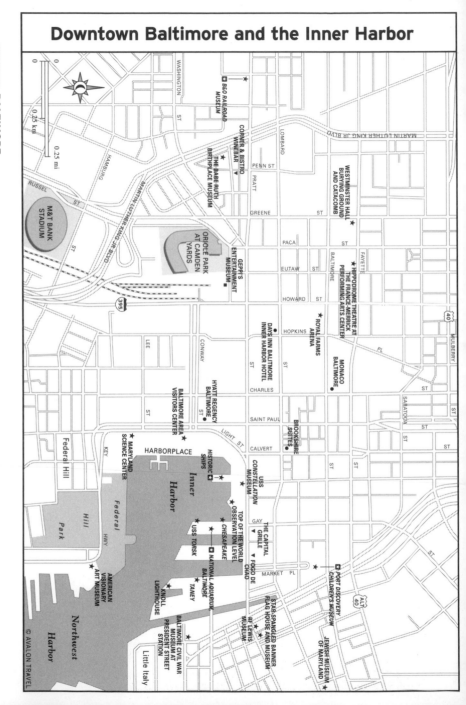

# Harbor Pass

Many of the popular sights in Baltimore can be accessed with a single ticket that offers discounted entry over individual admission prices. A four-day **Harbor Pass** (877/225-8466, www.baltimore.org, $53.95) includes admission over four consecutive days into four top attractions. Different options are available for the pass, but all include visitation to the National Aquarium and the Top of the World (Observation Level), plus two additional museums such as the Port Discovery Children's Museum, the American Visionary Art Museum, the Reginald F. Lewis Museum of Maryland African American History & Culture, and the Babe Ruth Birthplace Museum.

13-foot-deep tropical reef tank in the Atlantic Coral Reef exhibit. Another breathtaking experience can be found in the Upland Tropical Rain Forest. This world-renowned exhibit expertly mimics a real rain forest with live tropical birds, sloths, tamarin monkeys, and even poison dart frogs. A diverse selection of authentic rain forest plant life is also part of this habitat.

The aquarium's award-winning habitats are expertly designed and instantly engage visitors by drawing them into the world of the animals they feature. They also offer demonstrations such as the Dolphin Discovery where visitors can see dolphins feeding, training, and enjoying playtime.

4-D Immersion films ($5) are shown at the aquarium, and behind-the-scenes tours ($15-220) are available. Overnight dolphin and shark sleepovers, in which guests can spend the night at the aquarium ($115), are two of the more popular activities. Reservations for all the behind-the-scenes activities should be purchased well in advance. Tickets to the aquarium are issued on a timed-entry system (allow at least three hours for your visit), so you can purchase tickets online for the time you'd like to visit. The aquarium is a popular attraction year-round, but can be especially crowded during the hot summer days when school is out of session. Try to avoid this time if your schedule allows for it, or visit late in the day after the crowds have thinned out.

## ★ Historic Ships

The **Historic Ships** (Inner Harbor Piers, 301 E. Pratt St., 410/539-1797, www.historicships. org, one ship $11, two ships $15, four ships $18, lighthouse free) in the Inner Harbor form one

National Aquarium, Baltimore

of the most impressive military ship collections in the world. Visitors can not only see four ships and a lighthouse (all within easy walking distance of one another), but also 50,000 photographs, documents, and personal items that relate to the ships. Hours vary between ships and days, but all are open daily March-December (the *Taney* and lighthouse are closed Mon.-Thurs. Jan.-Feb.) 10am-3:30pm at a minimum, with longer hours in the summer months.

The first, the **USS Constellation** (Pier 1), was a sloop-of-war ship from 1854 to 1955. The USS *Constellation* was the last all-sail ship built by the U.S. Navy, and it was the flagship of the U.S. African Squadron 1859-1861. Visitors can begin their tour in the museum gallery at the pier to learn about the ship's history through artifacts and personal items that once belonged to the crew. From there, grab a complimentary audio tour wand and go aboard. The "Plan of the Day" will be posted with a list of activities taking place on the day of your visit. If you're lucky, you may get to witness the live firing of the Parrott rifle. Uniformed crew members are on board to answer questions as you explore the ship's four decks.

The second, the submarine **USS Torsk** (Pier 3), is the most exciting to visit. It was commissioned in 1944 and was one of just 10 Tench Class submarines to serve in World War II. Visitors can tour the entire boat including the torpedo rooms, operation station, engine room, crew quarters, and navigation station. It is difficult and unnerving to believe that more than 80 navy personnel lived aboard the sub at one time.

The third ship is the lightship *Chesapeake* (Pier 3), built in 1930. A lightship is a ship that is moored on a permanent or semipermanent basis and has beacons mounted to it. It is used as a navigational aid. Lightship duty meant long days sitting in place on the water and scary times riding out storms. Visitors can see a unique exhibit on sailors' canine companions.

USS *Constellation*

The fourth ship is the USCG cutter *Taney* (Pier 5), built in 1935. A cutter is defined as a Coast Guard ship that is over 65 feet in length and has accommodations for a crew to live aboard. Visitors can tour this authentic cutter that was decommissioned in 1986 and remains pretty much the same as it was when in use.

The **Knoll Lighthouse** (Pier 5), which stands at 40 feet, is one of the oldest Chesapeake Bay-area lighthouses and was erected at the mouth of the Patapsco River on a shallow shoal known as Seven Foot Knoll. It offers a detailed exhibit on how the lighthouse was built back in 1856.

Guided walking group tours of the USS *Constellation* ($14) are available for groups of 10 or more people over age six. Tours include museum admission, presentations, hands-on activities, and a Civil War-era sailor as your guide through the ship. Powder Monkey Tours are offered to children over six. These interactive tours teach the little ones about the young boys (ages 11-18) who served on fighting ships during the Civil War and were responsible for moving gunpowder from the powder magazine of the ship to the artillery pieces. Powder Monkey Tours are available every Saturday and Sunday at 1pm.

## The Babe Ruth Birthplace Museum

The **Babe Ruth Birthplace Museum** (216 Emory St., 410/727-1539, www.baberuthmuseum.com, daily 10am-5pm, closed Mondays Sept.-Mar., $7) is located three blocks west from Oriole Park at Camden Yards. It is inside the home where Babe Ruth was born in 1895 (you can even visit the bedroom where he first entered the world). From the west side of the stadium, look down and follow the 60 painted baseballs on the sidewalk, which will lead you to the museum. Babe Ruth memorabilia is on display in the museum, and visitors can learn little-known information on this legend's private life. The museum also screens a film on the Star-Spangled Banner and has a courtyard for events.

## ★ Port Discovery Children's Museum

The **Port Discovery Children's Museum** (35 Market Pl., 410/727-8120, www.portdiscovery.org, Memorial Day-Labor Day Mon.-Sat. 10am-5pm, Sun. noon-5pm, shorter hours the rest of the year, $14.95) is one of the top five children's museums in the country and is geared toward children up to age 10. The museum offers three floors of interactive exhibits with the goal of connecting learning and play. Exhibits focus on art, science, and health.

Interactive exhibits draw children into a learning adventure. The Adventure Expeditions area is "part physical adventure and part mental obstacle course," in which children decipher hieroglyphics, look for clues, and are eventually led to a lost pharaoh tomb in Egypt. Another fully interactive exhibit is Kick It Up, an indoor soccer and games stadium. In the stadium, children either play soccer or get involved in interactive, electronic games

during which they can compete in a dance competition, ride a bike, and sharpen their balance. Kids and adults can enjoy the KidWorks exhibit together, which is a three-story urban treehouse with rope bridges, slides, and many other exciting surprises. Toddlers (age 2 and up) can "cook" and serve their parents food in Tiny's Diner, a realistic 1950s-style diner.

The museum is geared completely toward children, so adults can take pleasure in the joy on their little ones' faces, but shouldn't expect a lot of exhibits that will capture their own interests. Also, children are free to run through the halls and explore the many fun and entertaining exhibits, so things can get a bit chaotic on busy days. Sneakers are the recommended footwear in order to participate in all the activities. The museum is just north of the Inner Harbor. It gets crowded in the summertime, so going early or late in the day is a good option.

## Maryland Science Center

The **Maryland Science Center** (601 Light St., 410/685-2370, www.mdsci.org, Sat.-Thurs. 10am-6pm, Fri. 10am-8pm, shorter hours in winter, $20.95) is a great place to bring the kids for a hands-on learning experience. The Dinosaur Mysteries exhibit is a must-see and will amaze the little ones with life-size models of prehistoric creatures. Your Body: The Inside Story takes kids on an adventure to learn what happens inside a human body in a 24-hour period. In this unique exhibit, visitors can go inside a heart and lungs and feel the heart beat and the lungs breathe. They can also hear a loud concert of digestive noises and interact with germs. Other exhibits include topics such as animal rescue, life on other planets, and a kids' room for children under eight. Other features in the center include Science Encounters, where visitors can see animated data projected on a sphere, or look at the night sky through a telescope in the on-site observatory (free on Fri. nights). There are also a planetarium and an IMAX theater on-site.

# The Poe Toaster

Edgar Allan Poe was one of Baltimore's most famous and mysterious citizens. He led a life of tragedy plagued by poverty, illness, and death. Poe was born in 1809 in Boston. The grandson of a Revolutionary War patriot, David Poe Sr., Edgar Allan Poe was orphaned at the age of three. Although he went to live with the Allan family in Richmond, he was never legally adopted and never really accepted fully into the family.

Poe enlisted in the army and after his discharge came to Baltimore to live with his widowed aunt in the neighborhood now known as Little Italy. He left for a brief time to attend West Point, but returned to live with his aunt and a few other family members again, although this time in West Baltimore on Amity Street. It was while here that Poe began writing short stories (prior to that time he had focused primarily on poetry).

Poe was awarded a $50 prize by a Baltimore newspaper for his short story, "MS Found in a Bottle." Many short stories followed including "Berenice," which caused a stir for being too gruesome. In 1835 Poe returned to Richmond. The following year, he married his 13-year-old cousin, Virginia, in Richmond.

In 1847, Virginia died of tuberculosis. Poe only lived another two years before dying a mysterious death back in Baltimore and was buried with his wife and aunt in **Westminster Hall Burying Ground & Catacomb** (519 W. Fayette St., 410/706-2072, www.westminsterhall.org, daily 8am-dusk, free).

The author is still shrouded in mystery, even after death: For 60 years (1949-2009), an unidentified visitor made a yearly trip to Poe's grave in the early hours on his birthday. The visitor was called the "Poe Toaster" because he made a toast of cognac on the grave and left three roses. Although he ended his visits in 2009 for reasons unknown, the Toaster had such an influence that the tradition was resurrected in 2016 with a new Toaster as part of a staged daytime event.

The **Edgar Allan Poe House & Museum** (203 N. Amity St., 410/462-1763, www.poeinbaltimore.org, June-Dec. Sat.-Sun. 11am-4pm, $5) is the house Poe lived in for a short time in West Baltimore. The house itself, which is a 2.5-story, five-room brick duplex (now part of a line of row houses) is the primary attraction of the museum. A few of Poe's personal items including a telescope are featured in the home. The immediate surrounding area is not recommended for sightseeing for safety reasons.

## Geppi's Entertainment Museum

### Geppi's Entertainment Museum
(301 W. Camden St., 410/625-7060, www.geppismuseum.com, Tues.-Sun. 10am-6pm, $10) is a privately owned museum featuring rare collections of American pop culture. The museum showcases a timeline of popular culture and its history in America. Some of the best comic books, cartoons, and memorabilia dating back to the colonial period can be viewed along with posters from 20th-century movies. The museum is in the same building as the Sports Legends Museum at Camden Yards.

## Top of the World

For the best view of Baltimore, visit the **Top of the World** (401 E. Pratt St., 410/837-8439, www.viewbaltimore.org, June-Sept. Mon.-Thurs. 10am-6pm, Fri.-Sat. 10am-7pm, Sun. 11am-6pm, reduced hours the rest of the year, $6) on the 27th floor of **Baltimore's World Trade Center.** The Top of the World is a 360-degree observation area with a spectacular view of the city skyline, the harbor, and surrounding areas through expansive windows. Stationary binoculars and photo map guides are available. Visitors are subject to manual searches of personal belongings.

## ★ B&O Railroad Museum

The **B&O Railroad Museum** (901 W. Pratt St., 410/752-2490, www.borail.org, Mon.-Sat. 10am-4pm, Sun. 11am-4pm, $18) is a National Historic Landmark and the birthplace of the American railroad system. The Baltimore & Ohio Railroad (yes, the one on the Monopoly game board) originated on Pratt Street in Baltimore in 1828. The facility was a station and repair shop that took up 100 acres. Visitors can go inside the 123-foot-tall roundhouse built in the early 1870s that was the turn-around area for large steam engines (they rolled onto a large turntable to reposition). The roundhouse is now a museum for historic train cars. Museumgoers can look at the cars and also take a short ride on the original rail tracks. An exhibition space called the Annex Gallery displays railroad-related artifacts from the museum's collection and those of other institutions such as the Smithsonian. The gallery features small objects such as lanterns, dining car china, tools, fine art, and clocks. Displays on the B&O Railroad's critical role in the Civil War show how the railroad changed the tactics for war and tells personal stories of the people who kept the railroad running during the conflict.

## Westminster Hall Burying Ground & Catacombs

What came first, the church or the cemetery? In the case of the **Westminster Hall Burying Ground & Catacombs** (519 W. Fayette St., 410/706-2072, www.westminsterhall.org, daily 8am-dusk, free), the answer is the cemetery by more than 65 years. The cemetery was first used in 1786. Many famous Baltimore residents are interred in the burying ground including Edgar Allan Poe (who was actually buried there twice—his coffin was relocated from his family plot to its current spot near the cemetery gate), General James McHenry, and Francis Scott Key's son, Philip Barton Key. Westminster Hall was built in 1852, at the intersection of Fayette and Greene Streets. The church was constructed above some of the graves on top of brick piers. The result was the creation of catacombs under the church, which visitors can tour. The outside burying ground, where Poe's grave is, is free to tour from 8am-dusk. There is a fee ($5) to tour Westminster Hall and the Catacombs; public tours are offered on the 1st and 3rd consecutive Friday (at 6:30pm) and Saturday (at 10am) of the month, from April to November. At least 15 people are required for a tour.

## Baltimore Visitors Center

The **Baltimore Visitors Center** (401 Light St., 877/225-8466, www.baltimore.org, Apr.-Sept. daily 9am-6pm, Oct. 1-Nov. 15 daily 9am-5pm, Nov. 16-Mar. 14 Wed.-Sun. 10am-4pm) is on the waterfront on the Inner Harbor. This large, 8,000-square-foot facility offers information on sights, events, harbor cruises, and other activities to do in Baltimore. Visitors can even purchase tickets here for local attractions. There's a walk-in fountain next to the center where kids of all ages can cool off on hot days.

## FELL'S POINT AND LITTLE ITALY

### Fell's Point Visitor's Center

A good place to begin exploring Fell's Point and Little Italy is at the **Fell's Point Visitor's Center** (1724 Thames St., 410/675-6750, www.preservationsociety.com/about-us/visitor-center.html, daily 10am-4pm). They offer a great brochure for a walking tour of the neighborhood as well as information on the sights in the area. Seasonal guided historic walking tours also leave from the center, and there is a gift shop.

## Frederick Douglass-Isaac Myers Maritime Park

The **Frederick Douglass-Isaac Myers Maritime Park** (1417 Thames St., 410/685-0295, www.douglassmyers.org, Mon.-Fri. 10am-4pm, Sat.-Sun. noon-4pm, $5) is a national heritage site/museum dedicated to African American maritime history. A series of exhibits chronicle the lives of Frederick

# Fell's Point and Little Italy

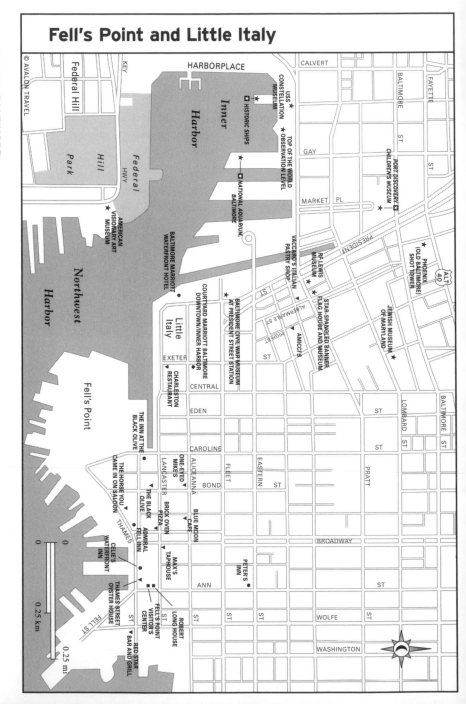

© AVALON TRAVEL

KEY

HARBORPLACE

Federal Hill

Inner Harbor

CALVERT

BALTIMORE

FAYETTE

ST

USS CONSTELLATION MUSEUM

HISTORIC SHIPS

TOP OF THE WORLD OBSERVATION LEVEL

GAY

ST

PORT DISCOVERY CHILDREN'S MUSEUM

Federal Hill Park

HWY

NATIONAL AQUARIUM, BALTIMORE

MARKET PL

AMERICAN VISIONARY ART MUSEUM

Northwest Harbor

BALTIMORE MARRIOTT WATERFRONT HOTEL

VACCARO'S ITALIAN PASTRY SHOP

PRESIDENT

R.F. LEWIS MUSEUM

PHOENIX (OLD BALTIMORE) SHOT TOWER

ALT 40

COURTYARD MARRIOTT BALTIMORE DOWNTOWN/INNER HARBOR

ST

STAR-SPANGLED BANNER FLAG HOUSE AND MUSEUM

JEWISH MUSEUM OF MARYLAND

Little Italy

ALBEMARLE ST

HIGH ST

AMICCI'S

BALTIMORE CIVIL WAR MUSEUM AT PRESIDENT STREET STATION

EXETER

CHARLESTON RESTAURANT

CENTRAL

ST

EDEN

LOMBARD ST

BALTIMORE ST

Fell's Point

THE INN AT THE BLACK OLIVE

CAROLINE

ST

PRATT

ALICEANNA

FLEET

EASTERN

ST

LANCASTER

ONE-EYED MIKE'S

BOND

THE HORSE YOU CAME IN ON SALOON

THE BLACK OLIVE

BRICK OVEN PIZZA

BLUE MOON CAFE

BROADWAY

ADMIRAL FELL INN

CELIE'S WATERFRONT INN

THAMES

MAX'S TAPHOUSE

PETER'S INN

ANN

ST

THAMES STREET OYSTER HOUSE

FELL'S POINT VISITOR'S CENTER

ROBERT LONG HOUSE

ST

ST

ST

WOLFE

ST

0

0

0.25 km

0.25 mi

FELL ST

ST

RED STAR BAR AND GRILL

WASHINGTON

# The Johns Hopkins Hospital: Pioneering Modern Medicine

The **Johns Hopkins Hospital** (1800 Orleans St.) is known as one of the best hospitals in the world. In the heart of Baltimore, north of Fell's Point and east of Mount Vernon, this teaching hospital and biomedical research facility for the Johns Hopkins University School of Medicine forms with that institution a $5 billion system of physicians, scientists, and students.

Funding for the hospital and school originally came from a wealthy Baltimore banker and merchant, Johns Hopkins, who willed $7 million in 1873 for their founding.

Both the university and hospital set the standard for many modern American medical practices. Numerous specialties were developed here, including endocrinology and neurosurgery. From the beginning, the goal was to combine research, teaching, and patient care. This concept developed into the first model of its kind, and led to unmatched success and an international reputation for excellence.

The Johns Hopkins Hospital is currently ranked third in the nation overall out of more than 4,700 hospitals. For additional information, visit their website at www.hopkinsmedicine.org.

Douglass and Isaac Myers. Douglass was a leader in the abolitionist movement, a former slave, and a successful statesman and orator. He lived and worked on the docks in Baltimore. Myers was a mason and labor leader who created a first-of-its-kind union for African American caulkers just after the Civil War. Union members ultimately formed a cooperative, and that cooperative purchased a shipyard and railroad in Baltimore called the Chesapeake Marine Railway and Dry Dock Company. The site encompasses 5,000 square feet of gallery space and features interactive exhibits, maps, photos, and artifacts that share the history of the African American community and how it influenced Baltimore in the 1800s. Forty-five-minute guided tours are available for parties of 10 or more for $8 per person.

## Robert Long House

The **Robert Long House** (812 S. Ann St., 410/675-6750, www.preservationsociety. com, Mon.-Wed. 9:30am-1:30pm, Thurs. 9:30am-2:30pm, Fri. 9:30am-12:30pm, tours daily Apr.-Nov. at 1pm and 2:30pm, $3) is the oldest city row house in Baltimore, having been built in 1765. It is a symmetrical Georgian-style brick row house with a pent roof and now serves as the headquarters for

the Preservation Society of Fell's Point and Federal Hill. The home belonged to Robert Long, who was a quartermaster for the Continental Navy. Visitors can see this restored building and its garden. The interior is furnished as it would have been during the Revolutionary War period.

## Baltimore Civil War Museum at the President Street Station

The **Baltimore Civil War Museum** (601 President St., 410/220-0290, Thur.-Mon. 10am-4pm, free) is a great stop for Civil War buffs. The museum is housed in a restored freight and passenger train depot that was known as the **President Street Station.** The depot is the oldest surviving city railroad terminal in the country and was built in 1850. It was an important rail stop during the Civil War and was the location of a famous riot that took place in April 1861 when the first Union troops stopped there on the way to Washington. The altercation marked the first bloodshed of the Civil War and more than a dozen people died in the riot (both soldiers and civilians were among the dead). The museum displays artifacts and pictures that detail Baltimore's involvement in the Civil War. Tours are available by appointment.

## Star-Spangled Banner Flag House and Museum

The **Star-Spangled Banner Flag House and Museum** (844 E. Pratt St., 410/837-1793, www.flaghouse.org, Tues.-Sat. 10am-4pm, $8) was the home of Mary Pickersgill, the woman who made the enormous and famous flag that flew over Fort McHenry on September 14, 1814, during the War of 1812 and inspired the poem written by Francis Scott Key that eventually became the U.S. national anthem. The house was built in 1793, and visitors can see what it looked like back when Mary lived there. The museum depicts the daily life in the home (that was also used as a business) around 1812, and living-history staff portray members of the Pickersgill family.

## Jewish Museum of Maryland

The **Jewish Museum of Maryland** (15 Lloyd St., 410/732-6400, www.jewishmuseummd.org, Sun.-Thurs. 10am-5pm, $10) offers visitors the opportunity to learn about regional Jewish history, culture, and the community. One of the country's leading museums on regional Jewish history, its displays include photographs, papers, and artifacts that are rotated regularly. The museum does a wonderful job of relating Jewish life in early Baltimore and other small towns in Maryland. The museum oversees a modern museum facility and two historic synagogues: the B'nai Israel Synagogue, built in 1876, and the Lloyd Street Synagogue, built in 1845.

## Reginald F. Lewis Museum of Maryland African American History & Culture

The **Reginald F. Lewis Museum of Maryland African American History & Culture** (830 E. Pratt St., 443/263-1800, www.africanamericanculture.org, Wed.-Sat. 10am-5pm, Sun. noon-5pm, $8) is the largest museum on the East Coast dedicated to African American culture. Visitors can learn about the contributions of African Americans in Maryland throughout the

the Star-Spangled Banner Flag House and Museum

state's history. The museum includes galleries, a genealogy center, recording studio, theater, café, and gift shop.

## Phoenix Shot Tower

The **Phoenix Shot Tower** (801 E. Fayette St., 410/837-5424, $5), which is also known as the **Old Baltimore Shot Tower,** stands nearly 235 feet tall near the entrance to Little Italy. It was built in 1828 out of one million bricks and, at the time, was the tallest structure in the country. The tower was used from 1828 to 1892 to produce lead shot, done by dropping molten lead from a platform at the top of the tower. The lead ran through a sieve and landed in cold water. It is a National Historic Landmark. Tours of the Shot Tower are offered Sat.-Sun. at 4pm.

# CANTON
## Patterson Park

**Patterson Park** (27 S. Patterson Park Ave., 410/276-3676, free) is one of the oldest parks in Baltimore. It encompasses 155 acres and has

Phoenix Shot Tower

the pagoda in Patterson Park

a great view of the harbor. On **Hampstead Hill** inside the park, a pagoda designed in 1890 stands at the site where local residents rallied in 1814 to protect their city from the British. British troops had come up the Patapsco River and attacked Fort McHenry, and on land, they had forces just east of the city at North Point. As they entered Baltimore, the British saw 20,000 troops and a hundred cannons facing them on Hampstead Hill. This caused them to retreat from Baltimore and go back to their ships. The area became a park in 1853, but saw more military activity during the Civil War when a military camp and war hospital were built there.

Today the park offers recreation trails, a lake, pavilions, playgrounds, an ice-skating rink, a public swimming pool, a recreation center, a stadium, and an adult day-care center.

## Captain John O'Donnell Monument

The **Captain John O'Donnell Monument** (O'Donnell St. and S. Curley St.) is in the center of Canton Square. John O'Donnell was an Irish sea captain who purchased 1,981 acres in the 1780s in the area that is now Canton. He allegedly named the area after the cargo from his ship, which contained goods from Canton, China. Captain O'Donnell's land included a house near the current-day Boston Street and all the waterfront land east of the northwest branch of the Patapsco River between Colgate Creek and Fell's Point.

## SS *John W. Brown*

The **SS *John W. Brown*** (Pier 1, 2000 S. Clinton St., 410/558-0646, www.ssjohnw-brown.org, Wed. and Sat. 9am-2pm, free, donations appreciated) is one of two remaining Liberty ships out of the 2,700 that were produced by the Emergency Shipbuilding Program during World War II. They were designed for swift construction, and the SS *John W. Brown* was built in just 56 days. The ships were used for sealifts of troops, arms, and gear to all war locations.

The SS *John W. Brown* made 13 voyages and was awarded several honors during the war. Oddly, after the war, the ship served as a vocational high school in New York City from 1946 to 1982. It was acquired in 1988 by the current owner, Project Liberty Ship, and fully restored as a museum and memorial. As the only Liberty ship in operation on the East Coast, the boat hosts six-hour Living History Cruises several times a year. During these cruises, it visits other ports on the East Coast. The ship is part of the National Register of Historic Places and also a recipient of the World Ship Trust's Maritime Heritage Award.

# FEDERAL HILL
## American Visionary Art Museum

The **American Visionary Art Museum** (800 Key Hwy., 410/244-1900, www.avam.org, Tues.-Sun. 10am-6pm, $16) holds a collection of visionary art—slightly different from folk art in nature, but which to the untrained eye can look similar. The museum defines it as "art produced by self-taught individuals, usually without formal training, whose works arise from an innate personal vision that revels foremost in the creative act itself." In a nutshell, it seems like anything goes in this funky, interesting, and inspiring museum. It has art in all mediums—oil, mosaic, watercolor, toothpicks, and even bras.

## ★ Baltimore Museum of Industry

The **Baltimore Museum of Industry** (1415 Key Hwy., 410/727-4808, www.thebmi.org, Tues.-Sun. 10am-4pm, $12) is housed in the original 1865 Platt Oyster Cannery building, the only remaining cannery structure in the city, and has exhibits on the history of industry and manufacturing in the Baltimore area. Baltimore has traditionally been a key industrial center and was home to the first passenger train, the world's biggest copper refinery, the first traffic light, and the first gas company. Collections include 100,000 artifacts relating to small business, factory workers, and other citizens whose hard work helped shape the country. Featured fields include the garment industry, automobile industry, pharmaceutical industry, newspaper industry, food industry, and the Maryland Lottery. Many of the exhibits are interactive for both adults and children.

The museum is easy to find—just look for the large red crane out front. Be sure to watch the short introductory video near

a cannon in Federal Hill Park

# Federal Hill

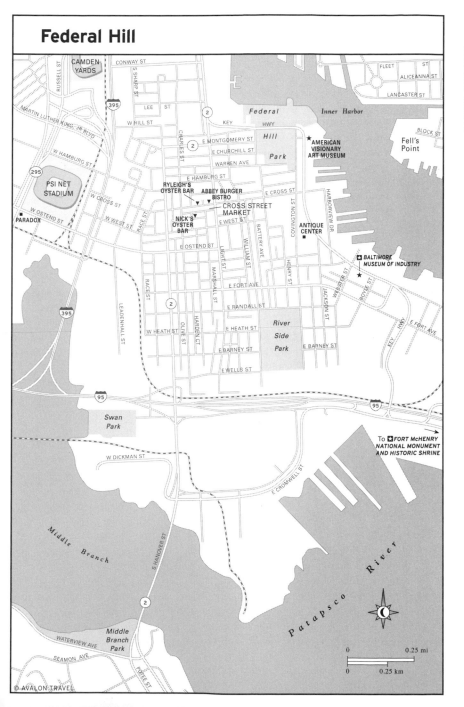

CAMDEN YARDS

RUSSELL ST
CONWAY ST
FLEET ST
ALICEANNA ST
LANCASTER ST

S SHARP ST
LEE ST
KEY HWY

*Federal*
*Hill*
Inner Harbor

BLOCK ST
Fell's Point

MARTIN LUTHER KING JR BLVD

395

W HILL ST
E MONTGOMERY ST

*Park*

CHARLES ST

2

★ AMERICAN VISIONARY ART MUSEUM

W HAMBURG ST

2

E CHURCHILL ST

WARREN AVE

W HAMBURG ST
FEDERAL ST

295

PSI NET STADIUM

E HAMBURG ST

RYLEIGH'S OYSTER BAR
W CROSS ST
ABBEY BURGER BISTRO
E CROSS ST

E CROSS ST

COVINGTON ST

HARBORVIEW DR

CROSS STREET MARKET

W OSTEND ST
■ PARADOX

NICK'S OYSTER BAR
W WEST ST
E WEST ST

ANTIQUE CENTER ■

RACE ST

E OSTEND ST

BATTERY AVE
WILLIAM ST
HENRY ST

LIGHT ST

★ BALTIMORE MUSEUM OF INDUSTRY
★

ISREM ST

BOYLE ST

395

LEADENHALL ST

2

MARSHALL ST

E FORT AVE

JACKSON ST

KEY HWY
E FORT AVE

W HEATH ST
OLIVE ST
HARDEN CT

E RANDALL ST

E HEATH ST

*River*
*Side*
*Park*

RACE ST

E BARNEY ST
E BARNEY ST

E WELLS ST

95

95

*Swan*
*Park*

To ✪ FORT McHENRY NATIONAL MONUMENT AND HISTORIC SHRINE

W DICKMAN ST

E CROMWELL ST

S HANOVER ST

*Middle*
*Branch*

*Patapsco*
*River*

2

WATERVIEW AVE

*Middle*
*Branch*
*Park*

SEAMON AVE

POTEE ST

0          0.25 mi
0          0.25 km

© AVALON TRAVEL

the museum entrance; it provides good insight into the background of the museum. Demonstrations are offered on Saturday and include topics such as printing (you can see how a real Linotype machine operates) and the job of a blacksmith. Exhibits aren't limited to the indoors; visitors can also see the coal-fired SS *Baltimore*, a restored and operational steam tugboat from 1906, just outside the museum. Free 45-minute tours of the museum are available. This is an interesting place for both adults and children over age 10. Plan on spending approximately two hours.

## Federal Hill Park

**Federal Hill Park** (300 Warren Ave., 410/396-5828) is a lovely spot right off the harbor that offers great views of the Inner Harbor and downtown from atop Federal Hill. The park is on the south side of the harbor, and the terrain rises steeply. During the colonial era, the grassy hill was a mine for paint pigment, and the drooping hillside and footpaths indicate where old tunnels remain underground. The area has been a park since the late 1700s and remains a nice recreation and picnic area. There is also a playground on-site. On the northern side of the park are cannons from the Civil War that are symbols of those

positioned by Union troops to face the city as a warning to Confederate sympathizers.

## ★ Fort McHenry National Monument and Historic Shrine

The **Fort McHenry National Monument and Historic Shrine** (2400 E. Fort Ave., 410/962-4290, www.nps.gov/fomc, daily 9am-5pm, extended summer hours, free admission to park, $10 fee for Star Fort/historical area) is a 43-acre national park with a historical area that houses Fort McHenry. It is east of Federal Hill and sticks out into the harbor. The fort was built between 1799 and 1802 and named after James McHenry, who was the secretary of war between 1796 and 1800, and constructed in the shape of a star with five points (aka the Star Fort). The star-shaped design was popular at the time since each point was within view of others to the left and right and the entire fort and surrounding area could be guarded with only five sentries.

Fort McHenry is known as the inspiration for the "Star-Spangled Banner." Francis Scott Key wrote the words to the anthem during the War of 1812 when he was held on a truce ship during the British attack on Baltimore. As the battle went on, Key watched from the water

Fort McHenry National Monument and Historic Shrine

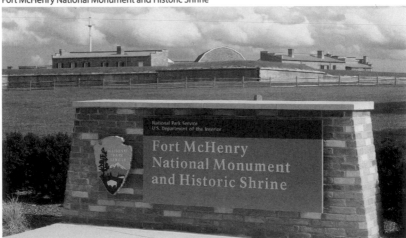

and through a smoke-filled landscape, and at "dawn's early light" on September 14, 1814, he could see the huge 30-by-42-foot American flag still flying above Fort McHenry as a symbol that Baltimore had not surrendered.

Begin your exploration at the visitors center and view the 10-minute video on the fort's history (shown on the hour and half hour). Exhibits on the fort, a gift shop, and restrooms are at the center. Then take a self-guided tour (approximately one hour) of the fort. Inside the fort is a large grassy area, and the rooms of the fort feature displays and authentic artifacts. Continue into the barracks (which include exhibits such as the Enlisted Men's Quarters, weapons, uniforms, Junior Officer's Quarters, the Powder Magazine, Commanding Officer's Quarters, and the 1814 Guard House). Children can participate in the Flag Change Program daily at 9:30am and 4:20pm, when they can assist rangers in raising and lowering a reproduced Star-Spangled Banner flag. Living-history interpreters are available on the weekends in the summer and tell stories about the fort and the people who lived in Baltimore while the facility was active. Allow two hours for your visit. There is no charge to visit the grounds.

# MOUNT VERNON
## ★ The Walters Art Museum

**The Walters Art Museum** (600 N. Charles St., 410/547-9000, www.thewalters.org, Wed.-Sun. 10am-5pm, Thurs. until 9pm, free) showcases the personal art collection of two men: William Thompson Walters, an American industrialist and art collector, and his son, Henry Walters. Both collected paintings, antiques, and sculptures. Upon Henry Walters's death, their joint collection of more than 22,000 works of art was left to the city of Baltimore for the benefit of the public.

The Walters Art Museum houses a fascinating collection that spans 5,000 years and five continents. It includes pieces from ancient Egypt, Roman sarcophagi, Renaissance bronzes, Chinese bronzes, and art nouveau jewelry. Some must-see items are an ancient Egyptian mummy from 1000 BC, two Fabergé eggs, and one of the best collections of armor in the country (including a child's set of armor).

Be sure to visit the Chamber of Wonders, where the museum has brought to life an intricate scene from a 1620 painting that came from the area that is now Belgium. The scene replicates the painting in detail and

The Walters Art Museum

34

# Mount Vernon

## Washington Monument and Museum at Mount Vernon Place

The **Washington Monument and Museum at Mount Vernon Place** (699 N. Charles St., 410/962-5070, www.mvconservancy.org, Wed.-Fri. 2pm-5pm, Sat.-Sun. 10am-1pm and 2pm-5pm, free) is the site of the first monument planned to honor George Washington. Completed in 1829, the white marble monument stands 178 feet tall and has a rectangular base, a relatively plain column, and a statue of Washington on the top. The monument looks even more imposing than its 178 feet because it sits on a hill. It was a landmark for boats making their way up the river from the Chesapeake Bay. Today, visitors can climb 228 narrow stone stairs to the top and enjoy a great view of Baltimore ($6.35). There is a little museum at the base of the monument.

is a re-creation of a chamber of natural history wonders that taps into human ingenuity from all over the globe. A highlight of the room is a 12-foot stuffed alligator. Although general admission to the museum is free, purchased tickets are required for special exhibits.

## Baltimore Streetcar Museum

The **Baltimore Streetcar Museum** (1901 Falls Rd., 410/547-0264, www.baltimorestreetcar.org, Sun. Mar.-Dec. noon-5pm, Sat. June-Oct. noon-5pm, $10) details the history of streetcars in the city and their evolution

the Baltimore Streetcar Museum

from horse-drawn transportation to an electricity-driven system. The fun part of this interesting little museum is that a number of original historic streetcars have been salvaged and visitors can actually ride in them (accompanied by volunteer conductors) down the old tracks. Unlimited rides are included with the admission fee. For a taste of what you'll find in the museum, visit the website and click on "Streetcar Memories."

## Basilica of the Assumption

The **Basilica of the Assumption** (409 Cathedral St., 410/727-3565, www.baltimorebasilica.org, Mon.-Fri. 7am-4pm, Sat.-Sun. 7am to the conclusion of mass at 5:30pm and 4:30pm respectively, $2 donation for tours) was the first Catholic cathedral built in the United States after the Constitution was ratified, and the building quickly became a symbol of the new country's religious freedom. It was constructed between 1806 and 1821 and the design and architecture were overseen by John Carroll, the first bishop in the country (and later archbishop of Baltimore), and Benjamin Henry Latrobe, who designed the U.S. Capitol. The basilica sits on a hill above the harbor and features a grand dome and what was considered cutting-edge neoclassical architecture to match that of the new federal city of Washington DC. Great effort went into creating an architectural symbol of America rather than using a European gothic design. At the time the cathedral was built, its only architectural rival in terms of scale and size was the U.S. Capitol, and the basilica was considered the most architecturally advanced structure in the country.

The full name of the cathedral is the Basilica of the National Shrine of the Assumption of the Blessed Virgin Mary, in Baltimore. It is ranked as a minor basilica, but is also a national shrine. The basilica is a cultural institution in Baltimore and offers services, tours, concerts, and lectures. It also has a prayer garden nearby on the corner of Franklin and North Charles Streets. The basilica recently underwent an extensive two-year restoration. Forty-five minute tours are offered Monday-Saturday at 9am, 11am, and 1pm, although Saturday tours are sometimes not possible due to weddings and special services. Tours are not required for visitation, but sightseeing is not permitted during mass.

## Brown Memorial Presbyterian Church

The **Brown Memorial Presbyterian Church** (1316 Park Ave., 410/523-1542, www.browndowntown.org, daily 9am-6pm, free) is a historic gothic revival-style Presbyterian church that was built in 1870. A unique feature is its 11 Tiffany stained glass windows representing scenes from the Bible, several of which are nearly three stories tall. The windows were added in the early 1900s, which made the church a local art treasure.

## The National Great Blacks in Wax Museum

The **National Great Blacks in Wax Museum** (1601 E. North Ave., 410/563-3404, www.greatblacksinwax.org, hours vary throughout season, $13) is the first wax museum in Baltimore and the first African American-oriented wax museum in the country. It was established in 1983 and displays more than 100 figures. The museum does a nice job of telling the history behind each figure through audio and text displays. Several famous Baltimore residents are depicted in the museum, including Frederick Douglass and singer Billie Holiday.

## The Maryland Historical Society

The **Maryland Historical Society** (201 W. Monument St., 410/685-3750, www.mdhs.org, Wed.-Sat. 10am-5pm, Sun. noon-5pm, museum only with no library hours on Sun., $9) is a great starting point for discovering Baltimore. You can view more than one million objects on display in two museum buildings including photographs, paintings, manuscripts, and lithographs. It also includes a huge library with more than 7 million items, including the most treasured: the historical manuscript to the "Star-Spangled Banner." Exhibits cover a diversity of topics including the War of 1812, African American history, women's history, maritime history, the history of Fell's Point, immigration, furniture, and mining. The Historical Society is easy to spot—the 1,700-pound, 14-foot statue of Nipper the RCA Dog sits on its rooftop facing Park Street.

# HAMPDEN AND HOMEWOOD
## Druid Hill Park

**Druid Hill Park** (2600 Madison Ave., 443/281-3538, www.druidhillpark.org, daily dawn to dusk, free) is a 745-acre park developed in 1860. It is approximately two miles from Hampden. It is one of the country's oldest landscaped public parks, along with Central Park in New York City and Fairmount

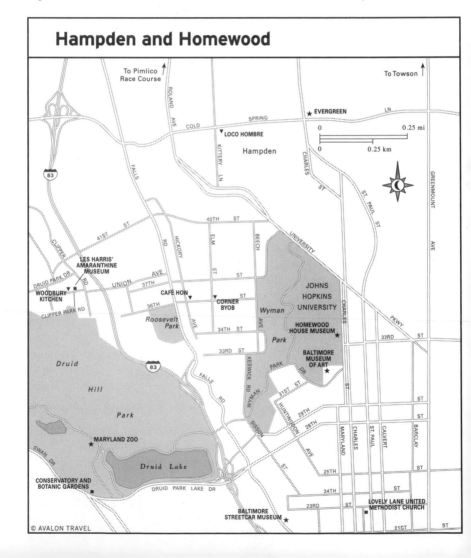

## Hampden and Homewood

© AVALON TRAVEL

Park in Philadelphia. Druid Park has something else in common with Central Park: It was formed at the northern edges of the city at the time it was established. To this day, the northern end of the park features forest that is some of the oldest in Maryland. The southern end of the park, however, has always been a popular area for those living in the city. Druid Hill Lake was built in 1863 and is one of the biggest earthen dammed lakes in the nation. Many fountains and artificial ponds that were original features in the park have been drained and reclaimed by nature, although their remains can still be found. The park also features tennis courts, a pool, disc golf, and workout equipment. There is also a zoo in the middle of the park, accessible only through the official zoo entrance. Safety can be a concern in the park at any time, but mostly after dark. Be aware of your surroundings, and if you feel uncomfortable, cut your visit short.

## THE MARYLAND ZOO IN BALTIMORE

The Maryland Zoo in Baltimore (Druid Park Lake Dr., 410/396-7102, www.

marylandzoo.org, Mar.-Dec. daily 10am-4pm, shorter hours Jan.-Feb., $18) is inside the large Druid Hill Park to the west of Hampden. The zoo opened in 1876 and is one of the oldest zoos in the country. It houses more than 1,500 animals. One of the premier exhibits in the zoo is the Polar Bear Watch, where visitors can take a large viewing buggy (like they use on the tundra) to watch three polar bears in their habitat. The zoo also offers other hands-on experiences such as camel rides and a Children's Zoo, where the little ones can pet certain animals. A family camping experience is also available in the spring.

## HOWARD PETERS RAWLINGS CONSERVATORY AND BOTANIC GARDENS

The **Howard Peters Rawlings Conservatory and Botanic Gardens** (3100 Swan Dr., Druid Hill Park, 410/396-0008, www.rawlingsconservatory.org, Wed.-Sun. 10am-4pm, free) within Druid Hill Park is the only remaining public conservatory in Baltimore. The complex dates back

Howard Peters Rawlings Conservatory and Botanic Gardens

# The Dog Who Found His Way Home

You'll find Nipper on the roof of the Maryland Historical Society.

The 14-foot, 1,700-pound RCA Dog, known as Nipper, that sits atop the Maryland Historical Society roof has a long history of adventure. The original Nipper was a stray terrier adopted in the 1880s by a man named Mark Barraud. He named the little black-and-white dog Nipper because he nipped at people's legs. When Barraud passed away, his brother, Francis, who was a painter, adopted the dog.

At the time, the phonograph was the latest technology. Nipper was captivated by the sound of the machine and would sit with his head tilted near its trumpet, listening. Francis thought this would make a great advertisement, and he painted a picture of Nipper and sold it to the Gramophone Company (which made phonographs). A United States patent was issued for the trademark of the image, and after two sales of the company, RCA ended up with the image in 1929.

In 1954, The Triangle Sign Company of Baltimore made the statue of Nipper, and it was placed on top of the D&H Distributing building. D&H Distributing was an RCA distributor. But when the company moved in 1976, they left the statue behind.

A collector from Fairfax, Virginia, wanted the statue and after he spent six years trying to convince D&H Distributing to let him buy it, they finally sold it to him for $1. Baltimore residents and officials were outraged. They felt Nipper was a Baltimore landmark, but a sale is a sale, and Nipper left Baltimore and was moved to Virginia where he sat on the collector's front lawn for 20 years.

In 1996, the collector decided to move, and he sold Nipper to the Baltimore's City Life Museum for $25,000. Two years later, the museum closed, and the Maryland Historical Society took over its collections and, in turn, inherited Nipper and placed him on the roof. Today visitors can still enjoy the 1,700-pound pooch, who found his way home to Baltimore and seems to be here to stay.

to 1888 and consists of two buildings from the Victorian era. There are also three newer buildings. Five different climates are represented in the buildings and there are also beautiful outdoor gardens. The Palm House is one of the most interesting buildings. The Palm House was built in 1888 and was designed by George Frederick (who also designed Baltimore's City Hall). Towering palms reach the upper windows of the impressive five-story house and block some of the natural sunlight in the conservatory.

# Les Harris' Amaranthine Museum

It would be a challenge to find another museum comparable to **Les Harris' Amaranthine Museum** (2010 Clipper Park Rd., 410/456-1343, www.amaranthinemuseum.org, Sun. noon-3pm and by appointment, closed July-Aug., $5). This unusual museum, which is open during very limited hours, takes visitors through a maze of the late Baltimore artist Les Harris's work while telling the history of art in chronological order, starting with prehistoric times and going out into the future. The museum is a labyrinth of art history and the creative process, made up of rooms, chambers, and passages, decorated from floor to ceiling with Harris's art. The Amaranthine Museum (the word *amaranthine* means eternally beautiful) itself is a unique art form and a fun deviation from traditional museums.

# Baltimore Museum of Art

The **Baltimore Museum of Art** (10 Museum Dr., 443/573-1700, www.artbma.org, Wed.-Fri. 10am-5pm, Sat.-Sun. 11am-6pm, free) is a cultural destination in Baltimore and one of two great art museums in the city (the other is the Walters Art Museum in Mount Vernon). The museum is adjacent to the Homewood campus of Johns Hopkins University.

The museum was founded in 1914 and grew from housing one single painting to offering 90,000 pieces on display. Its collection of 19th-century, modern, and contemporary art is internationally known and includes the famous Cone Collection of over 3,000 pieces by world-famous artists donated by wealthy socialite sisters Claribel and Etta Cone. The Cone Collection is worth approximately $1 billion. The Cone Collection includes the largest single collection of works by Henri Matisse in the world (500 total); 42 oil paintings, 18 sculptures, and 36 drawings are among the Matisse pieces. It also amasses work by Cézanne, Picasso, Degas, Manet, Van Gogh, and Gauguin.

In addition to the Cone Collection (housed in the Cone Wing), the museum features many other galleries. The West Wing for Contemporary Art contains 16 galleries with 20th- and 21st-century art including abstract expressionism, minimalism, conceptual art, and works by Andy Warhol. American galleries feature paintings, sculptures, decorative arts, and works on paper. There is also an African art collection of more than 2,000 pieces with works spanning from ancient Egypt to contemporary Zimbabwe.

The museum also offers visitors two lovely outdoor gardens with 20th-century sculptures.

# Johns Hopkins University

**Johns Hopkins University** (410/516-8000, www.jhu.edu) is a private not-for-profit research university that was founded in 1876 and named for philanthropist Johns Hopkins, its benefactor. The university maintains two main campuses in Baltimore: the Homewood Campus (3400 N. Charles St.) and the Medical Institution Campus (600 N. Wolfe St.). There are secondary campuses in Washington DC, Italy, Singapore, and China. Johns Hopkins developed the concept of a modern research university in the United States and is known throughout the world as one of the best. At least 37 Nobel Prize winners are affiliated with Johns Hopkins.

The Homewood Campus has a parklike setting even though it is located in a large city, with lovely old trees, large grassy areas, stately brick academic buildings, and redbrick residence halls. The Medical Institution Campus is located north of Fell's Point in east Baltimore.

## HOMEWOOD HOUSE

The **Homewood House** (3400 N. Charles St., 410/516-5589, www.museums.jhu.edu, Tues.-Fri. 11am-4pm, Sat.-Sun. noon-4pm, $8) on the eastern side of Johns Hopkins University is a wonderful example of federal architecture. Completed in 1808, the house is decorated with well-researched colors, patterns, and furniture from the period, much of it original. The country home was owned by wealthy Baltimore residents during the colonial era and then by the son of Charles Carroll, a signer of the Declaration of Independence.

### EVERGREEN MUSEUM & LIBRARY

The **Evergreen Museum & Library** (4545 N. Charles St., 410/516-0341, www.museums.jhu.edu, Tues.-Fri. 11am-4pm, Sat.-Sun. noon-4pm, $8) is a beautiful mansion that was built in the mid-19th century and purchased by the president of the B&O Railroad, John W. Garrett, in 1878. This wonderful exemplar of the Gilded Age sits surrounded by Italian-style gardens on 26 acres. The museum and library hold a collection of rare books, manuscripts, and artwork. The estate's 48 rooms, housing more than 50,000 items from the Garrett family (including a 24K gold-leafed toilet), can be viewed by the public only on guided tours. Tours begin every hour on the hour with the last tour starting at 3pm. Concerts and lectures are also given on the property. The museum is 4.5 miles north of the Inner Harbor.

## WALKING TOURS

Historic walking tours around Baltimore are given by the **Preservation Society of Fell's Point and Federal Hill** (410/675-6750, www.preservationsociety.com).

# Entertainment and Events

## NIGHTLIFE

Whether you're looking for delicious cocktails, a large wine selection, or a wild night of dancing, Baltimore has it all.

One block from the Inner Harbor is a great collection of bars and clubs in an entertainment complex called **Power Plant Live!** (34 Market Place, www.powerplantlive.com). The complex opened in sections between 2001 and 2003 and was named for a neighboring former power plant on Pier 4 that faces the Inner Harbor. Restaurants, bars, and nightclubs line an outdoor plaza where free music is offered May-October on the plaza stage. A popular venue in the complex is **Rams Head Live** (20 Market Pl., 410/244-1131, www.ramsheadlive.com). This general admission, standing-room-only venue features five full-service bars and two food kiosks. A wide variety of groups have played here including Patti Smith, Big Head Todd and the Monsters, They Might Be Giants, and Citizen Cope.

Two blocks north of the Inner Harbor near Power Plant Live! is a slightly upscale nightclub that caters to an older crowd. The **Havana Club** (600 Water St., 410/468-0022, www.havanaclub-baltimore.com, Wed.-Sat.

6pm-2am) is above Ruth's Chris Steak House and features a more intimate atmosphere with leather seating areas, private seating options, an extensive wine list, and a notable cigar selection. They also offer salsa dancing on Friday nights. The dress code is business casual.

Hidden in an industrial warehouse area southwest of the Inner Harbor is a thriving dance club called **Paradox** (1310 Russell St., 410/837-9110, www.thedox.com). People come from all over the region to be part of the serious parties that take place on the wooden dance floor. They feature all types of dance music and do not serve alcohol.

Those looking for a terrific place to catch live jazz won't be disappointed by **An Die Musik Live** (409 N. Charles St., 2nd Fl., 410/385-2638, www.andiemusiklive.com), downtown on the second floor of a town house. This intimate concert venue is for true music lovers. The cool renovated building offers great acoustics, comfortable seating, and a high caliber of artists. There is no elevator, so be prepared to climb some stairs.

Not far away is a popular old-school drinking establishment called **Club Charles** (1724

N. Charles St., 410/727-8815, www.club-charles.us, Mon.-Sun. 6pm-2am). This art deco bar is dark and crowded, but the bartenders are fantastic and the drinks are strong. There's even a resident ghost that plays pranks at the bar.

A classy place to linger over a drink and soak in a gorgeous view of the city is the **13th Floor** (1 E. Chase St., 410/347-0880, www.13floorbelvedere.com, Tues.-Wed. 5pm-10pm, Thurs. 5pm-11pm, Fri.-Sat. 5pm-1am). This Mount Vernon establishment is housed in the historic Belvedere Hotel building, which was known during the early part of the 20th century as the premier hotel in the city; it hosted U.S. presidents, foreign dignitaries, and movie stars. Today, the newly renovated restaurant and bar feature dark hardwood floors, white tabletops, live jazz, and a 360-degree view of the city. This is another place with a dress code, so be prepared so you're not disappointed.

One of the first modern lounges in the city, Mount Vernon's **Red Maple** (930 N. Charles St., 410/547-0149, www.930redmaple.com, Tues.-Fri. 5pm-2am, Sat. 6pm-2am) is still a popular hot spot. It features Asian-inspired tapas and other small plates, and guests can relax in lounge-style seating on the first floor or table seating on the second floor. The indoor dance floor and outdoor patio are popular nightspots.

A local landmark in Fell's Point is the **Cat's Eye Pub** (1730 Thames St., 410/276-9866, www.catseyepub.com, daily noon-2am). It is known for nightly live music despite the close and often crowded space. Music at this cozy pub includes blues, jazz, and folk.

A charming little wine bar on the waterfront in Fell's Point is **V-NO** (905 S. Ann St., 410/342-8466, www.v-no.com, Mon.-Wed. 4:30pm-9pm, Thurs. noon-10pm, Fri.-Sat. noon-midnight, Sun. noon-6pm). They offer indoor and outdoor seating and a lovely wine list with enough of a selection to keep things interesting. This is a great place to unwind away from the crowds.

## The Horse You Came In On Saloon

(1626 Thames St., 410/327-8111, www.thehorsebaltimore.com, open daily at 11:30am, $8-15) is America's oldest continuously operated saloon (it operated before, during, and after Prohibition). It first opened in 1775 and is allegedly the last place Edgar Allan Poe was seen alive. It may be where Poe had his last drink, and it's been rumored that his ghost haunts the saloon. The saloon originally had hitching posts out back to park horses. Menu items include traditional bar food, and there's nightly live entertainment (rock and roll). The saloon's slogan is "Where no one's ugly at 2am." It also has Maryland's only Jack Daniel's club (Old No. 7), where members purchase their own bottles of Jack Daniel's and the saloon stores them in a coveted space in their custom Jack Daniel's case. The saloon sells more Jack Daniel's than any other bar in Maryland.

The Horse You Came In On Saloon

# PERFORMING ARTS

## Hippodrome Theatre at France-Merrick Performing Arts Center

The **Hippodrome Theatre at France-Merrick Performing Arts Center** (12 N. Eutaw St., 410/837-7400, www.france-merrickpac.com) is a well-known circa 1914 stage performance theater on the west side of Baltimore. In the 1940s, this part of town had a flourishing arts scene and saw big-time acts such as Frank Sinatra, Bob Hope, and Benny Goodman, but the neighborhood declined in the following decades. This performing arts center is part of the rebirth of the area, and the Hippodrome Theatre was beautifully restored as part of that project. The center now offers musicals, holiday performances, and many other types of performances.

## Centerstage

**Centerstage** (700 N. Calvert St., 410/332-0033, www.centerstage.org) in Mount Vernon is a historic venue with two intimate performance spaces, two rehearsal halls, and three lobbies. The six-story building is a local landmark that has roots as the former Loyola College and High School. It offers a close-up theater experience for classical and contemporary performances and lends itself well to audience interaction. There are no bad seats in the house.

## Royal Farms Arena

The **Royal Farms Arena** (201 W. Baltimore St., www.royalfarmsarena.com) is showing its age a bit (it was built in the 1960s), but still hosts musical artists such as Carrie Underwood, well-known shows such as Cirque Du Soleil and Disney on Ice, and sporting events.

## Patricia & Arthur Modell Performing Arts Center at the Lyric

The **Patricia & Arthur Modell Performing Arts Center at the Lyric** (140 W. Mount Royal Ave., 410/900-1150, www.

lyricoperahouse.com) is a music hall that originally opened in 1894. Today it plays host to a wide variety of talent from kids' shows to top musical artists.

## Arena Players

The longest continuously running African American community theater in the country is the **Arena Players** (801 McCulloh St., 410/728-6500, www.arenaplayersinc.com). Founded in 1953, this respected theater supports local actors and writers.

## Joseph Meyerhoff Symphony Hall

The **Joseph Meyerhoff Symphony Hall** (1212 Cathedral St., 410/783-8000, www.bsomusic.org) is a 2,443-seat music venue in the Mount Vernon neighborhood. The venue is named for a former president of the Baltimore Symphony, Joseph Meyerhoff, who made a sizable donation for the construction of the hall. The venue is currently home to the **Baltimore Symphony Orchestra.**

# EVENTS

The **Baltimore Fun Guide** (www.baltimorefunguide.com) is a great online resource that lists local events throughout the city.

Hundreds of boats (both power and sail) can be found at the **Baltimore Convention Center** (1 W. Pratt St., 410/649-7000, www.bccenter.org) for four days in mid to late January during the **Baltimore Boat Show** (www.baltimoreboatshow.com, $14). The show features exhibits and activities for all ages.

April brings the **Preakness Crab Derby** (400 W. Lexington St, 410/685-6169) to the Lexington Market where fans can watch Baltimore celebrities race crabs for charity. The winner is awarded $500 for donation to their favorite charity.

For something completely different, attend the American Visionary Art Museum's annual **Kinetic Sculpture Race** (www.avam.org/kinetic-sculpture-race/), which takes place on a Saturday in early May. This race showcases completely human-powered works of art that can travel on the land, water, and through mud. These "machines" are often made of old bicycle parts, gears, etc. and can be "driven" by one person or a team. Fun awards are given out such as the "Grand Mediocre East Coast Champion Award (to the vehicle finishing in the middle of the pack)," the "Next to Last Award," and the "Best Bribe" award.

A more serious race that also takes place in May is the **Preakness Stakes** (www.preakness.com). With more than a 140-year history, this second leg of the Triple Crown of Thoroughbred Racing (which consists of the Kentucky Derby, the Preakness Stakes, and the Belmont Stakes) is a big deal in Baltimore and in horse racing overall.

**Honfest** (www.honfest.net) in Hampden is a major city festival that started out as a neighborhood celebration and blossomed to an international following. The festival takes place in mid-June along 36th Street. The "Hon" is short for "honey" ("hon" is a commonly used term of endearment in Baltimore) and refers to a ladies fashion that evolved in the 1960s. The style included large, brightly colored horn-rim glasses, loud prints, spandex and leopard-print pants, thick makeup, and beehive hairdos. The festival features many Hons in full attire and one is crowned "Miss Hon." There is also the running of the Hons. Hair and makeup can be done by vendors right in the street.

Baltimore's **Fourth of July** celebration (www.baltimore.org) is an annual favorite in the Inner Harbor. It features live music and a fireworks display. The fireworks celebration can be viewed from many vantage points around the city including, Federal Hill, Fell's Point, and Canton.

America's largest free arts festival, **Artscape** (Mount Royal Avenue, www.artscape.org) is held for three days each July and attracts more than 350,000 people. The festival is a rare opportunity for visitors and people from all neighborhoods in Baltimore to interact. More than 150 artists display their craft at this well-known event that began in the early 1980s.

**Miracle on 34th Street** (www.christmasstreet.com) is the premier holiday extravaganza in Hampden. Throughout December, one block of 34th Street becomes a magical, although somewhat over-the-top display of lights, reindeer, and really any type of decoration you can think of. It's quite the spectacle, but also quite festive, and definitely worth checking out if you don't mind sitting in traffic with the other spectators.

The **Night of 100 Elvises** (www.nightof100elvises.com) is actually a two-day event held in the beginning of December that benefits the Johns Hopkins Children's Center and the Guardian Angels. This ticketed party held at Lithuanian Hall (851-3 Hollins St.) features a dozen bands and multiple Elvis tribute performances.

# Shopping

## DOWNTOWN AND THE INNER HARBOR
### Harborplace

**Harborplace** (201 E. Pratt St., 410/332-4191, www.harborplace.com, Mon.-Sat. 10am-9pm, Sun. 11am-7pm) is the premier shopping market in downtown Baltimore. It was created in 1980 as a main attraction during the rebirth of the Inner Harbor. The market consists of two pavilions, the **Pratt Street Pavilion** and the

**Light Street Pavilion.** National stores and restaurants are abundant at Harborplace, but specialty shops such as **Life in Charm City** (Pratt Street Pavilion, 410/230-2652, Mon.-Sat. 10am-9pm, Sun. noon-6pm), which sells Baltimore-related merchandise; **Sock It To You** (Pratt Street Pavilion, 443/286-8889, Mon.-Sat. 10am-9pm, Sun. noon-6pm), which sells socks; and **Destination Baltimore** (Pratt Street Pavilion, 443/727-5775, Mon.-Sat.

10am-9pm, Sun. noon-6pm), which sells apparel, gifts, and seasonal items, are some of the independent stores located in the market.

## The Gallery

**The Gallery** (200 E. Pratt St., 410/332-4191, www.thegalleryatharborplace.com, Mon.-Sat. 10am-9pm, Sun. noon-6pm) opened a few years after Harborplace in a glass building across Pratt Street (attached to the Renaissance Hotel). The two shopping areas are connected by a skywalk. Many upscale national stores and restaurants are located in the four-story structure, but local merchants running Maryland-themed shops can also be found there.

## FELL'S POINT

Some of the most charming shops in Baltimore can be found in Fell's Point. Whether you're in the market for jewelry, home items, music, or clothing, you should turn up plenty to keep you interested if you poke around the historic streets and venture up some side alleys. **B'More Betty** (1500 Thames St., 443/869-6379, www.onlybetty.com, Wed.-Sun. 11am-7pm) is a trendy buyer and seller of designer handbags, shoes, and accessories. **Killer Trash** (602 S. Broadway, 410/675-2449, daily 11am-7:30pm) is a vibrant vintage shop with an eclectic selection of jewelry and clothes for wearing and for costumes. If you are looking for a special piece for your home, or just need a lamp rewired, **Brasswork Co., Inc.** (1641 Thames St., 410/327-7280, www.baltimorebrassworks.com, Mon.-Fri. 8:30am-5pm, Sat. 10am-6pm, Sun. noon-6pm) is the place to go. They offer gifts, lighting, timepieces, candleholders, and many other brass merchandise.

For all types of hats, visit **Hats in the Belfry** (813 S. Broadway, 410/342-7480, www.hatsinthebelfry.com, Mon.-Thurs. 10am-6pm, Fri.-Sat. 10am-8pm, Sun. 10am-7pm).

## FEDERAL HILL

Charles Street and Light Street are the best areas in Federal Hill to do some window browsing. Small boutiques and shops selling clothes and home goods are scattered through the charming neighborhood. Favorites include **Phina's for the Home** (919 S. Charles St., 410/685-0911, www.phinas.com, Tues.-Sat. noon-6pm, Sun. noon-3pm), a boutique linen store selling home and spa items and gifts; and **Brightside Boutique & Art Studio** (1133 S. Charles St., 410/244-1133, www.shopbrightside.com, Mon.-Sat. 11am-7pm, Sun.11am-5pm), selling clothes, accessories and home items.

## HAMPDEN

The "happening place" in Hampden is 36th Street, known locally as "The Avenue." This is especially true for shoppers since there are four blocks of retail stores offering clothing, furniture, antiques, beauty supplies, and some funkier items. The stores are locally owned, and the merchants are helpful if you're looking for a specific item. For starters, visit **Atomic Books** (3620 Falls Rd., 410/662-4444, www.atomicbooks.com, Sun.-Tues. 11am-7pm, Wed.-Thurs. 11am-9pm, Fri. 11am-10pm, Sat. 11am-9pm, Sun. 11am-7pm) to find unique titles and comics, or visit **Ma Petite Shoe** (832 W. 36th St., 410/235-3442, www.mapetiteshoe.com, Mon.-Thurs. and Sat. 11am-7pm, Fri. 11am-8pm, Sun. noon-5pm) for designer shoes and artisan chocolate.

# Sports and Recreation

## SPECTATOR SPORTS

### Oriole Park at Camden Yards

**Oriole Park at Camden Yards** (333 W. Camden St., 888/848-2473, http://baltimore. orioles.mlb.com) is the home of Major League Baseball's **Baltimore Orioles.** The park opened in 1992 in downtown Baltimore, just a short walk from the Inner Harbor. Camden Yards is consistently rated one of the top professional baseball parks in the country. The train station at the intersection of Howard and Camden Streets services the stadium for the Baltimore Light Rail.

### M&T Bank Stadium

A stone's throw from Camden Yards is the **M&T Bank Stadium** (1101 Russell St., 410/261-7283, www.baltimoreravens.com), home to the **Baltimore Ravens** of the National Football League. The multipurpose venue opened in 1998. The Hamburg Street Station of the Baltimore Light Rail services the stadium.

### Royal Farms Arena

The **Royal Farms Arena** (201 W. Baltimore St., www.royalfarmsarena.com) is the location for the **Baltimore Blast** (www.baltimore-blast.com) professional indoor soccer team's home games. The team was founded in 1992 and is part of the Major Indoor Soccer League.

## BIKING

Baltimore has a large biking community that is working hard to make the city more bike-friendly. Since 2006, 42 on-street bike lane miles have been created in the city, and there are 39 miles of off-road trails.

The **BWI Bike Trail** (www.bikewashington.org) is a 11-mile, asphalt surface, loop trail that circles BWI Airport. It has short sections on city streets, but is mostly level with a few bridge hills and one tougher hill. The trail runs past a light-rail station where a drinking fountain, restrooms, and vending machines are accessible. Parking is available in several spots including the **Dixon Aircraft Observation**

## Pimlico Race Course

The second leg of the famed Triple Crown horse races, **The Preakness Stakes,** is held on the third Saturday in May at **Pimlico Race Course** (5201 Park Heights Ave., 410/542-9400, www. pimlico.com), northwest of Hampden. The historic racecourse is the second-oldest in the country, having opened in 1870. The course was built after the governor of Maryland, Oden Bowie, made a proposition over dinner in 1868 to racing gurus in Saratoga, New York. The proposition included a race, to be held two years after the dinner, between horses that were yearlings at the time of the dinner. The American Jockey Club wanted to host the race, but Bowie pledged to build a state-of-the-art racetrack in Baltimore if the race was held there. After the pledge was made, plans were put in place for the birth of Pimlico.

Pimlico (originally spelled "pemblicoe") was a name given to the area west of the Jones Falls, an 18-mile-long stream that runs through the city of Baltimore and into the Inner Harbor, during the colonial era. The Maryland Jockey Club bought 70 acres in the area for $23,500 and constructed the racetrack for $25,000. Race day was always a big event at Pimlico, and horse-drawn carriages made their way through Druid Hill Park toward the course before additional roads were built directly to the track.

Pimlico quickly became an institution. It has survived wars, recession, the Great Depression, fire, and storms. The first Preakness Stakes was held here in 1873 and remains a time-honored tradition.

Area (Route 176 on Dorsey Road) and at the light-rail station (on the west side of Route 648).

The **Baltimore and Annapolis Trail** (410/222-6244) is a 15.5-mile paved trail that runs along a railroad route from Dorsey Road (near BWI Airport) and ends at the Annapolis waterfront. At the north end of the trail is a short connector to the BWI Bike Trail.

The **Gwynns Falls Trail** (www.gwynns-fallstrail.org) covers 15 miles between the I-70 Park and Ride trailhead and the Inner Harbor. The trail connects 30 neighborhoods in west and southwest Baltimore.

Bikes can be rented at **Light Street Cycles** (1124 Light St., 410/685-2234, Mon.-Fri. 10am-7pm, Sat. 10am-6pm, hybrids $30 per day, mountain bikes and road bikes $60 per day).

## PADDLEBOATS

Most kids get wide-eyed when they see the lineup of brightly colored "Chessie" the sea monster paddleboats at **Paddleboats Team Chessie** (301 E. Pratt St., www.baltimorepaddleboats.org, Memorial Day-Labor Day daily 11am-10pm, mid-Apr.-day before Memorial Day and day after Labor Day-mid-Nov. daily 11am-6pm, $20 per half hour) on the waterfront. Renting a paddleboat for a half hour or

an hour is a fun way to get a new perspective on the harbor. Regular paddleboats are also available for rent ($12 per half hour).

## CRUISES
### Urban Pirates

Bring the family on a unique 1.5-hour adventure in the harbor. The **Urban Pirates** (Ann Street Pier, Fell's Point, 410/327-8378, www.urbanpirates.com, $22-25) offers pirate cruises out of Fell's Point. Three pirates lead an interactive adventure where guests can dress up, get their faces painted, get a tattoo, and then depart on a cruise complete with songs, games, water cannons, and treasure. Adult cruises are also offered.

### Paddle Wheeler Cruise

*The Black-Eyed Susan* (2600 Boston St., 410/342-6960, www.baltimorepaddlewheel.com) is an authentic paddle wheeler that is docked in Canton but can board passengers at the Maryland Science Center, Pier 5 Hotel, and Broadway Pier in Fell's Point. It is designed for entertainment and can be chartered for corporate or private events, but public events (such as murder mystery dinner cruises for $70) are also offered.

Paddleboats Team Chessie

# Food

## DOWNTOWN AND THE INNER HARBOR

### American

**The Capital Grille** (500 E. Pratt St., 443/703-4064, www.thecapitalgrille.com, Mon.-Thurs. 11:30am-10pm, Fri. 11:30am-11pm, Sat. 5pm-11pm, Sun. 4pm-9pm, $29-50) on Pratt Street is part of a national chain of restaurants, but still offers a superb dining experience in a great location on the Inner Harbor. Steak and seafood make up the bulk of the menu in this traditional steak house, but the good service and pleasant atmosphere add to its overall appeal.

The **Corner & Bistro Winebar** (213 Penn St., 410/727-1155, www.cbwinebar.com, lunch Tues.-Thurs. 11am-2pm, Fri. 11:30am-2:30pm, dinner Sun. 4pm-10pm, Mon.-Thurs. 5pm-midnight, Fri. 5pm-10pm, Sat. 4pm-1am, $10-17) is a casual little bistro and wine bar that serves a bar menu of tasty appetizers and a small lunch and dinner menu of salads, burgers, and ciabattas. Try the Chesapeake, a ciabatta with grilled marinated chicken breast, crab dip, and grilled tomato and a side of sweet potato fries. The bistro is easy to walk to from attractions such as the Babe Ruth Birthplace Museum and is about a half block off Pratt Street.

### Asian

**Ban Thai Restaurant** (340 N. Charles St., 410/727-7971, www.banthai.us, Mon.-Thurs. 11am-10:30pm, Fri.-Sat. 11am-11pm, Sun. noon-9:30pm, $13-21) opened in 1993, and the same chefs that were here then are still cooking delightful Thai dishes in the kitchen today. The modest restaurant is known for its made-to-order food. They do a nice job with spices and can make each dish as hot or mild as you like. The menu includes a variety of classic and more daring dishes so both beginners and those experienced with Thai cuisine should have no problem finding a suitable dish. Vegetarian dishes are on the menu as well, but some have fish sauce. Try for a seat by the window so you can people-watch on Charles Street.

### Brazilian

For die-hard carnivores, it's hard to beat the Brazilian steak house **Fogo De Chao** (600 E. Pratt St., 410/528-9292, www.fogodechao.com, lunch Mon.-Fri. 11:30am-2pm, dinner Mon.-Thurs. 5pm-10pm, Fri. 5pm-10:30pm, Sat. 4pm-10:30pm, Sun. 4pm-9pm, lunch $34.95, dinner $51.95). This dining experience includes a large salad bar with more than 30 items, then an onslaught of 15 cuts of fire-roasted meats brought tableside. Each guest has a card to turn to green when you'd like more meat offered or red when you are taking a break or have had enough. This is a fun place to bring business guests (if they are not vegetarian) and a good place for groups. Although this restaurant is part of a small chain out of Dallas, Texas, this is the only location in Maryland.

### Turkish

**Cazbar** (316 N. Charles St., 410/528-1222, www.cazbar.pro, Mon.-Thurs. 11am-11pm, Fri.-Sat. 11am-midnight, Sun. 4pm-11pm, $16-27) is Baltimore's first authentic Turkish restaurant. They offer consistently good food, a warm and pleasant atmosphere, and friendly staff. As one person sitting close by commented, "I will eat here until my mouth burns like the fires of hell. It's that good." Although the food isn't generally that spicy, it's always good to know someone will take one for the team. The servers know the menu well and can help with tough decisions. Try their hummus or Mohamra walnut dip for a starter. They also have Turkish beer and sangria. On Friday and Saturday nights there are free belly dancing shows—not many places can say that.

# FELL'S POINT AND LITTLE ITALY
## American

**Peter's Inn** (504 S. Ann St., 410/675-7313, www.petersinn.com, Tues.-Sun. 6:30pm-10pm, Fri.-Sat. 6:30pm-11pm, $11-30) is a casual contemporary eatery that is known for its innovative dishes and fresh ingredients. It is housed in a farmhouse built in 1799 and the owners live upstairs. The restaurant was mainly known as a biker bar throughout the 1980s and early 1990s but has since transformed into a great food-focused restaurant. The menu changes weekly (look for the chalkboard next to the men's washroom) with the exception of salad, steaks, and garlic bread, which are staples. The restaurant is crowded on weekends so expect a wait (perhaps at their bar). They do not take reservations.

Beer lovers will think they've won the lottery after stepping inside ★ **Max's Taphouse** (737 S. Broadway, 410/675-6297, www.maxs.com, daily 11am-2am $10-12.50). With 140 rotating drafts, 102 taps, 5 casks, and 1,200 bottles in stock, you could spend a lifetime here searching for your favorite beer. This beer-lover's institution is Baltimore's premier beer pub and has been featured in countless magazines and "best of" lists. The friendly owner, expert "beertenders" (many of whom have been here for more than a dozen years), and delicious pub menu make this well-known establishment in the heart of Fell's Point not just a great drinking spot, but also a great place to eat and hang out with new and old friends. For the sports minded, they offer numerous televisions, pool tables, foosball, and dartboards. Private rooms are available with large-screen TVs, custom beer lists, and great sound systems with iPod connections. Weekday specials such as "Monday sucks happy hour" and "Friday big ass draft happy hour" occur weekly in addition to great annual events such as Max's Annual German Beer Fest and the Hopfest.

If you are looking for a classy restaurant with a lovely atmosphere and delicious food, and you don't mind paying for it, then make a reservation at the acclaimed ★ **Charleston Restaurant** (1000 Lancaster St., 410/332-7373, www.charlestonrestaurant.com, Mon.-Sat. 5:30pm-10pm, $79-212). They offer an extensive prix fixe tasting menu with three to six courses and an award-winning wine list of more than 800 labels. Chef Cindy Wolf has been a James Beard Award finalist for best chef, mid-Atlantic, on multiple occasions, and as recently as 2016. She is one of the best-known chefs in the city. Wolf's cooking is a blend of French fundamentals and South Carolina's Low Country cuisine. The restaurant is in Harbor East near Fell's Point. A jacket and tie are recommended but not required.

The **Blue Moon Café** (1621 Aliceanna St., 410/522-3940, www.bluemoonbaltimore.com, daily 7am-3pm, weekends 24 hours, $5-16) is a well-known breakfast café that was featured on Guy Fieri's show *Diners, Drive-Ins and Dives*. Open 24 hours on weekends, this small eatery inside a converted row house has a line out the door on the average Saturday or Sunday. The reason couldn't be that they're serving Captain Crunch—or could it? Captain Crunch french toast is one of their most popular dishes, but Maryland Eggs Benedict and delightful homemade biscuits and gravy are other very convincing reasons.

Exposed brick and beams, high ceilings, and dark wood add to the charm of the **Red Star Bar and Grill** (906 S. Wolfe St., 410/675-0212, www.redstarbar.us, Mon.-Thurs. 11:30am-midnight, Fri. 11:30am-2am, Sat. 10am-2am, Sun. 10am-midnight, $7-20). This fun eatery is a little off the beaten path in Fell's Point but still within easy walking distance of all the action. They serve great sandwiches, pizza, and burgers and also offer a nice selection of beer. This is a fun, casual place with a good vibe and tasty menu. They also have full bar, which is a comfortable place to stop in for a drink or meet friends.

A unique find is **One-Eyed Mike's** (708 S. Bond St., 410/327-0445, www.oneeyedmikes.com, Mon.-Fri. 11am-2am, Sat.-Sun. 10am-2am, $7-35). This lovely little treasure is one of the oldest operating taverns in Baltimore. It's housed in a tiny space on the edge of Fell's Point in an off-the-beaten-path row house. Walk through the bar and to the lovely little restaurant in the back, where they serve delicious crab cakes and stuffed filet. The staff is fun, the atmosphere is comfortable, and the food is good. The backbar was hand-carved, and they still have the original tin ceiling, both of which were put in during the 1860s. They also offer courtyard seating in nice weather. Ask about their Grand Marnier Club, the world's first.

## British Pub

The **Wharf Rat** (801 S. Ann St., 410/276-8304, www.thewharfrat.com, daily 11am-2am, $9-20) harkens back to a day when old seaport taverns were filled with visiting sailors. The name itself is a term used in the 18th century for seafarers and pirates when they came ashore. This is a fun place for great beer and pub food (their specialty is crab dip pizza and fish-and-chips). The bartenders are also the cooks, so be patient with your food. The atmosphere is friendly and inviting, and the pub is allegedly haunted.

## Seafood

**Thames Street Oyster House** (1728 Thames St., 443/449-7726, www. thamesstreetoysterhouse.com, lunch Wed.-Sun. 11:30am-2:30pm, dinner Sun.-Thurs. 5pm-9:30pm, Fri.-Sat. 5pm-10:30pm, raw bar open until 1am, $12-27) is a slightly upscale gem amid the bar scene in Fell's Point. They offer a fun staff and a lively nighttime atmosphere, but can also be a great place for a romantic seafood dinner if you reserve a table early in the evening. This is a classic oyster house with a great raw bar. There's a large bar area, and a water view from the upstairs.

## Italian

There is no shortage of great Italian restaurants in Little Italy and the surrounding area. ★ **Amiccis** (231 S. High St., 410/528-1096, www.amiccis.com, Sun.-Thurs. 11am-11pm,

Fri.-Sat. 11am-midnight, $14-19) has been a tradition in Baltimore since 1991. It's a self-proclaimed "Very Casual Eatery" whose mission is to provide great homemade Italian comfort food in a relaxed environment. All the menu items are wonderful, but first-timers should try the signature appetizer, the Pane' Rotundo. People in the know call it "that great shrimp and bread thing," and you'll see why after you try it. Amiccis also has a nice bar area that was added as the restaurant expanded from 25 seats to 300, and the original two friends who bought it are still running it today. The atmosphere is lively, and the patrons are a mix of locals and visitors.

★ **Vaccaro's Italian Pastry Shop** (222 Albemarle St., 410/685-4905, www.vaccaros-pastry.com, café menu $5-10) is *the* place to go in Baltimore for Italian pastries. They are widely known for their incredible cannoli filling but also offer many other delectable baked goods such as rum cake, biscotti, and cheesecake. They also offer a café menu of salads and

Amiccis

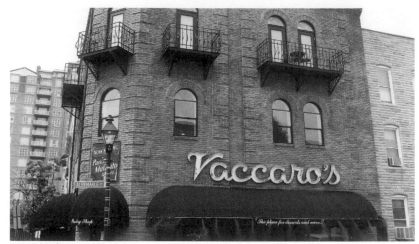

Vaccaro's Italian Pastry Shop

sandwiches and make cakes, cookie trays, and other items such as tiramisu for parties and other occasions. There are three additional locations throughout the Baltimore area (2919 O'Donnell St., 118 Shawan Rd., and 696A Bel Air Rd.).

For a great slice of pizza pie, stop in **Brick Oven Pizza** (800 S. Broadway, 410/563-1600, www.boppizza.com, Sun.-Thurs. 11am-11pm, Fri.-Sat. 11am-3am, $9-24), another fun, casual restaurant that was featured on *Diners, Drive-Ins and Dives*. The crispy-crust pizza and the list of more than 40 toppings including crab, gyro meat, and even Spam are reason enough dine here, but they also offer wraps, pasta, and salads.

## Greek

**The Black Olive** (814 S. Bond St., 410/276-7141, www.theblackolive.com, $27-40) serves authentic organic Greek food in a cozy section of Fell's Point. This elegant restaurant is family-owned and uses organic produce, dairy, flours, and sugars in all dishes. They have relationships with local farms and also serve fresh fish from all over the world including black sea bass, barbouni, and turbo. They boast the largest wine list in Baltimore. The wine cellar and dining rooms are available for private parties.

# CANTON
## American

The raven handrails are just one of many "Poe" details at **Annabel Lee Tavern** (601 S. Clinton St., 410/522-2929, www.annabelleetavern.com, Mon.-Sat. 4pm-1am, Sun. 3pm-midnight, $11-25). Baltimore is a natural setting for a restaurant and bar done in "Edgar Allan Poe." This unique little restaurant is a warm, funky place to have a good meal or a house cocktail off the Poe-themed drink list. The walls are inscribed with Poe's work. The tavern serves affordable upscale comfort food from an interesting but not over-the-top menu (try the rosemary beef tenderloin gyro or the roasted orange roughy tacos). They offer many daily specials and nice vegetarian options, but are known for their duck fat fries, which are worth a try if you've never had them.

The **Blue Hill Tavern** (938 S. Conkling St., 443/388-9363, www.bluehilltavern.com, brunch Sat.-Sun. 10:30am-2:30pm, lunch Mon.-Fri. 11:30am-2:30pm, dinner Mon.-Wed. 5pm-9pm, Thurs.-Sat. 5pm-10pm, Sun. 4pm-9pm, $13-29) is a great little modern tavern a few blocks off O'Donnell Street in Canton. Presentation is key in this trendy restaurant, and the food tastes as good as it looks. The menu includes a variety of American food with a heavy lean toward seafood. Try the mushroom Wellington, surf and turf, or yellowfin tuna and shrimp roulade. They also offer a hearty burger and salads. There's a rooftop patio for summertime dining that is one of the best in the city, even though it isn't on the water. They offer free valet parking.

## Greek

The **Sip and Bite Restaurant** (2200 Boston St., 410/675-7077, www.sipandbite.com, open 24/7, $5-28) is a Baltimore landmark that was featured on *Diners, Drive-Ins and Dives*. This 1948 original between Fell's Point and Canton is owned by a husband-and-wife team that are the third generation in one family to run this diner. They offer a huge menu of breakfast, lunch, and dinner with a slant toward Greek dishes. They serve classic Greek specialties like gyros, but also have killer crab cakes made from a 60-year-old family recipe.

## Seafood

**Mama's on the Half Shell** (2901 O'Donnell St., 410/276-3160, www.mamasmd.com, Mon.-Fri. 11am-2am, Sat.-Sun. 9am-2pm, $23-35) opened in 2003 and quickly became a tradition in Canton. This classic seafood house sits on the corner of O'Donnell Street and South Linwood Avenue in the heart of the neighborhood. They specialize in large, succulent oyster dishes (oyster stew, fried oysters, grilled oysters—you get the picture) but also have wonderful crab dishes, other seafood favorites, and a filet mignon selection. The two-story restaurant has a dark wood interior, a long bar on the first floor, and patio seating. The staff is warm and friendly, and they offer daily specials.

## Mediterranean

The **Speakeasy Saloon** (2840 O'Donnell St., 410/276-2977, Mon.-Thurs. 4:30pm-11pm, Fri.-Sat. 11:30am-11pm, Sun. 10am-10pm, bar daily until 2am, $12-22) is a an elegant saloon with a throwback decor to the Roaring Twenties. A 150-year-old staircase, large murals, mirrors, and a tin ceiling help visitors visualize what things were like when

gangsters and flappers frequented the original corner establishment. The upstairs patio boasts beautiful ironwork railings accented with flower boxes and a redbrick exterior. The food is surprisingly good for the reasonable prices they charge, with both seafood and Mediterranean dishes (examples include Mediterranean chicken, veal marsala, lamb scampi, and pork Athena). If you're looking for a quiet spot, sit on the patio, since it can get loud inside on a busy night.

## Mexican

If you like good Mexican food and you can put up with a few house rules, such as "Report any Elvis sightings to server," "Be nice or leave," and "Don't feed kitchen staff," then take a table at **Nacho Mama's** (2907 O' Donnell St., 410/675-0898, www.nachomamas-canton.com, Mon.-Sat. 11am-2am, Sun. 9am-2am, $11-30) in the heart of Canton. Nacho Mama's has been a hot spot in Baltimore since it opened on Elvis's birthday in 1994. The decor is a mix of the King, Natty Boh,

Mama's on the Half Shell

Speakeasy Saloon

the Orioles, the Baltimore Colts, and everything else Baltimore. The food is delicious, the portions are large, and they have more than a dozen kinds of margaritas. This is a great place to bring visitors to share some Baltimore tradition.

# FEDERAL HILL
## American

Peanut butter burgers, waffle fry nachos, pretzel roll buns, and homemade chips are just some of the items to try at **The Abbey Burger Bistro** (1041 Marshall St., 443/453-9698, www.abbeyburgerbistro.com, kitchen hours Tues.-Sun. 11:30am-midnight, Mon. 5pm-midnight, $6-17.50). This burger-and-beer-focused eatery has a great menu for both, including a build-your-own burger section and a rotating beer list (they even take requests online). This is a great place to stir your creativity, fill your burger appetite, and wash it all down with a cold brew.

**Hull Street Blues Cafe** (1222 Hull St., 410/727-7476, www.hullstreetblues.com, lunch Tues.-Sat. 11am-5pm, Mon. 11am-10pm, Sun. brunch 10am-2pm, dinner Tues.-Thurs. 5pm-10pm, Fri.-Sat. 5pm-11pm, Sun. 4pm-9pm, $16-29) has a long history. It got its start as a saloon back in 1889 and is now a lovely neighborhood café. Nestled amid the blocks of row

houses in Locust Point, the café is named for its side street address on Hull Street (which was named after a naval hero of the War of 1812, Isaac Hull). The restaurant has two sides: one is a casual barroom (where bar fare is served) with a 40-foot-long bar, and the other is the nautical-themed Commodore Room, where guests can enjoy gourmet meals off linens and stemware in front of the fireplace. Seafood, beef, and poultry are at the heart of the menu, but other options such as the chipotle-lime barbecue pork loin are local favorites.

## Seafood

When you're craving good seafood and aren't looking for an upscale atmosphere, **Nick's Oyster Bar** (1065 S. Charles St., 410/685-2020, www.nicksoysterbar.com, Sun.-Thurs. 11am-7pm, Fri. 11am-10pm, Sat. 11am-9pm, $10-22) is the place to go. It is in the west end of the Cross Street Market area and has been in business since 1972. It has cement floors, bottles of beer on ice, televisions tuned to sports, and all the local seafood favorites (including a raw bar). The menu includes steamed shrimp, crab, fish-and-chips, mussels, and the famous crab soup. They also have a sushi bar. Pull a stool up to the counter, order a beer, and chat with the crowd that forms on weekends.

# Natty Boh

The one-eyed, handlebar-mustached Mr. Boh pictured on a gold-and-white National Bohemian Beer can is not just the symbol for **National Bohemian Beer** (aka "Natty Boh"), but also a treasured icon in Baltimore. National Bohemian Beer was first brewed in Baltimore in 1885 by the National Brewing Company. After Prohibition, National Bohemian introduced Mr. Boh, who wears a distinctive smile that has delighted the people of Baltimore for decades.

Now make no mistake, Natty Boh is a cheap, domestic beer (think Pabst Blue Ribbon and Miller High Life); in fact the brand is now owned by Pabst Brewing Company. The beer's slogan is "From the Land of Pleasant Living," which refers to the Chesapeake Bay.

In 1965, Natty Boh became the Baltimore Orioles' official sponsor, and the beer was served at their former home, Memorial Stadium, as "the official beer of Baltimore."

The brand has been sold several times (the first in 1979 to Heileman Brewing Company), and in 1996 its production was moved out of the state. The beer was no longer available on tap in Baltimore. Disappointed fans went for years without their favorite beer being offered fresh from the keg (almost 90 percent of Natty Boh sales are in Baltimore), but in 2011, good news came. Pabst Blue Ribbon announced the return of the famous brew to Baltimore and the rest of Maryland on tap.

Nacho Mama's in Canton was one of the first to tap the newly available kegs, and did so on February 3, 2011. A packed house welcomed Natty Boh back. A total of eight official keg-tapping parties were held throughout the area, and it looks like the people of Baltimore can enjoy their beer on tap for the foreseeable future.

Another great seafood restaurant is **Ryleigh's Oyster Bar** (36 E. Cross St., 410/539-2093, www.ryleighs.com, Mon.-Sun. 11am-10pm, $8-29). The atmosphere is more upscale than a bar scene, and they offer really fresh oysters on their old slate oyster bar. There is a gourmet seafood menu with items such as crab cakes, tuna, and shrimp and grits. The crab pretzels are a great way to start, and they also offer salads and sandwiches and other items that aren't seafood.

## MOUNT VERNON
### Afghan
**The Helmand** (806 N. Charles St., 410/752-0311, www.helmand.com, Sun.-Thurs. 5pm-10pm, Fri.-Sat. 5pm-11pm, $13-17) looks like a simple restaurant but has been serving incredible Afghan food since 1989. It is one of a handful of eateries owned by a prominent Afghan family that helped bring the cuisine to the United States. Considered by many to be a local treasure, the *kaddo borawni,* a pumpkin appetizer, is a must-try before making the difficult entrée decision.

### American
The tuxedoed servers, stuffed leather seats, live piano music, and stiff drinks haven't changed a bit at ★ **The Prime Rib** (1101 N. Calvert St., 410/539-1804, www.theprimerib. com, Mon.-Thurs. 5pm-10pm, Fri.-Sat. 5pm-11pm, Sun. 4pm-9pm, $28-63) since its opening in 1965. Jackets are required, and the place looks like an establishment Sinatra would have frequented. The best part, however, is the food. The Prime Rib has been named one of the best in the country by *Esquire* magazine for its steaks, and it is easy to believe. This is a place to come when you want first-class food and service to match, and you don't mind paying for it.

The funky little pizza shop **Joe Squared** (33 W. North Ave., 410/545-0444, www.jo-esquared.com, Sun.-Wed. 11am-midnight, Thurs.-Sat. 11am-2am, $11-25) offers coal-fired square pizza, 17 varieties of risotto, an extensive rum list, good beer, and free live music (funk, soul, jazz, old time, etc.). Featured on *Diners, Drive-Ins and Dives,* the restaurant is family-owned, and the food is delicious. The clientele is mainly college-aged, and the area isn't ideal after dark. There is also a location in the Inner Harbor (30 Market Pl.).

## Italian

A great choice for pizza in Mount Vernon is **Iggies** (818 N. Calvert St., Ste. 1, 410/528-0818, www.iggiespizza.com, Tues.-Thurs. 11:30am-9pm, Fri.-Sat. 11:30am-10pm, Sun. 11:30am-8pm, $10-18). The pizza has a thin, crispy crust and a multitude of interesting topping options (think peaches, gorgonzola, rosemary, etc.). The place is very casual, and you must BYOB if you'd like to drink. When you enter, wait to be seated. Once seated, leave your plate on the table and get in line to order. When your food is ready, the staff will call your name and order number. The pizza is excellent, and the crowd is young and lively. It's a great place to grab a bit before heading to Centerstage.

# HAMPDEN AND HOMEWOOD
## American

★ **Woodberry Kitchen** (2010 Clipper Park Rd., 410/464-8000, www.woodberrykitchen. com, brunch Sat.-Sun. 10am-2pm, dinner Mon.-Thurs. 5pm-10pm, Fri.-Sat. 5pm-11pm, Sun. 5pm-9pm, $15-48) is a hip little restaurant in the historic Clipper Mill west of Hampden. They serve local meats and seafood and use fresh organic ingredients. The menu is based on what is seasonal and includes many regional dishes (think brined pork chops and oysters roasted in a wood-burning oven). The atmosphere is contemporary in design, and the space, a renovated 19th-century industrial mill, offers the warm ambience of exposed brick, wood, and soft lighting. On nice evenings, diners can also enjoy patio seating under market umbrellas and white lights. Reservations are a must on weekends and should be made weeks in advance if possible.

The **Corner Charcuterie Bar** (850 W. 36th St., 443/869-5075, www.cornerchar-cuteriebar.com, lunch Wed.-Fri. at 11 am,

dinner daily at 4pm, brunch Sat.-Sun 11am-2:30pm, $9-19) is a treasure in Hampden. They offer Belgium-influenced fare with interesting dishes such as roasted bone marrow and ostrich tartare and a great selection of meats and cheeses. A chef's $20 meal option changes daily as does the discount cocktail of the day. They have a convenience charge on credit card sales.

It's hard to find a more local dining institution in Hampden than **Café Hon** (1002 W. 36th St., 410/243-1230, www.cafehon. com, Mon.-Thurs. 11am-9pm, Fri. 11am-10pm, Sat. 9am-10pm, Sun. 9am-8pm, $7-19), and it's hard to miss the two-story pink flamingo that stands over its front door. The café name is a tribute to the "hon" culture in Hampden (see Honfest in the events section of this chapter), and the café serves a mix of comfort food and seafood. The adjoining Hon Bar offers live music and oyster shucking. This purely Baltimore establishment even has a Baltimore, Maryland, dictionary (or Bawlmer, Murlin, if you will) on the website.

Café Hon is a local institution in Hampden.

# Accommodations

## $100-200

If you want to be where the action is in Fell's Point, book a room at the **Admiral Fell Inn** (888 S. Broadway, 410/522-7380, www.admiralfell.com, $169-289). This historic European-style hotel includes seven buildings, some of which date back to the 1770s. Many stories surround the inn, as the building has served many purposes such as a ship chandlery, boardinghouse, theater, and YMCA. No two rooms are alike at the inn but each is decorated in modern furnishings with a cozy decor. Two specialty rooms are available, one with two levels and the other with a balcony overlooking the waterfront. The Tavern at the Admiral Fell Inn is open Wednesday-Saturday evenings to serve beer, wine, cocktails, and traditional spirits.

Travelers looking for a charming boutique hotel near bustling O'Donnell Street in Canton will be thrilled with the **Inn at 2920** (2920 Elliott St., 410/342-4450, www.theinnat2920.com, $175-215). This five-room inn is inside a rather regular-looking row house on Elliott Street. Look for the pale-green door on the corner. Once inside, the rooms are lovely, unique, and contemporary. They have exposed brick walls and modern furnishings. This hip little hotel is definitely something special, and you'll feel like a local stepping out onto the street. The water is within walking distance, but Fell's Point is a good 15-20 minutes by foot.

Budget-conscious travelers can have a great stay at the **Brookshire Suites** (120 E. Lombard St., 410/625-1300, www.brookshiresuites.com, $107-199) just a block away from the Inner Harbor on Lombard Street. The 11-story, 97-room hotel has a distinct exterior with a large black-and-white geometric pattern that can't be missed. The interior is contemporary with traditional-style rooms. The hotel caters to business travelers and offers a nice business center and laundry facilities, but its central location makes it a good choice for pleasure travel as well.

## $200-300

The **Monaco Baltimore** (2 N. Charles St., 443/692-6170, www.monaco-baltimore.com, $209-309) is consistent with other Kimpton Hotels as a top-notch choice for accommodations. This warm and friendly hotel is housed in the restored B&O Railroad building on Charles Street a few blocks northwest of the Inner Harbor. The personal service and attention to detail they offer is hard to beat. The hotel has Tiffany stained glass windows, a marble staircase, and vaulted ceilings. The rooms are large and modern with high ceilings and a hint of funky styling that's unique to Kimpton. The staff is wonderful, and the location is convenient to many restaurants and attractions even though it's not right on the water. They offer bikes and bike route maps to guests and a hosted wine hour in the evenings. They have 24-hour valet parking with in-and-out services for $38. The hotel is pet friendly.

The ★ **Hyatt Regency Baltimore** (300 Light St., 410/528-1234, www.baltimore.hyatt.com, $239-439) offers one of the best locations in the Inner Harbor. Situated right across Light Street from Harborplace and connected to it by two skywalks, the hotel offers tremendous harbor views. The rooms are modern and comfortable with large bathrooms and contemporary furniture. The building's lit-up, glass-enclosed elevators seem to shoot through the lobby roof and along the outside of the hotel. They are beautiful to look at and afford incredible views to the people inside. The hotel staff is also extremely helpful and pleasant. Bistro 300 on the third floor serves breakfast, lunch, and dinner (and has a nice bar). There is a small gift shop on-site, a fitness room, and pool. Ask for a harbor-view room on an upper floor; the corner rooms

# Traveling with Fido

Baltimore is surprisingly pet friendly for such a large and industrial city. Many hotels throughout the city allow your best friend to accompany you in your room. Additional fees and rules may apply to your four-legged friend, so ask when you make a reservation. Some hotels that allow dogs include:

- **Admiral Fell Inn** (888 S. Broadway, 410/522-7380)
- **Biltmore Suites** (205 W. Madison St., 410/728-6550)
- **Brookshire Suites** (120 E. Lombard St., 410/625-1300)
- **Four Seasons Hotel Baltimore** (200 International Dr., 410/576-5800)
- **Hilton Baltimore Convention Center Hotel** (401 W. Pratt St., 443/573-8700)
- **Holiday Inn Express Baltimore—Downtown** (221 N. Gay St., 410/400-8045)
- **Holiday Inn Inner Harbor Hotel** (301 W. Lombard St., 410/685-3500)
- **Hotel Monaco** (2 N. Charles St., 443/692-6170)
- **Intercontinental Harbor Court Hotel** (550 Light St., 410/234-0550)
- **Pier 5 Hotel** (711 Eastern Ave., 410/539-2000)
- **Lord Baltimore Hotel** (20 W. Baltimore St., 410/539-8400)
- **Residence Inn Downtown Baltimore/Inner Harbor** (17 Light St., 410/962-1220)
- **Sheraton Inner Harbor Hotel** (300 S. Charles St., 410/962-8300)
- **Sheraton Baltimore North** (903 Dulaney Valley Rd., 410/321-7400)
- **Sleep Inn & Suites Downtown Inner Harbor** (301 Fallsway, 410/779-6166)

offer spectacular floor-to-ceiling windows overlooking the water.

The ★ **Inn at Hendersons Wharf** (1000 Fell St., 410/522-7777, www.hendersonswharf. com, $197-325) is a lovely boutique hotel sitting directly on the water on the eastern side of Fell's Point. The hotel is located in a large brick building dating back to 1893, which it shares with condos and a conference center. The inn's 38 cozy rooms have exposed brick walls, colonial décor, feather beds, and 30-inch televisions with satellite service. There's a pretty interior courtyard. Rooms include a continental breakfast, access to a fitness center and pools, and high-speed Internet. Self-parking is available for $10 per night. The hotel is close to restaurants and shops in Fell's Point but far enough away to filter the noise. Ask for a harbor view.

The **Courtyard Marriott Baltimore Downtown/Inner Harbor** (1000 Aliceanna St., 443/923-4000, www.marriott.com, $249-304) has 195 rooms and 10 suites not far from the waterfront. The staff at this hotel is exceptionally friendly and helpful. They also offer great packages for family members of patients at Johns Hopkins Hospital, which include a discounted room rate, breakfast, and cab vouchers to and from the hospital. There is a small indoor swimming pool, a small fitness room, and an on-site restaurant and bar serving breakfast, lunch, and dinner. High-speed Internet is included. Ask for an upper-floor room on the harbor side of the hotel, where limited water views are available.

For a less expensive stay that is still convenient to the Inner Harbor, the **Days Inn**

**Baltimore—Inner Harbor Hotel** (100 Hopkins Pl., 410/576-1000, www.daysinnerharbor.com, $199-229) is the ticket. Just a few blocks from the stadiums and Inner Harbor, the 250 rooms are clean and convenient. Although the rooms aren't large, this is a well-located hotel with an affordable price tag.

## OVER $300

The **Inn at the Black Olive** (803 S. Caroline St., 443/681-6316, www.innattheblackolive.com, $289-439) is a boutique organic hotel offering 12 luxury guests suites along the waterfront on the border of Fell's Point and the harbor. All the suites are modern, with water views and spa bathrooms. Rooms include a basic organic breakfast. Other room amenities include balconies or sitting porches, king-size beds with organic mattresses, Sanijet pipeless hydrotherapy tubs, and high-speed Internet. All rooms are cleaned with natural chemical-free cleaners. There's an organic market and rooftop restaurant on-site called The Olive Room that serves Greek cuisine and has a large wine list. The Inn at the Black Olive is a LEED Platinum Inn.

A good choice on the waterfront in the Harbor East area of Baltimore between Fell's Point and the Inner Harbor is the **Baltimore Marriott Waterfront Hotel** (700 Aliceanna St., 410/385-3000, www.marriott.com, $269-489). This towering 31-story hotel is on the water's edge and offers stunning harbor views and great access to many of the best attractions. There are 733 modern rooms and 21 suites. Harbor-view rooms and city-view rooms are available.

Right near the Baltimore Marriott Waterfront Hotel is the **Four Seasons Hotel Baltimore** (200 International Dr., 410/576-5800, www.fourseasons.com, $509-2,500), which offers great views of the harbor and an elegant interior. There are 256 rooms and suites with views including the harbor, city, and marina. The rooms offer generous space, and the stunning Presidential Suite is more than 2,800 square feet. The corner suites offer stunning views. The service is on par with other Four Seasons hotels, which is to say much above average.

# Information and Services

Helpful tourist information on Baltimore can be found on the **Baltimore Area Convention and Visitors Association** website at www.baltimore.org. The website has details on events and attractions throughout the city and answers many common questions. Special offers are also available through the website. The **Baltimore Area Visitor Center** (401 Light St., 877/225-8466, Apr.-Sept. daily 9am-6pm, reduced hours the rest of the year) in the Inner Harbor is a great place to begin any trip to Baltimore. The 8,000-square-foot center offers information on nearly everything the city has to offer.

The most widely read paper in the city is the *Baltimore Sun* (www.baltimoresun.com).

It is also Maryland's largest daily newspaper and covers local and regional news. The Baltimore *City Paper* (www.citypaper.com) is a free alternative weekly paper that is distributed on Wednesday. It is known for having good coverage of clubs, concerts, restaurants, and theater. It also has political articles and covers subjects not featured in mainstream publications.

There are 31 hospitals in the metropolitan area of Baltimore. Top-ranking facilities include **Johns Hopkins Hospital** (1800 Orleans St., 410/955-5000, www.hopkinsmedicine.org) and the **University of Maryland Medical Center** (22 S. Greene St., 410/328-8667, www.umm.edu).

# Getting There

## AIR

The **Baltimore Washington International Thurgood Marshall Airport (BWI)** (410/859-7111, www.bwiairport.com) is just 10 miles south of Baltimore and a short 15-minute car ride from downtown Baltimore. This busy regional airport is a hub for Southwest Airlines and offers some of the best fares in the Washington DC/Baltimore area. Most other major airlines offer flight service to BWI as well. Parking is available at the airport by the hour or day, and there is a free cell phone lot for those who are picking up arriving passengers.

Car rentals are available at the airport from numerous national car rental companies, and courtesy shuttles run between the airport and major downtown hotels. The **SuperShuttle** (www.supershuttle.com, approximately $15 for a shared van) runs 24-hour service from the airport to locations throughout Baltimore and has a reservation counter on the lower level of the airport near baggage claims 1 and 10.

Cab service is also available from the airport, but this can be a costly option with fares running upward of $40 to downtown Baltimore.

Train service is available from the airport to downtown Baltimore through the Maryland Transit Administration (MTA) on their **Light Rail** (410/539-5000, www.mta. maryland.gov/light-rail, Mon.-Fri. 5am-11pm, Sat. 6am-11pm, Sun. 11am-7pm, $1.60). The BWI Marshall Light Rail station can be found outside the lower lever of the terminal near Concourse E.

## CAR

Baltimore is a very accessible city. Strategically located right on I-95, it can be reached easily by car from both the north and south. The drive from major cities such as New York (3.5 hours, 188 miles), Philadelphia (2 hours, 100 miles), Washington DC (1 hour, 39 miles), and Richmond (2.75 hours, 152 miles) is a straight shot and takes between one and four hours. I-83 also runs into the city from the north.

## TRAIN

**Pennsylvania Station** (1515 N. Charles St., 800/872-7245, www.amtrak.com) is centrally located on Charles Street near Mount Vernon and is less than two miles from the Inner Harbor. The stately 1911 building is nicely restored, and the station is one of the busiest in the country. Amtrak runs dozens of trains through Penn Station daily from all corners of the country. They offer ticket discounts for seniors, children, students, veterans, and conference groups.

A commuter rail service called **Maryland Area Rail Commuter (MARC)** (410/539-5000, www.mta.maryland.gov) operates trains on weekdays between Washington DC and Baltimore ($8 one way). This is another option for visitors traveling during the week.

## BUS

Just south of downtown Baltimore in an industrial section of the city is the **Greyhound** bus station (2110 Haines St., 800/231-2222, www.greyhound.com). Bus service runs daily from multiple destinations. It is advisable to take a cab from the station to points around Baltimore. Walking near the station is not advisable after dark.

A number of private bus lines provide service between cities in the mid-Atlantic and offer reasonable fares from cities such as Washington DC, Philadelphia, and New York City. An example is **Peter Pan Bus Lines** (800/343-9999, www.peterpanbus.com, $14 one-way from DC). Additional service can be found on www.gotobus.com.

# Getting Around

Although walking is a viable option for getting to many of the sights in Baltimore, depending on where you are staying, it is often easiest (and safest at night) to move around the city by car. Public transportation does provide other alternatives; however, most public transportation is geared toward commuters and isn't the most convenient for visitors wishing to explore major attractions.

The exception to this is the **Charm City Circulator** (www.charmcitycirculator.com, year round Mon.-Thurs. 7am-8pm, Fri. 7am-midnight, Sat. 9am-midnight, Sun 9am-8pm). This free, eco-friendly shuttle service has a fleet of 30 Hybrid electric shuttles that serve four routes in Baltimore City. The Green Route offers transportation from City Hall to Fell's Point and to Johns Hopkins. The Purple Route serves locations from 33rd Street to Federal Hill. The Orange Route runs between Hollins Market and Harbor East and the Banner Route goes from the Inner Harbor to Fort McHenry. Shuttles stop every 10-15 minutes at each designated stop.

## CAR

Downtown Baltimore is divided by two main streets. Baltimore Street runs east to west, and Charles Street runs north to south. All streets north of Baltimore Street (or above Baltimore Street if you're looking at a map) have the "north" designation (such as N. Highland Street). Likewise, those south (or below) Baltimore Street have a "south" designation. The same is true for the streets east and west of Charles Street (which is a one-way street running north downtown). Those streets to the east of Charles Street (or to the right) have "east" designations. Those to the west (left) have "west" designations.

When driving, it is very important to be aware that there are many one-way streets in Baltimore. Parking isn't too difficult in most parts of the city on weekends; however, garages right around the Inner Harbor can be expensive. Parking during the week is more of a challenge when commuters are in town and spaces are in short supply. There is on-street parking in many areas and pay lots are scattered throughout town. Be sure to read parking signs carefully, as many neighborhoods have resident-only parking and time restrictions.

Overall, driving in Baltimore is much as it is in other big cities. Drive with purpose and have a plan as to where you are headed. Sightseeing out the window in the middle of traffic can result in some less-than-friendly gestures from those in cars around you. When in doubt, or if you miss a turn, just drive around the block; it's difficult to get too lost if you keep an eye on the harbor.

## BUS

Bus service provided by the **Maryland Transit Administration (MTA)** (410/539-5000, www.mtamaryland.com, $1.60) includes 73 routes in Baltimore. Forty-seven of these routes are local routes inside the city. Bus routes primarily serve commuters on weekdays and are more limited on weekends, but it pays to check out the latest schedule online.

## RAIL

Two public rail systems serve Baltimore, although each only has one rail line. The first, called **Light Rail** (410/539-5000, www.mtamaryland.com, Mon.-Fri. 5am-12am, Sat. 6am-12am, Sun. 11am-7pm, $1.70), runs from BWI Airport north to Hunt Valley Mall (in northern Baltimore County). This is only a good option if you are traveling between two specific points on the line, such as Camden Yards to Mount Vernon (there are no east/west stops). The second is the **Metro Subway** (410/539-5000, www.mtamaryland.com, Mon.-Fri. 5am-12am, Sat.-Sun. 6am-12am, $1.70) that runs from the suburbs northwest of town and into downtown and Johns Hopkins. The line is 15.5 miles, and has 14 stations. Trains run every 8-10 minutes

# All Aboard the Water Taxi

Baltimore Water Taxi

For decades residents and visitors to Baltimore have enjoyed an alternative form of public transportation around the city. The **Baltimore Water Taxi** (410/563-3900, www.thewatertaxi.com) is a fun, easy way to travel between some of the best attractions, shopping areas, and restaurants in town. The famed blue-and-white boats can be seen zipping between 17 well-placed landings along the waterfront. The taxi service shuttles thousands of commuters and visitors alike on a daily basis, and local businesses rely on the service to bring their customers.

During the summer months, the taxi runs 10am-11pm Monday-Saturday and 10am-9pm Sunday. Hours are shorter during the remainder of the year. All-day adult passes are $14, and trip times range 10-20 minutes. Tickets can be purchased online with a credit card or on board with cash or a personal check. Landing areas are as follows:

- Landing 1: Aquarium
- Landing 2: Harborplace
- Landing 3: Science Center
- Landing 4: Rusty Scupper
- Landing 5: Pier Five
- Landing 7: Harbor East
- Landing 8: Maritime Park

- Landing 9: HarborView
- Landing 10: Locust Point
- Landing 11: Fell's Point
- Landing 14: Captain James Landing
- Landing 16: Canton Waterfront Park
- Landing 17: Fort McHenry

during rush hour, every 11 minutes on weekday evenings, and every 15 minutes on weekends. Again, this line is geared toward commuters and isn't too helpful for visitors wishing to move around town between sights.

## TAXI

Taxi service is available through three providers: **Yellow Cab** (410/685-1212), **Diamond** (410/947-3333), and **Royal** (410/327-0330). Hailing a cab on the street can be an impossible feat on busy nights in the city, so it's best to bring their phone numbers and try calling from your cell phone. Metered rates in Baltimore are $1.80 for the first one-eleventh of a mile or fraction thereof. Each additional one-eleventh of a mile is $0.20; $0.20 is also charged for each 30 seconds of wait time.

## WATER TAXI

**Water taxi service** (410/563-3900, www.thewatertaxi.com) is available around the harbor between many of the popular sights. This is a great service for visitors. The little boats with the blue awnings that can be seen scooting around the harbor are the taxi boats. They move between 17 stops that include all the prime waterfront destinations (including Fell's Point, Canton, and Fort McHenry in the summer). The boat captains are often chatting and make excellent tour guides.

## BIKE

Biking in Baltimore as a mode of transportation is becoming more popular. Many attractions have iron bike racks that look like bicycles stationed out front, so cyclists have a convenient place to lock up their bikes (yes, lock your bike). New bike lanes are being added around the city to encourage biking, although narrow roads and hills will always be a factor and riding in traffic can be risky when the streets are crowded.

# Excursions

If you have extra time and want to venture outside of Baltimore for a half- or full-day excursion, Havre de Grace and Westminster are two very different, yet equally alluring towns to visit. Havre de Grace provides the attractions of a historic bayside community, while Westminster offers Civil War history and a wonderful farm museum.

## HAVRE DE GRACE

Havre de Grace is a beautiful little town in Harford County that sits at the head of the Chesapeake Bay and the mouth of the mighty Susquehanna River. Its name in French means "Harbor of Beauty" or "Harbor of Grace."

The city was once seriously considered for the location of the nation's capital. Havre de Grace was incorporated in 1785 and has a population of around 13,000. Its seaside-like atmosphere makes it a popular tourist and outdoor recreation destination.

Havre de Grace is halfway between Baltimore and Philadelphia. It was, at one time, a popular stop for stagecoaches traveling between the two cities. Between 1912 and 1950, it was home to the Havre de Grace Racetrack, a popular horse-racing track. Famous horses such as Man o' War, his son War Admiral, Seabiscuit, and Challedon raced here during its heyday. For years, the Havre de Grace Handicap was one of the most highly regarded races in the northeast. The track was sold in 1951 to the owners of two other Maryland racetracks (Pimlico Race Course and Laurel Park Racecourse). The new owners closed the Havre de Grace course and moved the track's racing allotment dates to their own facilities.

Havre de Grace shelters well over 100 historic structures, and the town is designated a National Historic District. The town was first mapped in 1799, and the structures that

# Havre de Grace

Wed.-Sat. 10am-5pm, Sun. 1pm-5pm, Oct. 15-Mar. 31 Sat. 10am-5pm, Sun. 1pm-5pm, $3) is a small window into the history of the upper Chesapeake Bay and lower Susquehanna River. Exhibits explore topics such as fishing, waterfowl hunting, lighthouses, navigation, the Native Americans who lived in the region, European settlers, and wooden boat building.

## CONCORD POINT LIGHTHOUSE
The **Concord Point Lighthouse** (corner of Concord and Lafayette Sts., 410/939-3213, www.concordpointlighthouse.org, Apr.-Oct. Sat.-Sun. 1pm-5pm, free, donations appreciated) is a pretty little piece of history on the waterfront in Havre de Grace. The lighthouse was built in 1827 out of local granite and is one of the oldest lighthouses on the East Coast that has operated continuously. Now fully restored, it stands on a scenic stretch of the promenade. The climb up the 30-foot lighthouse tower is fairly short (as lighthouses go), so it's a fun activity to do with children (but they must be at least 42 inches tall). The lighthouse offers terrific views of the Susquehanna River and the Chesapeake Bay. There are a few informative exhibits at the Keeper's House (which used to be a bar) that give details on the lighthouse's first keeper, John O'Neil, and the history of the lighthouse. There is a gift shop.

## HAVRE DE GRACE DECOY MUSEUM
The **Havre de Grace Decoy Museum** (215 Giles St., 410/939-3739, www.decoymuseum. com, Mon.-Sat. 10:30am-4:30pm, Sun. noon-4pm, $6) is more than a showcase for wooden birds. Decoys have been part of the culture on the Chesapeake Bay for centuries. Originally, they were not considered art, but were made purely to lure waterfowl within hunting range. Today decoys are an art form. Carvers create sophisticated reproductions of birds using century-old skills. This pretty little museum is home to one of the best collections of functional and decorative Chesapeake Bay decoys in existence. Visitors can learn the history of waterfowling on the upper Chesapeake Bay

remain today are of many different ages and architectural designs. Simple Victorian duplexes stand side by side with single-family homes and Queen Anne estates built by wealthy residents.

## Sights
### HAVRE DE GRACE MARITIME MUSEUM
The **Havre de Grace Maritime Museum** (100 Lafayette St., 410/939-4800, www. hdgmaritimemuseum.org, April 1-Oct.14

## THE SUSQUEHANNA MUSEUM AT THE LOCK HOUSE

**The Susquehanna Museum at the Lock House** (817 Conesteo Street, 410-939-5780, www.thelockhousemuseum.org, mid-April-Oct. Fri.-Sun. 1pm-5pm, free) is a museum inside a historic house, which was built in 1840 and home to one of the lock tenders for the Susquehanna and Tidewater Canal (which ran 45 miles between Havre de Grace and Wrightsville, Pennsylvania). It also served as the office for the Toll Collector. The two-story brick building was almost twice the size of other lock houses on the Canal (there were 29 locks total). Exhibits in the museum recreate life along the canal and provide details on Havre de Grace's role in the growth of the country.

## Recreation

There are several **boat launch sites** in Havre de Grace. The first two are at the mouth of the Susquehanna River. One is north of the train bridge at the intersection of Otsego and Union Streets (on Water Street at Jean Roberts Memorial Park). The second is just downstream, off of Franklin Street by the Tidewater Grille (this is just for cartop boats since there is no ramp). A third launch site is at Tydings Park off Commerce Street, on the south side of town. This site is right on the Chesapeake Bay. It is important to know that boating near the Aberdeen Proving Ground south of the city is strictly forbidden. In addition to getting a fine for trespassing, landing anywhere on the proving grounds can be very dangerous because there are live munitions. Obey all signage in the area and respect the buoy markers.

Three miles northwest of Havre de Grace is the beautiful **Susquehanna State Park** (410/557-7994, www.dnr.state.md.us, daily 9am-sunset, Nov.-Feb. weekends only, $4). The park offers boating ($12 launch fee), hiking, mountain biking, kayaking, fishing, a playground, and picnicking. There are also several historic buildings on-site such as a 200-year-old gristmill (visitors can tour its four floors), a stone mansion, a barn, a tollhouse, and a miller's house. All buildings are

the Concord Point Lighthouse

and also how decoys are made through exhibits, lectures, tours, and demonstrations. More than 1,200 decoys are on display. Annual festivals are held at the museum, and there is a nice little gift shop with decoys, books, and other waterfowl-related items.

## TYDINGS PARK

**Tydings Park** (350 Commerce St. at the southern end of Union Ave., 410/939-1800) is a 22-acre park on the waterfront in Havre de Grace. It is situated at the head of the Chesapeake Bay and is the site of several annual festivals and concerts. The park facilities include a fishing pier, boat ramp, picnic area, tennis courts, gazebos, and a playground. It is also the starting point of the half-mile **Havre de Grace Promenade,** a waterfront walkway that goes past the Maritime Museum and continues to the Concord Point Lighthouse. The park is also known as the **Millard E. Tydings Memorial Park.**

open on weekends between Memorial Day and Labor Day from 10am-4pm. A section of the former **Susquehanna and Tidewater Canal** can be seen in the park. This canal was built in 1836 and connected Havre de Grace with Wrightsville, Pennsylvania. Mule-drawn barges made this an important commercial route for more than 50 years. To reach the park, take I-95 to exit 89, and then proceed west on Route 155 to Route 161. Turn right on Route 161 and then right again on Rock Run Road.

## Food

Cold beer, good pub food, and friendly service can be found at **Coakley's Pub** (406 St. John St., 410/939-8888, www.coakleyspub.com, Mon.-Sat 11am-10pm, Sun. 11am-9pm, $4-24) on St. John Street. This cozy spot offers quality fare with a Chesapeake Bay flair (try the crab pretzel). The food and service are consistent, and the atmosphere is casual and inviting.

The ★ **Laurrapin Grille** (209 N. Washington St., 410/939-4956, www.laurrapin.com, Mon.-Thurs. 4pm-10pm, Fri. 4pm-2am, Sat. 11am-2am, Sun. noon-6:30pm, $11-25) is a contemporary American restaurant that specializes in seasonally inspired food. They take fresh local ingredients and turn them into delicious and creative items that take advantage of the bounty of the surrounding area. The result is a wonderful menu with dinner entrées that include crab cakes, lamb, pasta, salmon, and steak. It is obvious that great care goes into developing each menu item, and the result is fresh and tasty. The atmosphere has a bit of a bar feel, but the back room is quieter.

The **Havre de Grace Ritz Gourmet Café** (421 St. John St., 410/939-5858, www. havredegraceritzgourmetcafe.com, Mon.-Sat. 11am-9pm, Sun. 11am-4pm, $9-14) makes superb sandwiches and panini. Kate's Kickin' Cajun Shrimp Panino, the New Yorker Deli Sandwich, and the prime rib tartine are just a few of the delectable choices. They also offer salads, seasonal selections, and breakfast on weekends.

A popular waterfront restaurant is the **Tidewater Grille** (300 Franklin St., 410/939-3313, www.thetidewatergrille.com, Mon.-Fri. 11am-10pm, Sat.-Sun. 9am-10pm, $8-44). They offer a traditional seafood menu with a great view of the Susquehanna and Chesapeake headwaters. Ask for a seat by the window or sit on the patio when it's nice out. Free docking is available for those coming by boat.

## Accommodations

The elegant **Vandiver Inn** (301 S. Union Ave., 410/939-5200, www.vandiverinn.com, $145-165) offers 18 guest rooms in three beautifully restored Victorian homes. Eight are in the Vandiver Inn mansion (built in 1886), and an additional 10 are in the adjacent Kent & Murphy Guest Houses. All have private bathrooms. Each guest is treated to a lovely breakfast, free in-room wireless access, and in-room cable television. The inn is within blocks of the Chesapeake Bay and within the city of Havre de Grace. Many special events are held at the inn, so if you are looking for a quiet stay with little activity, ask about events during your stay when you make a reservation.

The only Victorian mansion built of the stone in Havre de Grace is the **Spencer Silver Mansion** (200 Union Ave., 410/939-1485, www.spencersilvermansion.com, $85-160). This nicely restored 1896 home offers four guest rooms and a lovely carriage house for rent. A full breakfast is served each morning until 10:30am. The mansion is a short walk to the Chesapeake Bay and is near the attractions in downtown Havre de Grace. It is also pet friendly.

Five miles south of Havre de Grace is the **Hilton Garden Inn Aberdeen** (1050 Beards Hill Rd., 410-/272-1777, www. hiltongardeninn3.hilton.com, $179-189) in Aberdeen, Maryland. This modern hotel offers a fitness center and indoor pool. All rooms have 32-inch HD flat-screen televisions, microwaves, refrigerators, and complimentary wireless Internet.

## Camping

Camping is available at **Susquehanna State Park** (888/432-2267, www.dnr.state.md.us, Apr.-Oct., $22.49-51.49 plus $4 park fee and a nightly park facility fee $4.51-4.61). They have 69 sites (six have electric and six have camper cabins). There are two comfort stations with hot showers.

## Information and Services

For additional information on Havre de Grace, stop by the **Havre de Grace Office of Tourism & Visitor Center** (450 Pennington Ave., 410/939-2100) or visit www.explorehavredegrace.com.

## Getting There

Havre de Grace is approximately one hour by car (37 miles) north of Baltimore. It is off I-95, on the southern side of the M. E. Tydings Memorial Bridge. Exit onto Route 155 and follow that road past the Susquehanna Museum and into the historic district of Havre de Grace.

# WESTMINSTER

Westminster is the seat of Carroll County and has a population of around 18,000. It was founded in 1764 and incorporated in 1838. This picturesque town surrounded by primarily farmland and rolling terrain saw a cavalry battle known as Corbit's Charge fought right on the downtown streets during the Civil War. It was also the first locale in the country to offer rural mail delivery.

Westminster is also the home of the late Whittaker Chambers's farm. He hid the "pumpkin papers," which were the key to a controversial case concerning espionage during the Cold War, in a hollowed-out gourd here. The papers resulted in the 1950 conviction of former State Department official Alger Hiss. This evidence confirmed Hiss's perjury in front of Congress when he denied being a Soviet spy.

Westminster is also known for its above-average number of tornadoes. No fewer than four major tornadoes have touched down in Westminster in its recorded history, resulting in varying degrees of destruction.

Today, Westminster is a lovely little city with many artists and art galleries. It is also home to **McDaniel College** (2 College Hill, 410/848-7000, www.mcdaniel.edu), a private liberal arts and sciences college founded in 1867 with just under 3,000 students.

## Sights

### DOWNTOWN WESTMINSTER

Downtown Westminster offers a lovely historic district along Main Street with many old buildings and stories to surround them. The area is friendly to pedestrians and shelters many independent shops, galleries, and restaurants. Large trees line the streets, and there is plenty of parking in two parking decks and outdoor lots.

Many buildings on Main Street in Westminster have a long history, but none as varied as **Odd Fellows Hall** (140 E. Main St.). This plain, three-story brick building was erected in 1858 for $9,000 by the Salem Lodge No. 60 of the Independent Order of Odd Fellows. It was a central location for gatherings in Westminster.

Prior to the Civil War, the building was used by a local militia with Southern sympathies. Not long after the war, a comedian from Alabama performed at the hall and made jokes about President Grant and other officials in the government. As legend has it, the patrons did not appreciate the jokes and threw rocks at him. After being hit in the neck, the performer became upset and left the stage. The local sheriff offered him protection for the night, but the performer refused and went out back to saddle his horse. He was found dead behind the hall shortly after, having had his throat slit. Shortly after that day, and from then on, reports of people seeing a ghost behind the hall of a man engaged in monologue have been common. The building later became a town library, a saloon, a concert hall, and a newspaper office.

In 1912, the building was known as the Opera House, when the Odd Fellows created an opera room that became the first movie theater in town. In recent years it was home to the Opera House Printing Company, but at the time of writing, it was empty.

## HISTORICAL SOCIETY OF CARROLL COUNTY

The **Historical Society of Carroll County** (210 E. Main St., 410/848-6494), on the east end of Westminster's downtown area, has exhibits on the heritage of Carroll County and the surrounding Piedmont area.

## ★ CARROLL COUNTY FARM MUSEUM

The **Carroll County Farm Museum** (500 S. Center St., 410/386-3880, www.ccgovernment.carr.org, Mon.-Sat. 9am-4:30pm, Sun. noon-4pm, adults $5, family $10) offers visitors a unique opportunity to see what rural life in the mid-19th century was like. Part of a 142-acre complex, the museum demonstrates how families had to be self-sufficient by producing everything they needed (food, household items, soap, yarn, etc.) right on their own land.

The museum features a three-story brick farmhouse and authentic farm buildings built in the 1850s, including a log barn, smokehouse, saddlery, broom shop, springhouse, and wagon shed. A guided tour conducted by costumed interpreters of the farmhouse's seven rooms is included with admission, as is a self-guided walking tour of the various exhibit buildings. The wagon shed houses the buggy that was used for the first rural mail delivery route. The route ran between Westminster and Uniontown. Although the route signaled the development of a sophisticated mail delivery system, many residents were not happy about it because they felt cut off from the rest of the community when they were no longer forced into taking regular trips into town to get news and socialize.

There are also public buildings on-site such as a firehouse, schoolhouse, and general store. Artifacts and antiques from the period (many of which were donated by local families) are also on display. There are many live animals at the museum such as sheep, geese, pigs, goats, and horses, which make this a great place to bring children. There is also a gift store.

## ART GALLERIES

At the west end of the downtown area, the **Carroll Arts Center** (91 W. Main St., 410/848-7272, Mon., Wed., Fri., and Sat. 10am-4pm, Tues. and Thurs. 10am-7pm) houses two locally focused art galleries, the **Tevis Gallery** and the **Community Gallery.** It also has a 263-seat theater where it hosts concerts, plays, lectures, recitals, and films year-round. In addition, there are a handful of independent galleries along Main Street and Liberty Street.

The **Esther Prangley Rice Gallery** (410/857-2595), in Peterson Hall at McDaniel College, features work by students and local artists.

## WALKING TOURS

Walking tours are popular in Westminster, and brochures with self-guided tours are available at the **Visitor Center** (210 E. Main St., 410/848-1388). One of the most popular is the Ghost Walk brochure that tells tales of local hauntings. The **Carroll County Public Library** (50 E. Main St., 410/386-4488) also offers guided one-hour ghost tours.

## Shopping

Many national stores and chain restaurants can be found along Route 140, but the historic downtown area offers a mix of locally owned retail shops and restaurants. Westminster blends cultural experiences with the atmosphere of a small town.

The **Downtown Westminster Farmers Market** (Conaway Parking Lot, Railroad Avenue and Emerald Hill Lane) is held on Saturday mid-May through mid-November (8am-noon). It is a "producers-only" market and offers fresh produce, baked goods, flowers, and local honey.

## Food

### AMERICAN

A nice and cozy casual neighborhood restaurant is **Rafael's** (32 W. Main St., 410/840-1919, www.rafaelsrestaurant.com, Mon.-Thurs. 11am-9:30pm, Fri. 11am-10:30pm, Sat. noon-10:30pm, Sun. noon-9pm, breakfast Sat.-Sun. 8am-1pm, $7-19). They have good food and reasonable prices and are especially known for their hamburgers. They serve lunch and dinner daily and breakfast on weekends. The staff is friendly, and the food is consistent.

A popular local eatery with homebrewed beer is **Johansson's Dining House** (4 W. Main St., 410/876-0101, www.johanssonsdininghouse.com, Mon.-Thurs. 11am-10pm, Fri.-Sat. 11am-11pm, Sun. 10am-10pm, $8-31). This casual restaurant serves a varied menu (filet mignon, seafood, pizza, and sandwiches) and homemade desserts. The place has a lot of character, a good decor, and is in the heart of Westminster. The 1913 building opened as a restaurant in 1994.

### IRISH

**O'Lordans Irish Pub** (14 Liberty St., 410/876-0000, www.olordansirishpub.com, Sun. and Tues.-Thurs. 11am-10pm, Fri.-Sat. 11am-11pm, $8-30) is a lively spot on Liberty Street. The pub has a traditional Irish pub feel with a fireplace, murals, dark wood, plank floors, and a stone facade. The bartenders are witty, and the food portions are ginormous and delicious. The pub offers a great happy hour menu and has developed a loyal fan base.

### MEXICAN

**Papa Joe's Mexican Restaurant** (250 Englar Rd., 410/871-2505, www.papajoeswestminstermd.com, Mon.-Sat. 11am-10pm, $9-18) is the local favorite for Mexican food. They offer traditional Mexican dishes in a friendly, colorful atmosphere. The restaurant is family owned and operated, and they have fun specials such as a salsa bar night on Monday. The fajitas are a signature dish and come smothered in a wonderful cream sauce, which is a little different from

traditional fajitas. Seating is limited, but there is outdoor seating when the weather is nice.

### TEAROOM

The best tearoom in Westminster (okay, maybe it's the only tearoom in Westminster, but it's a good one) is **Gypsy's Tearoom** (111 Stoner Ave., 410/857-0058, www.gypsystearoom.com, Tues.-Sat. 10am-5pm, $9-30) in the oldest home in Westminster, which was built by town founder William Winchester. This English-style tearoom serves everything from tea with hors d'oeuvres to full-service dinners. They also offer event planning for special occasions. The tearoom is located in a rural setting near town. It also has a gift shop.

## Accommodations

Accommodations right in Westminster are mainly limited to chain hotels such as the **Westminster Days Inn** (25 S. Cranberry Rd., 410/857-0500, www.daysinn.com, $79-89), and the **Best Western Westminster Catering and Conference Center** (451 WMC Dr., 410/857-1900, www.book.bestwestern.com, $113-117).

Eight miles southwest of town on the way to New Windsor is the **Yellow Turtle Inn Bed and Brunch** (111 S. Springdale Ave., New Windsor, 410/635-3000, www.yellowturtleinn.net, $120-199). This lovely bed-and-breakfast sits on three acres in the country and offers eight guest rooms with private bathrooms and two whirlpool suites.

## Information and Services

Additional information on Westminster can be found at the **Carroll County Visitor Center** (210 E. Main St., 410/848-1388, www.carrollcountytourism.org, Mon.-Sat. 9am-5pm, Sun. 10am-2pm).

## Getting There

Westminster is 35 miles northwest of Baltimore and 56 miles north of Washington DC. Route 140 runs through Westminster from east to west and Route 97 runs north to south.

# Annapolis and Southern Maryland

C apital city Annapolis has been the crown jewel of Maryland throughout its rich history. The city is known as the sailing capital of the world, as the birthplace of American horse racing, and for having more 18th-century buildings than any other city in the United States. Annapolis has remained extremely well preserved as a colonial-era town despite its popularity with tourists and businesses. It is a fun place to visit, a great place to people-watch, and a fantastic place to eat seafood.

Southern Maryland offers a relaxed atmosphere compared to the bustle of Annapolis. The cities along the western shore of the Chesapeake Bay vary from sleepy seaside towns to active sailing communities. Crisscrossed with scenic roadways and state and national parks, this area makes for a lovely excursion.

## PLANNING YOUR TIME

Annapolis and Southern Maryland can be explored in a long weekend or over several day trips from Baltimore. The distance between Annapolis and Point Lookout is approximately 82 miles (about two hours by car). Annapolis and Solomons Island are good choices for overnight stays or for boating on the Chesapeake Bay.

The closest airport to Annapolis is **Baltimore Washington International Thurgood Marshall Airport (BWI)** (410/859-7040, www.bwiairport.com), but parts of Southern Maryland are actually closer to **Ronald Reagan Washington National Airport (DCA)** (703/417-8000, www.metwashairports.com), just outside Washington DC in Arlington, Virginia (Point Lookout is 79 miles from DCA and 99 miles from BWI). Normally, the lowest airfares can be obtained by flying into BWI, so it pays to explore both options. Once you arrive in the region, it is best to explore by car. Parking is plentiful except for right in downtown Annapolis, but even there, most hotels have parking available and public garages can be found.

---

**Previous:** the docks at Sandy Point State Park; Maryland State House. **Above:** Annapolis Harbor.

Look for ★ to find recommended
sights, activities, dining, and lodging.

# Highlights

★ **Annapolis City Dock:** This public waterfront boasts beautiful scenery, impressive yachts, and many shops and restaurants (page 72).

★ **U.S. Naval Academy:** More than 60,000 men and women have graduated from this prestigious school and gone on to serve in the U.S. Navy and Marine Corps (page 72).

★ **Calvert Marine Museum:** This wonderful museum shares the whole history of the Chesapeake Bay, focusing on prehistoric times, the natural environment, and the bay's unique maritime heritage (page 86).

★ **Calvert Cliffs State Park:** More than just a beautiful sandy beach with stunning cliffs, this park offers superb fossil hunting (page 88).

★ **St. Mary's City's Outdoor Museum of History and Archaeology:** This living re-creation teaches visitors about life in Maryland's original capital city during colonial times (page 90).

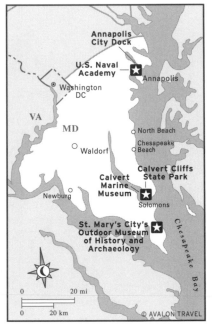

# Annapolis and Southern Maryland

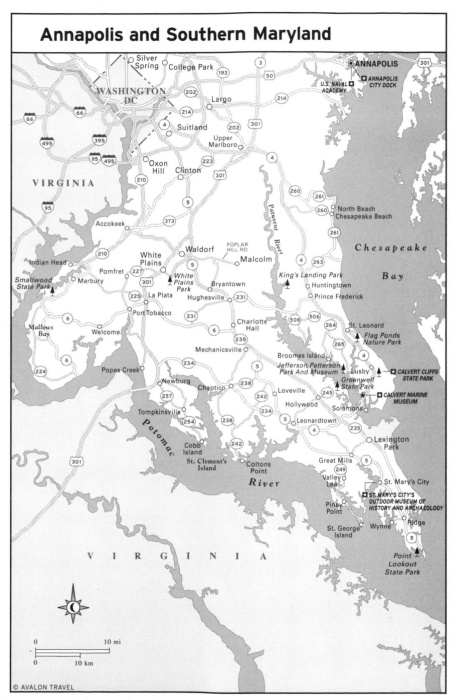

© AVALON TRAVEL

# Annapolis

Maryland's capital city of Annapolis is a picturesque and historic seaport on the Chesapeake Bay. It is widely known as the "Sailing Capital of the World," due to its popularity as a sailing port for both resident and international vessels. Literally hundreds of sailboats cruise the surrounding waters year-round, with regular races being held several times a week during the summer.

In 1649, a settlement named Providence was founded on the northern shore of the Severn River by Puritans exiled from Virginia. The settlement was later moved to the southern shore and renamed several times before finally becoming Annapolis, a tribute to Princess Anne of Denmark and Norway, who was in line to be the queen of Great Britain. The city was incorporated in 1708. Annapolis prospered as a port and grew substantially during the 18th century. It even served as the temporary capital of the United States in 1783.

From its earliest days more than 300 years ago, Annapolis was known as a center for wealth, social activities, and a thriving cultural scene. It was also known for its cozy pubs and abundant seafood restaurants, which welcomed prosperous visitors from all over the globe. Annapolis was also the birthplace of American horse racing—several of the original stock of the American Thoroughbred line entered through its port, and people came from all over the colonies to watch and bet on horse races. George Washington is even said to have lost a few shillings at the local track.

Annapolis is a great place to visit and explore. It has a vibrant waterfront with many shops and restaurants, and is quaint and historical, yet welcomes an international crowd. The city was designed more like the capital cities in Europe with a baroque plan, rather than the grid layout customary to U.S. cities. Circles with radiating streets highlight specific buildings, such as St. Anne's Episcopal Church (one of the first churches in the city) and the State House. Numerous magnificent homes were built in the city's early days and hosted many of the founders of our country for lavish social events. Today Annapolis it is home to the U.S. Naval Academy and St. John's College.

The most popular neighborhood for visitors is the Historic Downtown area. This is where the scenic waterfront and City Dock are located, as well as charming boutiques, fabulous restaurants, and historic homes. Another popular tourist area is Eastport, just south of Historic Downtown. This area is home to "Restaurant Row" and offers sweeping Chesapeake Bay views and a fun-loving, slightly funky atmosphere.

## SIGHTS
### ★ Annapolis City Dock
The **Annapolis City Dock** (Dock Street on the waterfront) is the heart of the downtown area. Annapolis boasts more 18th-century buildings than any other American city, and many of these charming structures line the dock area. Locally owned shops, boutiques, and souvenir stands beckoning shoppers off the busy streets and waterfront restaurants help fuel the energy of this hot spot. The public waterfront is where visitors can take in the beautiful scenery while getting a good look at many expensive yachts. The waterfront area is also known as **Ego Alley,** since a steady parade of high-end sailing and motor vessels can be seen going by on nearly every weekend and evening.

### ★ U.S. Naval Academy
The **U.S. Naval Academy** (121 Blake Rd., 410/293-1000, www.usna.edu) was founded in 1845 by the secretary of the navy. Since that time, more than 60,000 men and women have graduated from this prestigious school and gone on to serve in the U.S. Navy or the U.S. Marine Corps. The student body is referred

# Annapolis

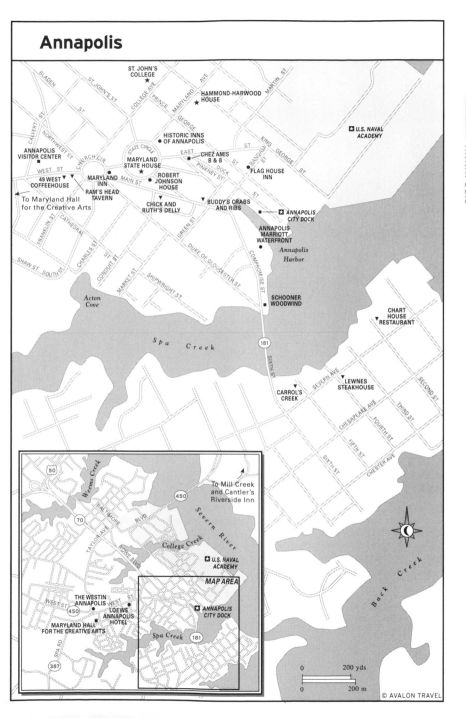

ST. JOHN'S COLLEGE

HAMMOND-HARWOOD HOUSE

U.S. NAVAL ACADEMY

HISTORIC INNS OF ANNAPOLIS

ANNAPOLIS VISITOR CENTER

CHEZ AMIS B & B

MARYLAND STATE HOUSE

FLAG HOUSE INN

49 WEST COFFEEHOUSE

MARYLAND INN

ROBERT JOHNSON HOUSE

RAM'S HEAD TAVERN

To Maryland Hall for the Creative Arts

CHICK AND RUTH'S DELLY

BUDDY'S CRABS AND RIBS

ANNAPOLIS CITY DOCK

ANNAPOLIS MARRIOTT WATERFRONT

Annapolis Harbor

Acton Cove

SCHOONER WOODWIND

CHART HOUSE RESTAURANT

Spa Creek

181

SIXTH ST

SEVERN AVE

LEWNES STEAKHOUSE

SECOND ST

CARROL'S CREEK

CHESAPEAKE AVE

THIRD ST

FOURTH ST

FIFTH ST

SIXTH ST

CHESTER AVE

50

Weems Creek

To Mill Creek and Cantler's Riverside Inn

450

BALTIMORE BLVD

70

Severn River

TAYLOR AVE

ROWE BLVD

College Creek

U.S. NAVAL ACADEMY

MAP AREA

Back Creek

THE WESTIN ANNAPOLIS

WEST ST

450

LOEWS ANNAPOLIS HOTEL

ANNAPOLIS CITY DOCK

MARYLAND HALL FOR THE CREATIVE ARTS

SPA RD

Spa Creek

181

387

0          200 yds

0          200 m

© AVALON TRAVEL

Annapolis City Dock

# The Life of the Chesapeake Bay

The Chesapeake Bay is the largest estuary in the country. Its drainage basin includes more than 64,000 square miles with more than 150 tributaries. The bay is approximately 200 miles long, starting at the mouth of the Susquehanna River on the northern end and the Atlantic Ocean on the southern end. At its widest point it is 30 miles across, and at its narrowest point it is 2.8 miles.

The Chesapeake Bay is part of the **Intracoastal Waterway,** a 3,000-mile navigable inland water route that runs along the Atlantic and Gulf coasts. The bay links the Delaware River with the Albemarle Sound in North Carolina.

More than 300 species of fish and countless shellfish live in the Chesapeake Bay. Maryland is known for its abundant local seafood, especially the famed blue crab, which can be found on nearly every menu in the region.

Many shorebirds live all or part of their lives on the Chesapeake Bay or in the bordering wetlands, including bald eagles, great blue herons, ospreys, peregrine falcons, and piping plovers.

The Chesapeake Bay is a prominent feature in Maryland. During the second half of the 19th century and the first half of the 20th, the bay was a vital link between major cities in Maryland and Virginia, such as Baltimore and Norfolk, and was home to passenger steamships and packet boats (boats that kept regular schedules and were originally designed to transport mail, passengers, and freight). When road crossings were built in the late 20th century, making the steamboat industry obsolete, the bay became known for its seafood production, with a focus on the blue crab and oyster industries. By the mid-20th century, nearly 9,000 full-time watermen worked on the bay. Plentiful oyster harvests were the inspiration for Maryland's state boat, the **skipjack,** which remains the only type of working boat in the country that operates under sail.

Today, the Chesapeake Bay produces less seafood than it did in the last century due to runoff from many mainland areas, overharvesting, and the invasion of foreign marine species. The **Chesapeake Bay Foundation** (www.cbf.org), headquartered in Annapolis, is the largest conservation organization dedicated to the well-being of the Chesapeake Bay watershed.

to as the "Brigade of Midshipmen." The academy is directly northeast of downtown Annapolis at the confluence of the Severn River and the Chesapeake Bay. Guided walking tours of the more than 300-acre campus led by professional guides are offered to visitors through the **Armel-Leftwich Visitor Center** (52 King George St., 410/293-8687, www.usnabsd.com, Mar.-Dec. daily 9am-5pm, Jan. and Feb. Mon.-Fri. 9am-4pm, Sat.-Sun. 9am-5pm, $10.50). Tours are 1.25 hours and are offered throughout most of the day while the visitors center is open; they cannot be booked in advance. Tours provide a close-up look at the imposing marble buildings and monuments on campus, and cover topics such as history, architecture, traditions, and life as a midshipman.

Access to the Naval Academy grounds is limited. Government-issued photo identification is required for admission. Parking is available at the stadium on Rowe Boulevard inside the Noah Hillman Parking Garage (enter from Duke of Gloucester or Main Street). There are also parking meters around City Dock.

## Maryland State House

The **Maryland State House** (100 State Circle, 410/260-6445, www.msa.maryland. gov, daily 9am-5pm, free, donations appreciated) is the oldest legislative house in the country that has been in continual use. It is also the oldest peacetime capitol. The State House was built in the 1770s, and the first Maryland legislature meeting was held here in 1779. The building is architecturally significant—its dome is the largest wooden dome constructed without nails in the United States.

During 1783 and 1784, when Annapolis served as the U.S. capital, the State House was home to the U.S. government. It was there that two significant events took place. The first was that George Washington resigned his commission before the Continental Congress on December 23, 1783, and the second was that the Treaty of Paris ending the Revolutionary War was ratified here on January 14, 1784. Self-guided tour information is available on the first floor of the State House.

## St. John's College

**St. John's College** (60 College Ave.,

the Maryland State House

410/263-2371, www.sjca.edu) is the oldest college in town, despite the misconception that this distinction belongs to the U.S. Naval Academy. The school was founded in 1696 as the King William's School. It is the third-oldest college in the country behind Harvard and William & Mary. One block from the State House (across King George Street from the Naval Academy), the school sits on 32 scenic acres adorned with stately brick buildings, tree-lined paths, and sprawling lawn. It is also a National Historic Landmark with several 18th-century buildings.

St. John's College offers a liberal arts curriculum. Because of its location at the confluence of the Chesapeake Bay and the Severn River, the school offers strong sailing, crew, and rowing opportunities. Each April, St. John's College and the Naval Academy play each other in a highly anticipated croquet match on the front lawn of the St. John's campus. Both teams dress for the event, which has become a spirited spectacle.

St. John's College adopted the "Great Books" program of study in 1937. This mandatory four-year program requires students to read Western civilization's prominent authors in philosophy, theology, math, science, poetry, music, and literature. Classes are then discussion based. The school uses a series of manuals in place of textbooks, lectures, and exams. Grades are only released at the student's request and are based on papers and class participation.

## Hammond-Harwood House

There are many historic homes in Annapolis. If you can only choose one to visit, the **Hammond-Harwood House** (19 Maryland Ave., 410/263-4683, www.hammondharwoodhouse.org, Apr.-Dec. Tues.-Sun. noon-5pm, Jan.-Mar. appointment only, $10) should be it. It is one of the most superb British colonial homes in the country and the most impressive in Annapolis. Designed in the Anglo-Palladian style (a variation of the classical Roman revival style), construction began on the house in 1774. It was completed

sometime after 1776, but the exact year is unknown. The home is special because it offers perfectly preserved architecture and one of the best collections of furniture and decorative art from the 18th century in Maryland. It is a National Historic Landmark.

Fifty-minute walk-in tours begin at the top of each hour and provide insight into the history of the house, information on its architect and the people who lived in the home, and the opportunity to learn about the collections, such as a large collection of the works of Charles Willson Peale, a painter well known for his Revolutionary War period portraits. Visitors can also tour the garden at no extra cost. In-depth, two-hour architectural tours of the home are offered by appointment for $20.

## St. Anne's Episcopal Church

**St. Anne's Episcopal Church** (1 Church Circle, 410/267-9333, www.stannes-annapolis.org, free) was the first church in Annapolis. The original structure was established in 1692 and completed in 1704 and was one of 30 original Anglican parishes in Maryland. Its bell was donated by Queen Anne. The original 65-foot-by-30-foot structure was razed in 1775 to make way for reconstruction of the second St. Anne's Episcopal Church on the same grounds. Building of the new church was delayed due to the Revolutionary War but was finally finished in 1792. The new church was larger and more structurally sound, but burned down on Valentine's Day in 1858 due to a furnace fire. The church that stands in Church Circle today was built in 1858 (although the steeple was finished in 1866). Its design incorporated part of the old tower. The clock in the church steeple actually belongs to the city due to a special agreement it made with the church when a city clock was needed. Visitors to St. Anne's can examine the church's Romanesque revival architecture with its original archways, pews, and stained glass windows. They can also visit the first cemetery in the city, which is located on the grounds. Four Sunday worship services are held weekly at 8am, 9:30am, 11:15am, and 5:30pm.

# ENTERTAINMENT AND EVENTS

## Nightlife

Annapolis harbors one of the best little venues in the mid-Atlantic for intimate concerts with big-name artists. **Rams Head on Stage** (33 West St., 410/268-4545, www.ramsheadonstage.com) is the performance venue at the popular **Rams Head Tavern** (www.ramsheadtavern.com), which has been a fixture in Annapolis for more than two decades. Rams Head on Stage is a reserved-seating venue with food and drink service during the shows. Nearly all shows at this venue are 21 and older. There are no bad seats in the house, and the bands play right in front of the tables. Samples of recent performances include the Smithereens, Cowboy Junkies, The English Beat, and Los Lobos.

The **49 West Coffeehouse, Winebar & Gallery** (49 West St., 410/626-9796, www.49westcoffeehouse.com) is a great place to kick back and enjoy coffee or a great martini (depending on the time of day) and listen to jazz. They host live music most nights and jazz for brunch on Sunday. The establishment is also an art gallery and features different artists monthly. They offer a neighborhood feel near the downtown area and serve breakfast, lunch, and dinner daily.

## Performing Arts

The **Maryland Hall for the Creative Arts** (801 Chase St., 410/263-5544, www.marylandhall.org) is an active center for the performing arts. Resident companies include a symphony, opera, ballet, and chorale, offering performances throughout the year in the 800-seat theater.

## Events

The **Maryland Renaissance Festival** (1821 Crownsville Rd., Crownsville, 410/266-7304, www.rennfest.com) is a long-standing tradition in Maryland. After passing through the entry gates to the festival, visitors become part of a wooded, 25-acre 16th-century English village named "Revel Grove." There are plenty of activities to keep the entire family busy, with shows on 10 major stages, a jousting arena, games, crafts, five pubs, and of course, tons of delicious food. The festival is open on Saturday, Sunday, and Labor Day Monday from the end of August through late October. The festival is held in Crownsville, eight miles northwest of Annapolis.

Many events are scheduled throughout the year in Annapolis, including several footraces such as the **Annapolis Ten Miler** (www.annapolisstriders.org), festivals, food celebrations, and art shows. For a list of events, visit www.downtownannapolis.org.

## SHOPPING

There are many boutiques and locally owned shops in downtown Annapolis. Maryland Avenue, Main Street, and West Street are great places to start a shopping adventure. Some examples of the types of stores you can browse include jewelry stores, maritime stores, home furnishings shops, women's boutiques, antiques stores, glass shops, and fine-art galleries.

---

# They'll Scare Ya Sober

Sometimes referred to as "a drinking town with a sailing problem," Annapolis has long known how to get its drink on. The city is filled with all kinds of history, including tales of hair-raising hauntings at local watering holes. **Annapolis Tours and Crawls** (443/534-0043, www.toursandcrawls.com, $18) offers a great two-hour haunted pub crawl through the downtown area. They take guests through some of the most haunted taverns, pubs, and bars while telling stories that are sure to give you goose bumps. Each stop is about 30 minutes and can be different each time. This drinking tour is a great way to learn the history of some of the best taverns in town, with an added twist. Tours meet at the top of Main Street and are for people 21 and over.

# SPORTS AND RECREATION

Two-hour sailing cruises can be booked on two beautiful, 74-foot wooden schooners through **Schooner *Woodwind* Annapolis Sailing Cruises** (410/263-7837, www.schoonerwoodwind.com, mid-Apr.-late Oct. daily, $44). Cruises depart from the **Annapolis Waterfront Hotel** (across from the City Dock) and sail by the U.S. Naval Academy and into the Chesapeake Bay. Private cruises can also be booked.

**Pirate Adventures on the Chesapeake** (311 3rd St., 410/263-0002, www.chesapeakepirates.com, mid-Apr.-Memorial Day and Labor Day-Oct. Sat.-Sun., Memorial Day-Labor Day daily, sail times at 9:30am, 11am, 12:30pm, 2pm, 3:30pm, and 5pm, $22) is a children's adventure aboard a pirate ship. Kids quickly become part of a pirate tale with face painting, costumes, and a lot of imagination. Once aboard, they learn the rules of the ship, read treasure maps, and find a message in a bottle. They even engage in battle using water cannons. Cruises leave from the company's office in Annapolis. Face painting and dress-up begin 30 minutes prior to departure; sailing time is 75 minutes.

The **Baltimore & Annapolis Trail** (www.traillink.com/trail/baltimore-and-annapolis-trail.aspx) is a 13-mile paved rail trail that is part of the former route of the Baltimore & Annapolis Railroad. It opened in 1990 and runs from Boulters Way in Annapolis to Dorsey Road in Glen Burnie. The southern part of the trail is primarily residential and winds through pleasant suburban neighborhoods. The northern part of the trail is much more urban.

An extremely popular nearby park right on the Chesapeake Bay is **Sandy Point State Park** (1100 E. College Pkwy., 410/974-2149, www.dnr.state.md.us, daily Jan.-Oct. 7am-sunset, Nov.-Dec. 7am-5pm, boating 24 hours year-round, $7). This lovely 786-acre park, 10 miles northeast of Annapolis at the western terminus of the Chesapeake Bay Bridge, used to be the site of a ferry that shuttled people and cars between the mainland and the Eastern Shore prior to completion of the bridge. Today it offers a wide sandy beach, swimming area, bathhouse, boat landing, picnic areas, and stunning view of the Chesapeake Bay. It is also a great place for bird-watching. The park is off Route 50 at exit 32.

# FOOD
## American

The premier steak house in Annapolis is ★ **Lewnes Steakhouse** (401 4th St., 410/263-1617, www.lewnessteakhouse.com, Sun. 4pm-10pm, Mon.-Thurs. 4pm-10pm, Fri.-Sat. 4pm-10:30pm, $19-44). This independent restaurant opened in 1921 and is still owned by the same local family. They serve prime steak that is properly prepared to sear in the flavorful juice while browning the exterior. Their menu includes filet, prime rib, porterhouse, New York strip, rib eye, and some non-beef selections such as tuna steak and lobster. They also have an extensive, well-selected wine list. The food and wonderful staff are the lure of this restaurant, and the atmosphere is well suited for a romantic evening. This is a restaurant that really cares whether the guests are satisfied.

A local institution, the **Rams Head Tavern** (33 West St., 410/268-4545, www.ramsheadtavern.com, Sun. 10am-2am with brunch, Mon.-Sat. 11am-2am, $9-30) has been serving tasty pub food since 1989. This friendly, multiroom tavern (including the original space in the cozy downstairs) serves sandwiches, burgers, and pub favorites such as shepherd's pie, brats and mash, chicken stuffed with crab imperial, and shrimp and grits. They have a terrific brunch menu on Sunday with a wonderful variety of entrées that are beautifully presented. They also serve beer from the Fordham Brewing Company, which used to be on-site. The atmosphere is classically "pub" with warm, friendly service and convivial patrons. This can be a busy place on concert nights at the adjoining Rams Head on Stage.

Quarter-pound crab cakes with no filler,

seasoned to perfection, are the calling card of a local favorite named ★ **Chick & Ruth's Delly** (165 Main St., 410/269-6737, www. chickandruths.com, daily 6:30am-11:30pm, $6-33). Just a block from the State House, the sandwich shop was opened by Chick and Ruth Levitt in 1965, and it has been growing ever since. Specialty sandwiches named after politicians augment the traditional Jewish deli fare, along with seafood, pizza, wraps, burgers, and tasty ice-cream treats. This is a touch of New York with an Annapolis flair. They are open for breakfast, lunch, and dinner.

**Vin 909 Winecafe** (909 Bay Ridge Ave., 410/990-1846, www.vin909.com, $12-19) is a wine-tasting café. They offer more than 35 types of wine by the glass and an extensive selection of beer. The café is in what once was a private residence, a bit off the beaten path south of the historic area of Annapolis (across Spa Creek). Prices for wine and food are reasonable, and there is frequently a wait for a table. They specialize in pizza, panini, and plates to share. The ambience is cozy and modern with wooden floors and low lighting. There is an outdoor patio with seating when the weather is nice.

## Crab Houses

If you like seafood, you can't visit Annapolis without eating local blue crabs. *The* place to go for the authentic crab house experience is ★ **Cantler's Riverside Inn** (458 Forest Beach Rd., 410/757-1311, www.cantlers.com, Sun.-Thurs. 11am-10pm, Fri.-Sat. 11am-11pm, $8-32), a short distance from the downtown area and accessible by both car and boat. It is situated on a cove right on the water in a mostly residential neighborhood and sells local steamed crabs by the dozen (in all sizes) as well as offering other fresh seafood like crab cakes, shrimp, and oysters. They also serve pizza and sandwiches for non-seafood eaters. This is not a fancy place; it is a place to relax, get messy picking crabs, and meet new friends. They have indoor seating, a covered deck, and outdoor picnic tables. This used to be where the locals went, but in recent years it has become a popular tourist restaurant also. They also have a large bar inside the dining room. Word of warning: Don't rub your eyes with Old Bay seasoning on your hands.

Another popular crab house right in the historic downtown area is **Buddy's Crabs and Ribs** (100 Main St., 410/626-1100, www.buddysonline.com, Mon.-Thurs.

the Reuben sandwich at Chick & Ruth's Delly, made with freshly baked rye bread

# Feeling Crabby?

Cantler's Riverside Inn in Annapolis offers an authentic crab house experience.

Maryland is known for its blue crabs, and the full "crab" experience can be enjoyed at a number of traditional crab houses throughout the bay region. For those new to the authentic crab experience, be prepared that this is a casual event, but not necessarily a cheap one. Traditional crab houses will often have long tables spread with brown paper and equipped with wooden mallets, claw crackers, and picks. Cold beer can accompany the appetizer, main course, and dessert. Patrons bring a lot of time, good cheer, and their appetites. Eating crabs is a social and messy event, but it is also one of the best experiences on the Chesapeake Bay.

Where to crack a claw:

- **Abner's Crab House** (3748 Harbor Rd., Chesapeake Beach, 410/257-3689, www.abnerscrabhouse.com)

- **Bo Brooks Crab House** (2780 Lighthouse Point, Baltimore, 410/558-0202, www.bobrooks.com)

- **Cantler's Riverside Inn** (458 Forest Beach Rd., Annapolis, 410/757-1311, www.cantlers.com)

- **Captain James Crab House** (2127 Boston St., Baltimore, 410/327-8600, www.captainjameslanding.com)

- **Hamilton's Canton Dockside** (3301 Boston St., Baltimore, 410/276-8900, www.cantondockside.com)

- **Mike's Restaurant and Crab House** (3030 Riva Rd., Riva, 410/956-2784, www.mikescrabhouse.com)

- **Thursday's Steak and Crabhouse** (4851 Riverside Dr., Galesville, 410/867-7200)

11:30am-9:30pm, Fri. 11:30am-10pm, Sat. 11am-11pm, Sun. 9:30am-9pm, $11-39). This lively icon on Main Street is a family-owned restaurant and also the largest restaurant in Annapolis. They specialize in serving large groups and also give special pricing to kids. Steamed crabs are the entrée of choice at Buddy's, but the homemade crab cakes are also a front-runner. Buddy's has a wide menu for both the seafood lover and the non-seafood eater and offers three all-you-can-eat buffets. The first is their soup, salad, and pasta bar for $8.95 (offered Mon.-Fri. 11:30am-3pm), the second is their seafood dinner buffet for $22.95 (Fri. 4pm-9pm and Sat. 11am-9pm), and the third is their Sunday brunch for $14.95 (Sun. 9:30am-1:30pm).

## Italian

If you're looking for good pizza in a family atmosphere and want to get away from the crowds of the downtown area, go to **Squisito Pizza and Pasta** (2625 Riva Rd., 410/266-1474, www.squisitopizzaandpasta. com, Sun.-Thurs. 11am-10pm, Fri.-Sat. 11am-11pm, $7-16). This casual restaurant serves delicious pizza, pasta, and sandwiches at very reasonable prices. They are a small franchised chain with a handful of locations (all in Maryland). Order at the main counter and then take a seat. A server will bring you your meal. This is a very casual restaurant that is popular with families with children.

## Seafood

A great place for local seafood and waterfront dining is **Carrol's Creek** (410 Severn Ave., 410/263-8102, www.carrolscreek.com, Mon.-Thurs. 11:30am-9pm, Fri.-Sat. 11:30am-10pm, Sun. 10am-8:30pm, $7-34). A short walk from the historic area across the Spa Creek Bridge, the bright-red building is easy to spot along Restaurant Row in Eastport. The menu offers local seafood, fresh fish, steak, chicken, and vegetarian dishes. Their Southwestern scallops are to die for. They also have a large wine list. The restaurant is locally owned and run, and much of the staff has been there

for decades. There is plenty of free parking. Reservations are recommended (ask for a seat by the windows).

The **Chart House Restaurant** (300 2nd St., 410/268-7166, www.chart-house.com, brunch Sun. 10am-2pm, dinner Mon.-Thurs. 4:30pm-9pm, Fri.-Sat. 4:30pm-10pm, Sun. 2pm-9pm, $20-43) offers fantastic waterfront views of the City Dock and is within walking distance of the historic district. The restaurant is a part of an upscale national chain and is housed in a nice historic building. The menu is heavily weighted toward seafood and steak, with fresh fish, crab, lobster, filet, and surf and turf. They also offer chicken and salads. The food and decor are above average, which is reflected in the prices, but the restaurant has a great location and the service is excellent. Reservations are recommended.

Another lovely waterfront restaurant is the **Severn Inn** (1993 Baltimore Annapolis Blvd., 410/349-4000, www.severninn.com, Sun. brunch buffet 10am-2pm, $36; lunch Mon.-Sat. 11:30am-2:30pm, dinner Mon.-Sat. 5pm-close, closed Mon. Jan.-Mar., $14-45), situated on the east side of the Naval Academy Bridge, overlooking Annapolis and the Severn River. They describe themselves as a "modern American seafood house" and serve local and nonlocal seafood and other dishes such as a wonderful filet mignon. They have a pleasant decor inside with white tablecloths and a comfortable, yet airy feel to the dining room as well as a large waterfront deck with pretty blue market umbrellas (open after April). Sunset is especially scenic, and if you're an oyster lover, grabbing a drink and a few oysters while watching the sun go down is a combination that's hard to beat.

## ACCOMMODATIONS
### $100-200

If you are looking for charming accommodations in a historic property, the **Historic Inns of Annapolis** (58 State Circle, 410/263-2641, www.historicinnsofannapolis. com, $120-270) offers three boutique hotels housed in 17th- and 18th- century buildings.

The **Maryland Inn** (16 Church Circle) has 44 guest rooms within view of the State House, Main Street, and the waterfront. The inn was built in the late 1700s and has hosted presidents, statesmen, and political dignitaries. The decor includes Victorian-era furnishings. It has a fitness center on-site, a restaurant, and a Starbucks. The **Governor Calvert House** (58 State Circle) is across the street from the Maryland State House and is one of the oldest buildings in Annapolis (built in 1695). It has 51 guest rooms, a colonial garden, meeting space, Internet, cable television, and views of the State House. Rooms are small, but this was originally a private home and was even the residence of two former Maryland governors. This property is where guests for all three historic properties check in. The **Robert Johnson House** (23 State Circle) is a smaller hotel with 29 guest rooms. This brick home was built in 1773 and has views of the Governor's Mansion and the State House. The house has Georgian-style architecture and is furnished with 19th-century furniture.

An alternative in this price range is the

**Hampton Inn & Suites Annapolis** (124 Womack Dr., 410/571-0200, www.hamptoninn3.hilton.com, $109-134). The hotel is in a business park four miles from the historic area of Annapolis. The 117 rooms are comfortable and come with complimentary wireless Internet, a mini fridge, 37-inch television, and free breakfast. The hotel is pet friendly.

## $200-300

For a comfy bed-and-breakfast stay, the lovely ★ **Chez Amis Bed and Breakfast** (85 East St., 410/263-6631, www.chezamis.com, $202-228) offers four beautiful rooms and wonderful service. Each room in this 1890s home has a private bathroom, a television, and free wireless Internet. A delicious three-course breakfast is served each day at 9am, and cookies and refreshments are available all day. The bed-and-breakfast is within walking distance to downtown Annapolis, but a complimentary shuttle is offered to restaurants. The owners live in the bottom floor of the home.

The **Flag House Inn** (26 Randall St., 410/280-2721, www.flaghouseinn.com,

Governor Calvert House

$189-350) is a wonderful bed-and-breakfast with off-street parking in historic Annapolis. Just a half block from the City Dock, this comfortable, friendly inn is a great home base for exploring Annapolis. They offer four guest rooms and a two-room suite with private bathrooms and a full hot breakfast each morning.

## Over $300

Fabulous waterfront views can be found at the **Annapolis Waterfront Hotel** (80 Compromise St., 888/773-0786, www. annapoliswaterfront.com, $335-599). This Marriott hotel is the only waterfront hotel in Annapolis, and many of the rooms overlook the Chesapeake Bay and some have balconies (other rooms view Annapolis Harbor and the downtown area). The hotel is walking distance to historic attractions, shopping, restaurants, and the Naval Academy. Allergy-free rooms are available. The hotel offers standard amenities such as a fitness center and meeting facilities. Valet parking and Internet service are available for an additional fee. Their waterfront restaurant, **Pusser's Caribbean Grille,** is a popular dining spot for seafood and also offers great views. This premium location doesn't come cheap, but if you are after a room with a view, it delivers.

The **Westin Annapolis** (100 Westgate Circle, 410/972-4300, www.westinannapolis. com, $299-459) is an immaculate, top-notch hotel a short distance from all the action in downtown Annapolis. The 225 guest rooms are spacious and modern, and there's a lovely, well-stocked bar in the lobby. Free shuttle service is available to the downtown area, and there is parking on-site. There are an indoor pool and fitness center, and the hotel is pet friendly.

The **Loews Annapolis Hotel** (126 West St., 410/263-7777, www.loewshotels.com, $309-409) is a lovely hotel in downtown Annapolis within walking distance to many attractions (10 minutes to the City Dock). The bright, nautical decor is perfect for the hotel's location, and the 216 guest rooms are

luxurious and large (there are also 18 suites). Parking is available on-site for an additional fee ($18 for self-parking and $22 for valet), and there is a complimentary local shuttle service operating throughout the historic district. There are a fitness room and spa (no pool) for hotel guests, and wireless Internet service is available in guest rooms for an additional fee. There is also a restaurant on-site.

## INFORMATION AND SERVICES

For additional information on Annapolis, stop in the **Annapolis & Anne Arundel County Conference and Visitors Bureau** (26 West St., 410/280-0445, daily 9am-5pm) or visit www.visitannapolis.org.

## GETTING THERE

Most people arrive in Annapolis by car. The city is a quick 45-minute drive east from Washington DC (32 miles) via U.S. 50 and about 30 minutes (26 miles) south of the Inner Harbor in Baltimore (via I-97).

Annapolis is 22 miles from **Baltimore Washington International Thurgood Marshall Airport (BWI)** (410/859-7040, www.bwiairport.com). Private shuttle service can be arranged from the airport to Annapolis through **Annapolis Airport Shuttle** (410/971-8100, www.annapolisairportshuttle. com) or by limousine through **Lighthouse Limousine** (410/798-8881, www. lighthouselimousines.com).

## GETTING AROUND

Parking can be challenging in the downtown area but **The Circulator** (410/216-9436, www.parkannapolis.com, every 10 minutes Sun.-Thurs. 6:30am-midnight, Fri.-Sat. 6:30am-2:30am) is a great way to move around Annapolis. It is a trolley service that provides free transportation around the central business district and stops at four downtown parking garages. The four garages are **Gotts Court Garage** (25 Northwest St., 410/972-4726, first hour $2, $15 maximum), the **Noah Hillman Garage** (150 Gorman St.,

410/267-8914, $2 an hour, $20 maximum), the **Knighton Garage** (corner of Colonial Ave. and West St., 410/263-7170, $1 first hour, $10 maximum), and the **Park Place Garage** (5 Park Pl., $1 an hour, $10 maximum). Stops are located along the trolley's loop route from Westgate Circle to Memorial Circle and start at the Westin Annapolis Hotel at Park Place. Trolleys also stop at popular areas such as Church Circle and City Dock. If you aren't at a stop but want to get on the trolley, simply raise your hand when one drives by and it will pull over to pick you up.

There is also metered parking at City Dock near Spa Creek, and there is a parking lot at the Navy Marine Corps Memorial Stadium

(off Rowe Blvd. on Taylor Avenue). Trolley rides from the stadium lot cost $2 since it is not within the central business district.

Two free shuttle buses also run from the stadium to downtown. The **Navy Blue Shuttle** runs to the historic area and west Annapolis with stops at the Naval Academy Main Gate and Church Circle. It leaves the stadium parking lot every half hour Monday-Friday 9am-6pm, and Saturday and Sunday 10am-6pm. The **State House Shuttle** operates on a loop between the stadium and the State Legislative Buildings. It leaves the stadium every 15 minutes (every 5 minutes during rush hour) Monday-Friday 6:30am-8pm.

# Southern Maryland

Southern Maryland contains a thousand miles of shoreline on the Chesapeake Bay and the Patuxent River. The region includes Calvert, Charles, and St. Mary's Counties and is a boater's playground, a bird-watcher's paradise, and a seafood lover's dream. Traditionally a rural agricultural area connected by steamboat routes, today Southern Maryland is traversed by scenic byways that connect charming towns and parks. The communities in the region have grown tremendously in recent decades and welcome tourists and those seeking outdoor recreation such as boating, fishing, crabbing, hiking, and biking.

## CHESAPEAKE BEACH

Chesapeake Beach is on the mainland in Calvert County about 45 minutes south of Annapolis (29 miles). The town was founded in 1894 by the Chesapeake Bay Railway Company and was intended to be a vacation destination for Washingtonians. The town thrived as such during the early 1900s when visitors arrived by train. Today, long after the railroad days, visitors can still enjoy nice views of the Chesapeake Bay, beach access, and charter fishing.

## Sights

A nice little museum that does a good job of presenting local history is the **Chesapeake Beach Railway Museum** (4155 Mears Ave., 410/257-3892, www.cbrm.org, hours vary by season, free). The small, three-room museum is housed in a restored train depot and provides information on the train that once ran between Chesapeake Beach and Washington DC. Artifacts, photos, maps, equipment, and postcards are on exhibit, and the volunteers are very friendly and helpful. The museum hosts many family events throughout the year.

If you're looking for summer fun and a break from the heat, bring the kids to the **Chesapeake Beach Water Park** (4079 Gordon Stinnett Blvd., 410/257-1404, www.chesapeakebeachwaterpark.com, daily mid-June-mid-Aug. Mon. 11am-6pm, Tues.-Sun. 11am-7pm, $21). It features eight waterslides, pools, fountains, waterfalls, and giant floating sea creatures to climb on. There are even "adult" swim times.

Surfing enthusiasts will enjoy spending an hour or two at **Bruce "Snake" Gabrielson's Surf Art Gallery and Museum** (Route 261, three miles south of Chesapeake Beach,

240/464-3301, www.hbsnakesurf.com, open evenings by appointment on Mon., Wed., and Thurs., free). Maryland's only surfing museum opened in 2012 and showcases the personal treasures collected by its founder, surfing legend Bruce Gabrielson, over the course of 60 years. Featured items include antique surfboards, photographs, and posters signed by various surfing legends. It is a little off the beaten path in the offices of the National Surf Schools and Instructors Association.

## Food

The two restaurants within the **Chesapeake Beach Hotel and Spa** (4165 Mears Ave., 410/257-5596, www.chesapeakebeachresortspa.com) are a couple of the best dining options in Chesapeake Beach. The **Rod 'N' Reel** (410/257-2735, daily 8am-2am, $10-33) serves breakfast, lunch, and dinner. They have a nice selection of sandwiches and seafood entrees and items from the land. They also have an extensive wine list. **Boardwalk Cafe** (Fri. 4pm-midnight, Sat. 11am-midnight, Sun. 11am-9pm, $8-25) is a casual restaurant on the resort boardwalk. They serve soup, salads, and casual seafood. It is a great spot to grab a drink and enjoy the scenery.

Another choice in Chesapeake Beach is the family-owned **Trader's Seafood Steak and Ale** (8132 Bayside Rd., 301/855-0766, www.traders-eagle.com, Sun. 7am-9pm, Mon.-Thurs. 8am-9pm, Fri.-Sat. 7am-10pm, $8-24), offering seafood, burgers, and other entrées for lunch and dinner and many traditional options for breakfast. The atmosphere is friendly and casual and they have a deck bar. They also have a breakfast buffet on Sunday (7am-1pm).

## Accommodations and Camping

The **Chesapeake Beach Resort and Spa** (4165 Mears Ave., 410/257-5596, www.chesapeakebeachresortspa.com, $169-382) is a well-maintained property with 72 guest rooms. The hotel is on the Chesapeake Bay waterfront, and some rooms have balconies overlooking the water. A full-service spa is on-site, and there is also a marina. There are two waterfront restaurants at the hotel, a fitness room, sauna, game room, and an indoor swimming pool. Complimentary continental breakfast is served on weekdays. Fishing charters can be arranged through the hotel.

**Breezy Point Beach and Campground** (5300 Breezy Point Rd., 410/535-0259, www.co.cal.md.us, May-Oct., $50 per night) is a public beach and campground six miles south of Chesapeake Beach at **Breezy Point Beach** (410/535-0259, May-Oct. daily 6am-dusk, $10). The half-mile beach has a swimming area, bathhouse, picnic area, playground, and a 300-foot fishing pier. The camping available May-October includes water and sewage. Multiple-night minimums may be required on certain days. No pets are allowed on the beach or in the campground.

## Information and Services

For additional information on Chesapeake Beach visit www.chesapeake-beach.md.us.

## SOLOMONS ISLAND

Solomons Island sits at the southern tip of Calvert County at the confluence of the Chesapeake Bay and the Patuxent River. It is about a 1.5-hour drive southeast from Washington DC (61 miles), a 1.75-hour drive south of Baltimore (81 miles), and an 80-minute drive (58 miles) south from Annapolis. It is connected to St. Mary's County by the **Governor Thomas Johnson Bridge,** a 1.5-mile bridge over the Patuxent River on Route 4.

Solomons was first settled by tobacco farmers, but a surge in the oyster industry following the Civil War led it into the oyster processing and boatbuilding trades. The town quickly became a shipbuilding, ship repair, and seafood harvesting stronghold. In the 1880s, the local fishing fleet counted more than 500 boats, and many of them had been built right in Solomons. Among these were "bugeyes," which were large, decked-over sailing canoes, mostly built from shaped logs. The

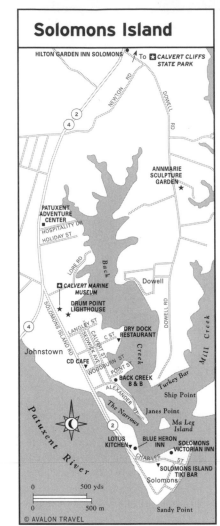

## Solomons Island

HILTON GARDEN INN SOLOMONS
To ◨ CALVERT CLIFFS STATE PARK
NEWTON RD
DOWELL RD
RD
2
4
ANNMARIE SCULPTURE GARDEN ★
PATUXENT ADVENTURE CENTER
HOSPITALITY DR
HOLIDAY ST
LORE RD
Back Creek
Dowell
◨ CALVERT MARINE MUSEUM
DRUM POINT LIGHTHOUSE ★
SOLOMONS ISLAND RD
DOWELL RD
4
LANGLEY ST
CALVERT ST
C ST
DRY DOCK RESTAURANT
Johnstown
SEDWICK AVE
CD CAFE ▼
WOODBURN ST
POINT ST
Creek
Mill Creek
BACK CREEK B & B ●
Turkey Bar
ALEXANDER ST
Ship Point
The Narrows
Janes Point
Patuxent
2
Ma Leg Island
LOTUS KITCHEN ▼
BLUE HERON INN ●
SOLOMONS VICTORIAN INN
CHARLES ST
River
▼ SOLOMONS ISLAND TIKI BAR
Solomons
0        500 yds
0        500 m
Sandy Point
© AVALON TRAVEL

recreation play an important role in Solomons' economy. It houses countless marinas, boat suppliers, charter boat companies, a pilot station, and other types of water-related business such as kayaking outfitters. Many restaurants and inns serve the influx of tourists to this beautiful waterside town.

## Sights
### ★ CALVERT MARINE MUSEUM
The **Calvert Marine Museum** (14200 Solomons Island Rd., 410/326-2042, www. calvertmarinemuseum.com, daily 10am-5pm, $9) does a wonderful job of sharing the story of the Chesapeake Bay, with exhibits on prehistoric times, the natural environment, and the bay's unique maritime heritage. There are three exhibit galleries totaling 29,000 square feet, including a discovery room with fossils, live animals (such as otters, fish, and rays), and a paleontology exhibit.

Behind the museum is a marsh walk that enables visitors to stroll over the salt marsh flats. Wildlife is abundant in the marsh, and you can expect to see signs of inhabitants such as raccoons, opossums, water snakes, crabs, herons, and ducks. This great natural exhibit is a living study of the local plant and animal life.

On the museum's waterfront is the iconic **Drum Point Lighthouse,** a "screwpile," cottage-style lighthouse that is one of only three that still stand out of an original 45 on the bay. The lighthouse is fully restored and houses early 20th-century furniture. Guided tours are available.

The museum's small-craft collection is housed in a 6,000-square-foot building that is open toward the boat basin. The collection has 19 boats in a range of sizes. Some boats are displayed on land, and others are in the water.

Those wishing to see an original seafood-packing house can visit the **Lore Oyster House** (May and Sept. weekends 1pm-4pm, June-Aug. daily 1pm-4pm, free). This restored National Historic Landmark is a little more than half a mile south of the museum campus on Solomons Island Road. It was built in 1934

city soon became the dominant commercial center in Calvert County.

By the late 1920s, oyster harvests began to decline. This was followed by the Great Depression and the worst storm to ever hit the island (in 1933), which left the lower half of it under water. World War II brought better times when the island became a staging area for training troops readying for amphibious invasions.

Today, tourism, boating, and outdoor

# Pirates of the Chesapeake

Although Blackbeard the pirate was best known for his ruthless handiwork in the Caribbean and his eventual beheading in Ocracoke, North Carolina, he often retreated to the Chesapeake Bay to repair his ship and prepare her for sea. He was not alone on the bay. The tobacco industry thrived along its shores for nearly 200 years (between roughly 1600 and 1800), bringing with it explorers from all parts of Europe as well as large populations of pirates.

Initially pirates settled in the southern part of the bay, but later they spread through most of the area. Although pirates often attacked colonial ships, the outlaws were tolerated by the colonies and in some ways helped them become independent from England. Pirates often sold goods to colonists that they could not purchase from England.

Despite their success, pirate life was very difficult, and most died young. Entire crews could be wiped out by disease, as living conditions were filthy on board their ships. Many also suffered fatal wounds during battle. Although some did go on to enjoy the riches they stole, this was the minority.

and now shares exhibits that explain oyster processing.

Sightseeing sailing cruises on the river leave from the museum dock weather permitting. They are one hour long and go through the inner harbor, underneath the Governor Thomas Johnson Bridge, and turn around at the Naval Recreation Center. The cost is $7. Trips can accommodate 40 passengers and leave the dock at 2pm Wednesday-Sunday (May-Oct.). On Saturday and Sunday in July and August additional 12:30pm and 3:10pm cruises are offered. Call 410/326-2042, ext. 41. Tickets can be purchased at the museum the day of the cruise.

The museum also has a woodworking shop and a reference library.

## ANNMARIE SCULPTURE GARDEN AND ARTS CENTER

The **Annmarie Sculpture Garden and Arts Center** (13480 Dowell Rd., 410/326-4640, www.annmariegarden.org, sculpture garden daily 9am-5pm, arts building daily

Calvert Marine Museum

10am-5pm, $5) features a lovely sculpture garden accessed by a quarter-mile walking path. The path goes through a wooded garden where sculptures both on loan and part of the center's permanent collection can be viewed. More than 30 sculptures are on loan from the Smithsonian Institution and National Gallery of Art. The Arts Building features a rotating exhibit space and a gift shop. The center offers many family activities throughout the year and also hosts annual festivals. This is a peaceful place to walk or bring the kids.

## ★ CALVERT CLIFFS STATE PARK

One of the prime recreation attractions in Calvert County is **Calvert Cliffs State Park** (10540 H. G. Trueman Rd., Lusby, 301/743-7613, www.dnr.state.md.us, daily sunrise to sunset, $5 per vehicle). This day-use park is about 7 miles north of Solomons Island, right on the Chesapeake Bay, and offers a sandy beach, playground, fishing, marshland, and 13 miles of hiking trails. The main attraction in this park, however, is fossil hunting along the beach. At the end of the Red Trail (1.8 miles from the parking lot), the open beach area gives rise to the dramatic Calvert Cliffs. More than 600 species of fossils have been identified in the cliff area, dating back 10 to 20 million years. The most common types of fossils found include oyster shells from the Miocene era and sharks teeth. Visitors can use sieves and shovels to look through the sand, but it is illegal to hunt fossils beneath the cliffs for safety reasons (dangerous landslides can occur). Swimming off the beach is allowed at your own risk, as there are no lifeguards on duty.

## Sports and Recreation

Those wishing to rent a kayak or paddleboard (starting at $35 for three hours) or take a guided kayak tour ($75 per person), can do so from **Patuxent Adventure Center** (13860 C Solomons Island Rd., 410/394-2770, www.paxadventure.com). They also sell bikes and kayaks and other outdoor gear and accessories.

## Nightlife

The **Solomons Island Tiki Bar** (85 Charles St., 410/326-4075, www.tikibarsolomons.com, mid-Apr.-mid-Oct.) is a local institution in Solomons. This well-known shack/tiki village near the harbor makes a killer mai tai and caters to pretty much anyone over 21 looking for a good time, good drink, and a fun island atmosphere. Visitors come by land and sea for this "adventure." Just be sure to decide ahead of time who is driving or sailing you home.

## Food

Relaxed waterfront dining can be found at **The Dry Dock Restaurant** (C St., 410/326-4817, www.zahnisers.com, hours vary by season, $19-32). This harborfront restaurant specializes in steaks and seafood and prides itself on using as much local produce and sustainable seafood as possible. Large windows overlook the harbor, and there is outside deck seating in the warmer months. This is a small, intimate establishment that has been part of the marina for many years. There is an interesting collection of antique wooden decoys around the bar that were part of a private collection.

The ★ **CD Café** (14350 Solomons Island Rd., 410/326-3877, www.cdcafe.info, Sun. lunch 11am-3:30pm, dinner 5:30pm-9pm, Mon.-Sat. lunch 11:30am-3:30pm, dinner 5:30pm-9:30pm, $9-26) is a small, 11-table restaurant with a large menu of simply delicious food. They are open daily and serve lunch (pasta, burgers, salad) and dinner (seafood, steak, pasta, burgers). This is a popular restaurant, so expect to wait at prime times (there is a nice bar and waiting area), but the atmosphere is warm and inviting, the staff is genuinely helpful and friendly, and the food keeps residents and tourists coming back. Try the hummus, the cheesecake appetizer, and the salmon.

The **Lotus Kitchen** (14618 Solomons Island Rd., 410/326-8469, www.lotuskitchen-solomons.com, Wed.-Thurs. 9am-8pm, Fri. 9am-10pm, Sat. 9am-6pm, Sun. 9am-4pm, under $10) offers healthy food and a scenic view in a charming converted house right in town. The offering includes breakfast sandwiches, deli sandwiches, quiche, soup, meat and cheese boards, beer, wine, and coffee drinks. With menu items with names such as the Good Karma, the Garden Unicorn, and the Pot of Gold, half the fun is picking out your order. They are also known for their famous Kim's Key Lime Pie.

## Accommodations

There is no shortage of wonderful bed-and-breakfasts in Solomons Island. The ★ **Back Creek Inn Bed and Breakfast** (210 Alexander Ln., 410/326-2022, www. backcreekinnbnb.com, $115-225) is a beautiful waterfront inn with seven clean and spacious guest rooms. They have two deepwater boat slips on their 70-foot pier (at mile marker 5 on Back Creek) and two bicycles for guest use. The inn is in a quiet part of town and can accommodate small business groups with indoor and outdoor meeting space. They also have free wireless Internet throughout the property. A full gourmet breakfast is served Monday-Saturday between 8:30am and 9:30am. Coffee, tea, juice, and coffee cake are available starting at 8am.

Another lovely waterfront bed-and-breakfast is the ★ **Blue Heron Inn** (14614

Solomons Island Rd., 410/326-2707, www. blueheronbandb.com, $179-249). The two suites have king-size beds, and the two guest rooms have queens. All rooms have private bathrooms and a water view (with either a private balcony or access to a common balcony). Wireless Internet and cable are included with all rooms.

Guests are treated to a gourmet breakfast each morning in a sunny breakfast room with access to the balcony (where breakfast can be served on nice days). A complimentary glass of wine is available each evening.

**Solomons Victorian Inn** (125 Charles St., 410/326-4811, www.solomonsvictorianinn. com, $135-250) offers great harbor views and a lush garden, and is within a short walk of shops and restaurants. At the southern tip of Solomons Island, on the western Chesapeake Bay shore, this gracious inn was built in 1906 and was the home of a renowned yacht builder. Several of the rooms are named after his boats. Six guest rooms and one carriage house with a separate entrance are available to rent, and each includes a private bathroom, television, wireless Internet, and a full breakfast. Most rooms have a harbor view.

A good option for hotel accommodations in Solomons Island is the **Hilton Garden**

Lotus Kitchen

**Inn Solomons** (13100 Dowell Rd., 410/326-0303, www.hiltongardeninn3.hilton.com, $159-195), which is a half mile from the downtown attractions. They have clean, comfortable rooms, a fitness center, indoor pool, seasonal outdoor pool, business center, and complimentary wireless Internet.

## Information and Services

For additional information on Solomons Island, visit www.solomonsmaryland.com or stop by the **Solomons Island Visitor Center** (14175 Solomons Island Rd., 410/326-6027).

## ST. MARY'S CITY

St. Mary's City is a small community an hour and 45 minutes south of Annapolis (73 miles) and two hours south of Baltimore (96 miles) in extreme Southern Maryland. It sits on the western shore of the Chesapeake Bay and the eastern shore of the St. Mary's River (a Potomac River tributary). Established in 1634, the area is the fourth-oldest permanent settlement in the country and is widely known as the "birthplace of religious tolerance."

St. Mary's City is in St. Mary's County, a beautiful rural area with abundant farmland and water access. St. Mary's County has many Amish and Mennonite communities, and

motorists are warned to be alert for horse-drawn carriages along the highways. Amish farms dot the landscape and are recognizable by their windmills and the lack of power lines running along their properties.

St. Mary's was Maryland's capital for 60 years. Roman Catholics founded the city in their quest for religious freedom. When the state capital moved to Annapolis, St. Mary's went into deep decline and had dropped out of existence by 1720. In 1840, St. Mary's College was developed by Maryland legislature to celebrate the state's founding site. In 1966, the state of Maryland started the process of preserving the site and created the Historic St. Mary's City Commission. Today the city is still home to St. Mary's College and the outdoor museum of history and archaeology known as Historic St. Mary's City. Today, St. Mary's City is home to **St. Mary's College of Maryland** (Route 5, www.smcm.edu).

### Sights
★ **ST. MARY'S CITY'S OUTDOOR MUSEUM OF HISTORY AND ARCHAEOLOGY**
Maryland's premier outdoor living-history museum, the **St. Mary's City's Outdoor Museum of History and Archaeology**

an Amish buggy near St. Mary's City

(18559 Hogaboom Ln., 240/895-4990, www. hsmcdigshistory.org, hours change by season, $10) is a re-creation of colonial St. Mary's City. The complex includes the *Dove* ship that first brought settlers to the area, an early tobacco plantation, the State House of 1676 (47418 Old State House Rd.), and a woodland Native American hamlet.

Although visitors should not expect the living museum to be on the same scale as Williamsburg, Virginia, the park is still a wonderful place to visit and has costumed interpreters, archaeological discoveries, a visitors center (18751 Hogaboom Ln.), outdoor living-history exhibits (where you can watch new buildings being erected in the town center, learn about Native American culture, and see the people and livestock at a tobacco plantation), reconstructed colonial buildings, the St. John's site museum, and a working 17th-century farm.

Visitors to St. Mary's City can participate in many hands-on activities and special events during the open season, such as a workshop on dinner preparation at the plantation and a hands-on pirate experience. Professional archaeologists are actively working to rediscover the city's past, and excavation sites can be seen throughout this National Historic Landmark.

# POINT LOOKOUT

**Point Lookout State Park** (11175 Point Lookout Rd., Scotland, 301/872-5688, www. dnr.state.md.us, daily 6am-sunset, $7) encompasses 1,042 acres at the southern tip of St. Mary's County near Scotland, Maryland. The park is two hours (82 miles) south of Annapolis on a beautiful peninsula at the confluence of the Chesapeake Bay and the Potomac River. It is managed by the Maryland Department of Natural Resources.

Captain John Smith was the first to explore the peninsula in 1612, but the park is best known as the location of a prison camp during the Civil War. In the years leading up to the war, the area was a thriving summer resort thanks to its sandy beaches and stunning location. The coming of the war brought financial hardship, and the area was leased by the Union army as the site of a hospital facility, and then later the largest Confederate prison camp.

Conditions were horrible at the camp, which was primarily for enlisted men, and many of the prisoners froze to death during the winter months. Those who survived

**SOUTHERN MARYLAND**

Point Lookout State Park

were plagued by filth. It is said that more than 52,000 Confederate soldiers were held at the camp during the war, and between 3,000 and 8,000 died there. There are two monuments and an on-site museum that recall this part of the park's past.

Whether or not you believe in ghosts, the park boasts countless incidents of unexplained phenomena and firsthand encounters with "ghosts" of soldiers. The most haunted location is said to be the lighthouse, which is no longer in use.

Today the park is primarily known as a wonderful recreation spot. It has several boat launch locations ($12), canoe rentals, a camp store, fishing, hiking trails, picnic areas, a playground, beaches, swimming, and a nature center. The park is also pet friendly.

In addition to being surrounded by water, there is a large lake in the center of the park (Lake Conoy), which is a perfect spot for boating and fishing. A water trail guide for the park is available for purchase at the park headquarters.

Camping is offered in the park April-October on 143 wooded sites ($21.49). Twenty-six have full hookups ($38.49) and 33 provide electricity (33.49). There are also a half-dozen four-person camper cabins for rent ($50.49) on a nightly basis. Off-season camping is available with limited services. Call 888/432-2267 for reservations.

# Maryland's Eastern Shore and Atlantic Beaches

Look for ★ to find recommended
sights, activities, dining, and lodging.

# Highlights

★ **Schooner *Sultana:*** This amazing replica of a British Royal Navy ship serves as an
educational center and the site of the annual
Chestertown Tea Party (page 98).

★ **Historic District in St. Michaels:**
Beautiful churches, colonial homes, interesting
shops, and great restaurants charm in this elegant downtown area (page 104).

★ **Chesapeake Bay Maritime Museum:**
This wonderful museum in St. Michaels fills 18
acres with all things Chesapeake Bay (page 104).

★ **Pickering Creek Audubon Center:**
This 400-acre farm in Easton includes forest,
marsh, meadow, a freshwater pond, wetlands,
and more than a mile of shoreline (page 109).

★ **Blackwater National Wildlife
Refuge:** This beautiful waterfowl sanctuary
features 27,000 acres of protected freshwater,
brackish tidal wetlands, meadows, and forest
(page 116).

★ **Assateague Island National
Seashore:** These 37 miles of protected coastline are a haven for migrating birds and home to
a herd of wild ponies (page 120).

★ **Ocean City Boardwalk:** Along three
miles of wood-planked boardwalk sit dozens
of hotels, motels, restaurants, shops, and
amusement parks (page 123).

★ **Ocean City Life-Saving Station
Museum:** Learn the history of rescues at sea
along the Maryland coast (page 123).

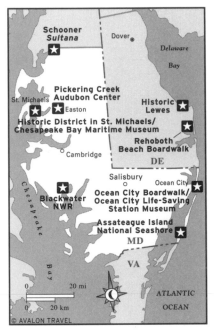

★ **Rehoboth Beach Boardwalk:** This
mile-long walkway offers stunning views of the
Atlantic and enough activity and food to keep a
family busy for days (page 135).

★ **Historic Lewes:** Victorian homes, upscale
restaurants, and cozy inns are the trademark of
this relaxing little coastal town (page 139).

# Maryland is blessed with thousands of miles of shoreline along the Chesapeake Bay and Atlantic Ocean. One of the most scenic areas in the state, the Eastern Shore is made up of a series of bayside towns that retain the charm of

yesteryear and are still partly supported by the local fishing industry.

Most travelers are welcomed to the Eastern Shore in the seafood haven of Kent Island after crossing the Chesapeake Bay Bridge. From there they head north to historic towns such as Chestertown and Rock Hall, or south to upscale St. Michaels or the quaint towns of Tilghman Island and Oxford. Easton and Cambridge offer their own special charm with bustling downtown areas and ample sports and recreation.

Maryland and Delaware share a thin strip of barrier island along the Atlantic coast, offering beachgoers many choices for a sun-filled vacation. On the very southern end, the Assateague Island National Seashore, which is shared with Virginia, is a quiet place to calm your spirits, view wildlife, and enjoy a long, pristine beach. Its northern neighbor is the bustling beachfront community of Ocean City. With its exciting boardwalk, active

nightlife, and plentiful activities, Ocean City never sleeps. Three popular Delaware beaches, Bethany, Rehoboth, and Lewes, stretch to the north.

## PLANNING YOUR TIME

The Eastern Shore of the Chesapeake Bay can be explored in a day or two, but many people choose to go there for extended relaxation and to spend a little downtime. Getting around by car is the best option, as public transportation is sparse. Route 301 is the major north/south route in the northern part of the Eastern Shore, while U.S. 50 is the major route in the middle and southern regions.

A good plan of action is to choose one or two towns to explore and spend a weekend enjoying them and learning about the Chesapeake Bay. The distance between Chestertown and Cambridge is about 52 miles, so the distances are not too cumbersome when traveling by car. Be aware,

**Previous:** Rehoboth Beach Boardwalk; Cambridge waterfront. **Above:** a sandpiper on Rehoboth Beach.

# The Eastern Shore and Atlantic Beaches

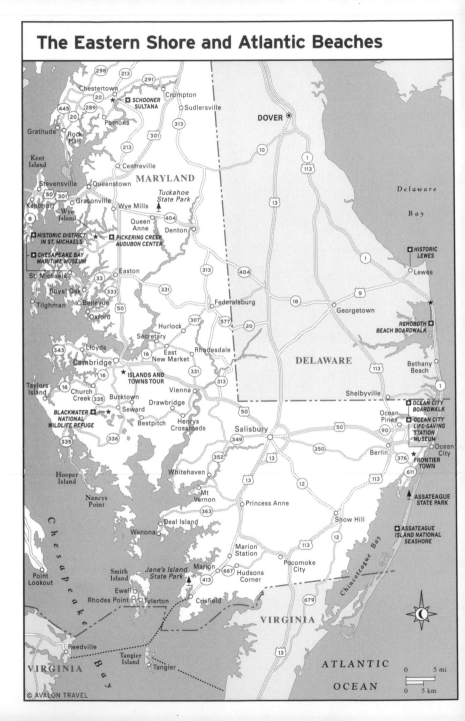

© AVALON TRAVEL

however, if you are traveling during the busy summer months, especially on a weekend, that traffic can back up on Route 50. Friday evening drives over the Bay Bridge (toll $4) can mean long wait times and bumper-to-bumper traffic.

The Atlantic beaches in Maryland and Delaware can be explored individually over a weekend, but they are often destinations that people spend a week at a time at over the summer months for a relaxing vacation. In the high season—generally, mid-June until Labor Day—many accommodations have minimum stays. The off-season is a great time to go if you don't have school constraints. Spring and fall offer cooler temperatures and fewer crowds at the beaches, and generally, prices for accommodations are reduced.

If you plan to just visit one of the beaches, keep in mind they all have unique characteristics. If you seek excitement, activity, and the bustling hubbub of a busy boardwalk, then Ocean City is a good choice. If you prefer the charm of a quaint, harborside historic town with close access to the beach, then Lewes, Delaware, may be a better option. If it's something in between that you are looking for, perhaps a more family-oriented beach

scene with fewer hotels and more beach house rentals, then Bethany Beach is a good choice. Finally, if you seek the activity of a boardwalk, but a scaled-down version is more your style, then Rehoboth Beach may suit you.

Regardless of where you end up, you will find good seafood and many excellent choices for restaurants at all the beaches. Keep in mind, "Maryland is for Crabs," and delicious blue crab dishes are available in many places. This is *the* place to eat them.

The vast majority of visitors to the Maryland and Delaware beaches drive there. Once you arrive, it's difficult to get too lost as long as you know where the beach is. One main road, the Coastal Highway, runs along the coast; it goes by Route 528 in Maryland and Route 1 in Delaware.

The **Ocean City Municipal Airport** (12724 Airport Rd., Berlin, 410/213-2471) is three miles west of the downtown area of Ocean City and can accommodate general aviation and charter aircraft. Commercial air service is provided at the **Salisbury-Ocean City Wicomico Regional Airport** (5485 Airport Terminal Rd., Salisbury, 410/548-4827) five miles from downtown Salisbury on Maryland's Eastern Shore.

**EASTERN SHORE**

the beach at Ocean City

# The Eastern Shore

The Eastern Shore holds a special place in many Marylanders' hearts. The wide peninsula between the Chesapeake Bay and the Atlantic Ocean contains endless miles of shoreline, beachfront resorts, nature preserves, and small seaside towns. Water is everywhere on the Eastern Shore and so are the culinary delights fished right from the bay. Amazing restaurants with million-dollar views, cozy inns, and plentiful outdoor activities welcome visitors nearly year-round.

## KENT ISLAND AND KENT NARROWS

The Chesapeake Bay Bridge stretches from Sandy Point near Annapolis on the mainland to Kent Island. Kent Island is the largest island in the Chesapeake Bay and the gateway to the Eastern Shore. The island is bordered on the east by a narrow channel called the Kent Narrows.

Kent Island welcomes Bay Bridge drivers to a gathering of easily accessible waterfront restaurants. Visitors traveling Route 50 are immediately thrown into a seaside atmosphere, and the urge to stop and sample some of the local cuisine is hard to resist.

### Food

The **Narrows Restaurant** (3023 Kent Narrows Way South, Grasonville, 410/827-8113, www.thenarrowsrestaurant.com, lunch Mon.-Sat. 11am-4pm, Sun. brunch 11am-2pm, dinner Mon.-Sat. 4pm-close, Sun. 11am-close, $10-36) is one of the most popular seafood restaurants on the island. It has a nice atmosphere and a great view. Patio seating is available.

Another local favorite is **Harris Crab House** (433 Kent Narrows Way, Grasonville, 410/827-9500, www.harriscrabhouse.com, daily lunch and dinner from 11am, $11-68). They have two levels of waterfront dining and outdoor seating. The views are great, and the

seafood is plentiful. This is a casual place with a crab house atmosphere.

The **Fisherman's Inn & Crab Deck** (3116 Main St., 410/827-8807, www.fishermansinn. com, daily 11am-10pm, $19-40) serves great seafood and also has a seafood market.

## CHESTERTOWN

Chestertown is a pretty waterfront colonial town with less than 5,000 residents. It is 40 minutes (29 miles) northeast of Kent Island on the Chester River, a tributary of the Chesapeake Bay. It is about 35 miles northeast of the Chesapeake Bay Bridge.

The town's history dates back to 1706, and it was known as one of Maryland's six "Royal Ports of Entry" (second only to Annapolis as a leading port). The town was a spot for the wealthy in its heyday, which is reflected in the numerous brick mansions and row houses that line the waterfront. The port is still a popular location for sailing ships and tourists. It is also home to **Washington College** (www.washcoll.edu), a private liberal arts college of which George Washington was a founding patron. The school was established in 1782, making it the tenth-oldest college in the country.

### Sights

#### HISTORIC CHESTERTOWN

Chestertown is worth exploring on foot. The state's second-highest concentration of colonial homes (after Annapolis) can be found in Chestertown, and there is a scenic waterfront promenade.

#### ★ SCHOONER *SULTANA*

The schooner *Sultana* (107 S. Cross St. on the waterfront, 410/778-5954, www.sultana-education.org) is a replica of a British Royal Navy ship that sailed during the 18th century and patrolled the North American coastline just before the Revolutionary War. The ship lives in the Chestertown Harbor and is used to

# William Preston Lane Jr. Memorial Bay Bridge

Once upon a time, Marylanders had to depend on boats to cross the Chesapeake Bay. The first plan to connect the mainland to the Eastern Shore came in 1927 but was abandoned first until 1938 and then again until 1947. Finally, under the leadership of Governor William Preston Lane Jr. the State Roads Commission began building the "Bay Bridge" in 1949.

The original span of the bridge, which is used for eastbound traffic today, cost $45 million and became the longest continuous over-water steel structure in the world at 4.3 miles. It first opened to traffic on July 30, 1952. The bridge is part of U.S. Routes 50 and 301 and quickly became an important connection to the Baltimore/Washington DC area from the Eastern Shore and Ocean City, Maryland.

The second span, which currently carries westbound traffic, was started in 1969 at a cost of $148 million. This span opened in 1973. This architectural marvel has a vertical clearance of 186 feet, and the suspension bridge towers are 354 and 379 feet tall. The bridge starts on the mainland next to Sandy Point State Park and stretches to Kent Island. The bridge can accommodate 1,500 vehicles per lane per hour.

teach students about the Chesapeake Bay history and environment. Two-hour public sails are held on weekends from the end of April to the beginning of November ($30). Many events are offered throughout the season on the ship; a list is available on the website.

## Events

The biggest annual event in Chestertown is the **Chestertown Tea Party** (www.chestertownteaparty.org), held at the end of May. In May 1774, five months after the famous Boston Tea Party when the British closed the port of Boston, residents of Chestertown resolved to prohibit the purchase, sale, or drinking of tea. Legend has it that they then held their own version of the Boston Tea Party staged on the schooner *Sultana* on the Chester River to show their colonial defiance. The annual festival celebrates this heritage through a reenactment of the tea party and a weekend of family events.

Aviation enthusiasts won't want to miss the annual **Potomac Antique Aero**

**Squadron's Antique Fly-In** (www.fly-ins. com, free but donations appreciated). This wonderful one-day antique aircraft show is held in June at the **Massey Aerodrome** (33541 Maryland Line Rd., Massey, www. masseyaero.org), approximately 17 miles northeast of Chestertown. It is sponsored by the Potomac Antique Air Squadron. More than 200 antique and rare aircrafts make up this impressive show. Visitors can see the airplanes up close, speak with the owners, and enjoy delicious food.

## Shopping

A dozen or so art galleries, studios, and shops feature the work of local, regional, and international artists in the historic waterfront district of Chestertown.

From April to December a local farmers market is held on Saturday mornings in the heart of the downtown area between Spring Avenue and Cross Street. It features fresh bakery items, produce, plants, herbs, and local artwork.

## Food

The most well-known eatery in town is the **Kitchen at the Imperial** (208 High St., 410/778-5000, www.imperialchestertown. com, Mon., Wed.-Sat. 11:30am-9pm, Sun. brunch 10am-3pm, dinner 3pm-9pm, $9-33). This wonderful restaurant was formerly located in Rock Hall but is now located in the Imperial Hotel, which first opened in 1903 and still offers three rooms for rent. The restaurant is open for lunch and dinner and offers a Bloody Mary brunch on Sunday. Their fresh menu varies seasonally but they usually have terrific local seafood dishes and meat from local farms.

Seafood, comfort food, and sophisticated choices can all be found at the **Lemon Leaf Café** (337 High St., 443/282-0004, www. thellcafe.com, Mon.-Wed. 11am-8pm, Thurs. 11am-9pm, Fri.-Sat. 7:30am-9pm, Sun. 7:30am-8pm, $7-30). This clean little gem has a signature dish of chicken and dumplings but also serves incredible authentic Maryland

# Tiki Bar Boat Stop

If you are exploring the Chesapeake Bay by boat and could use a taste of the islands and a party-hardy atmosphere, stop in **Jellyfish Joel's Tiki Bar** (22170 Great Oak Landing Rd., Chestertown, 410/778-5007, www.mearsgreatoaklanding.com, in-season Fri. starting 2pm and Sat.-Sun. starting 11am). This waterside bar sits on a peninsula by the beach on Fairlee Creek nine miles west of Chestertown and is a favorite boating stop. It offers a sandy beach, palm trees, and sunset beach parties every Friday during the summer. Boats can anchor or tie up on the floating docks. The bar is the main attraction, with cold beer and colder tropical drinks with names such as "Painkillers" and "Pain n'de Ass." They have live entertainment on the weekends and sell snacks and sandwiches.

crab soup, great crab cakes, and a delicious lemon meringue pie. The friendly service really makes diners feel like part of the "family," and makes for a relaxed dining experience even though the restaurant is usually full.

Right next door to the Lemon Leaf Café, and accessible through the restaurant or off the street, is **JR's Past Time Pub** (337 High St., 443/282-0055, www.jrspub.net, daily 11am-1am, $7-30). This 60-year-old pub has the same owner as its popular neighbor. It has a unique vintage clock motif and is decorated with signs from businesses in Chestertown's past. They serve traditional pub fare and share some dishes with their sister restaurant. The food menu is printed on paper grocery bags and their drink menu on wine bags. The pub is popular with students from Washington College and also has a piano bar with live music on Sunday evenings.

If you're looking for a water view with your meal, the only game in town is **The Fish Whistle** (98 Cannon St., 410/778-3566, www. fishandwhistle.com, Mon.-Wed. 11am-8pm, Thurs. 11am-8:30pm, Fri.-Sat. 11am-9pm, Sun. 11am-7pm, late-night bar menu daily until

11pm, $10-29). The location is excellent, right on the Chester River, and they serve a nice seafood menu with good daily specials. They have a large menu with bar food, sandwiches, and land and seafood entrées. Try the catfish fingers or the oyster potpie. Their slogan is, "It's all about the food," and they mean it.

Phenomenal oyster fritters are among the menu items at the **Blue Heron Café** (236 Cannon St., 410/778-0188, www.blueheron-cafe.com, dinner Mon.-Sat. from 5pm, $16-30). This consistently good restaurant serves regional American cuisine such as crab cakes, filet, and lamb. The desserts are amazing. Reservations are a must on weekend nights.

A great place to grab a drink in the summer and watch the sun set is at **The Sandbar at Rolph's Wharf** (1008 Rolph's Wharf Rd., 410/778-6389, www.rolphswharf.com). This is a small outdoor bar that is primarily open on weekends. It offers wonderful views of the Chester River, cold beer, and snacks.

The **Chestertown Farmers Market** is held every Saturday (late March-late December) from 8am to noon at **Fountain Park** (220 High St.).

## Accommodations

A pre-Revolutionary War landmark, the **White Swan Tavern** (231 High St., 410/778-2300, www.whiteswantavern.com, $150-280) is a cozy bed-and-breakfast in the historic district of Chestertown. The inn was built in 1733 and has been used for a number of purposes throughout its history, including a private home and a tavern. A special room in the inn houses many artifacts that were found when the building was restored in 1978. There are six guest rooms, one of which was the original one-room dwelling that housed shoemaker John Lovegrove prior to 1733. The rooms are large and comfortable, and the location of this inn couldn't be any better if you are looking to explore the downtown area and waterfront. A continental breakfast and afternoon tea are served to guests. The bed-and-breakfast can accommodate small weddings and conferences. Two additional apartments are available for long- or short-term stays near the inn.

A cute home away from home very convenient to Washington College (it's 100 yards from campus) and within a 15-minute walk to the riverfront is **Simply Bed and Bread** (208 Mount Vernon Ave., 410/778-4359, www.simplybedandbread.com, $129-149). They offer two allergy-friendly guest rooms in a 1947 Cape Cod-style home. One room has a queen bed, and the other has a

*THE EASTERN SHORE* **EASTERN SHORE**

White Swan Tavern

king. Each clean, cozy room has ample space. The innkeepers do a great job of making guests feel welcome. A continental breakfast is served each morning, and guests are treated to welcome sweets upon arrival.

One mile outside of Chestertown is the lovely **Brampton Bed and Breakfast Inn** (25227 Chestertown Rd., 410/778-1860, www.bramptoninn.com, $180-380), a restored plantation house built in 1860. It now has 13 guest rooms, suites, and cottages available to visitors. All accommodations have private bathrooms, sitting areas, fireplaces, flat-screen televisions with DVD players (no cable), bathrobes, and bath amenities. The estate is well cared for with beautiful gardens and a large front porch. A full à la carte breakfast is served in the dining area daily between 8:30am and 10am, although guests may opt to have breakfast delivered to their rooms. One cottage on the property is pet friendly.

A few chain hotels are options near the historic district in Chestertown. The **Holiday Inn Express Hotel & Suites Chestertown** (150 Scheeler Rd., 410/778-0778, www.ihg.com, $95-122) has 81 guest rooms, complimentary breakfast, and free wireless Internet, and the adjacent **Comfort Suites** (160 Scheeler Rd., 410/810-0555, www.choicehotels.com, $110-120) has 53 guest rooms, complimentary continental breakfast, and an indoor pool.

## Information and Services

For additional information on Chestertown visit www.chestertown.com or stop by the **Kent County Visitor Center** (corner of Rte. 213 and Cross St., www.townofchestertown.com, Mon.-Fri. 9am-5pm, Sat.-Sun. 10am-2pm).

## ROCK HALL

Fourteen miles southwest of Chestertown is the small waterfront town of Rock Hall. Rock Hall sits directly on the Chesapeake Bay and has a population of less than 1,500 people. Sometimes referred to as the "Pearl of the

Simply Bed and Bread

Chesapeake," this quaint maritime town has a history of fishing and boating and during the colonial era was a stop for passenger boats and shipping boats transporting tobacco and seafood. Today Rock Hall still has a working harbor and a fleet of professional watermen.

## Sights

There are three small museums in Rock Hall. **The Rock Hall Museum** (at the Municipal Building on S. Main Street, www.rockhallmd.com, Sat.-Sun. 11am-3pm, free, donations appreciated) is a two-room facility a short walk from the town center housing artifacts from the town's history and focusing on the lifestyle, economy, and traditions of the community. **The Waterman's Museum** (in the Haven Harbour Marina, 20880 Rock Hall Ave., 410/778-6697, www.havenharbour.com, daily 10am-4pm, free) features a unique collection of vintage photographs taken during the watermen era, as well as boats and local carvings. The third museum, **Tolchester Beach Revisited** (Main St.

behind the Shoppes at Oyster Court, www. rockhallmd.com, Sat.-Sun. 11am-3pm), is a unique little place with artifacts and memorabilia from a former amusement park that was at a nearby steamboat landing. In its prime, it included 155 acres of amusement space and brought in as many as 20,000 visitors during a weekend by six steamships and one ferry. The park included a dance hall, bowling alley, bingo parlor, roller coaster, pony carts, a roller-skating rink, and numerous vendors. The park closed for good in 1962.

A warm and friendly local theater, **The Mainstay** (5753 Main St., 410/639-9133, www.mainstayrockhall.org) is a cultural and artistic center in Rock Hall. It occupies a building that was constructed more than a century ago. With just 120 seats, this is an intimate theater that offers more than 50 blues, folk, classical, and jazz concerts every year. They sell beer, wine, soft drinks, and home-baked treats during performances.

## Food

The **Osprey Point Inn Restaurant** (20786 Rock Hall Ave., 410/639-2194, www.ospreypoint.com, dinner Wed.-Sun. starting at 5pm, Sunday brunch May-Sept. 10:30am-2pm, $18-25) features great water views from the Osprey Point Inn. The setting is comfortable and relaxing, and the young but highly skilled chef is truly passionate about his work. They have a fresh, seasonal menu with seafood and land-borne choices.

Another good choice in Rock Hall is **Uncle Charlie's Bistro** (834B High St., 410/778-3663, www.unclecharliesbistro.com, Mon.-Thurs. 11am-8pm, Fri. 11am-9pm, Sat., noon-9pm, $8-27). They offer American dishes, including seafood, salads, burgers, and sandwiches. The atmosphere and staff are very pleasant despite a not-so-impressive exterior.

## Accommodations

The serene waterfront setting of the ★ **Inn at Huntingfield Creek** (4928 Eastern Neck Rd., 410/639-7779, www.huntingfield. com, $185-325) is hard to beat. Guests can literally swim, kayak, and bike right from the front door of this beautiful farm estate that was once a high-end hunting club and horse racing track. Four guest rooms in the manor house and four private cottages allow for a variety of accommodations (pets are allowed in the cottages). The estate is a blend of old-world charm and modern conveniences. It has lovely grounds, a view of the Chesapeake Bay, a saltwater pool, wireless Internet, and a library. Gourmet breakfasts are served daily in the gorgeous manor house.

The **Osprey Point Inn** (20786 Rock Hall Ave., 410/639-2194, www.ospreypoint.com, $180-280) offers luxurious accommodations in three settings. There are seven guest rooms in the main inn, three rooms in the farmhouse, and five rooms at the marina annex. Guests in all three locations can enjoy the amenities at the inn, including a pool and daily continental breakfast. A marina provides boat access, docks, and a bathhouse. There is also a lovely on-site restaurant that features delicious food in a waterfront setting (dinner Wed.-Sun. starting at 5pm, Sunday brunch May-Sept. 10:30am-2pm).

## Information and Services

Additional information on Rock Hall can be found at www.rockhallmd.com or by stopping by the **Rock Hall Visitor's Center** (5585 Main St., 410/639-7611, www.rockhallmd. com, open daily).

# ST. MICHAELS

The historic waterfront town of St. Michaels is approximately one hour (51 miles) from Annapolis (from Route 50, exit on Route 322 and follow the signs for Route 33 to St. Michaels). This charming vintage port is a popular tourist destination and features manicured colonial, federal, and Victorian homes, stunning churches, and a scenic shopping area with specialty stores, restaurants, exclusive inns, and bed-and-breakfasts. Seafood lovers can eat their fill of local crab, fish, and oysters, and those looking to go out on the water can take a cruise or launch a kayak.

St. Michaels was founded in the mid-1600s as a trading stop for the tobacco and trapper industries. The town's name came from the Christ Episcopal Church of St. Michael Archangel parish that was founded in 1677. The historic center of St. Michaels, known as St. Mary's Square (between Mulberry Street and E. Chestnut Street), was created in 1778 when a wealthy land agent from England purchased 20 acres and created 58 town lots. Many of the homes in St. Michaels that were built in the late 1700s and 1800s still stand today.

St. Michaels earned the nickname "the town that fooled the British" during the War of 1812, when residents protected their town from British gunfire using trickery as their defense. Warned of a nighttime attack from British barges positioned in their waters, the townspeople strung burning lanterns in the treetops above the town to fool the attackers into overshooting their targets. The plan worked, and only one house, still known today as the "cannonball house," was hit in the attack.

In the late 1800s and early 1900s, St. Michaels's economy was primarily supported by seafood processing and shipbuilding. Slowly, toward the end of the 20th century, the town became a popular tourist destination and a weekend getaway spot for Washingtonians and other regional residents.

## Sights
### ★ HISTORIC DISTRICT IN ST. MICHAELS

The charming and historic downtown area of St. Michaels is a cornucopia of churches, colonial homes, shops, restaurants, and galleries. This elegant district was added to the National Register of Historic places in 1986 and is a destination for many tourists and area residents. The area includes a scenic harbor on the Miles River. South Talbot Street (Route 33) is the main artery through town, just a few blocks from the waterfront.

### ★ CHESAPEAKE BAY MARITIME MUSEUM

The **Chesapeake Bay Maritime Museum** (213 N. Talbot St., 410/745-2916, www.cbmm. org, daily May-Oct. 9am-5pm, Nov.-Apr. 10am-4pm, $15) is an 18-acre learning center for all things Chesapeake Bay. There are 10 exhibit buildings, a large display of traditional

Chesapeake Bay Maritime Museum

bay boats, and the Hooper Strait Lighthouse built in 1879.

The museum is a wealth of information on Chesapeake Bay history and the people who live there. Instead of relying on tour guides or reenactors to teach visitors about the bay, the Chesapeake Bay Maritime Museum employs real people of the Chesapeake who live and work on the bay and share their actual experiences. Examples include master decoy carvers, retired crab pickers, and ship captains. Visitors can also witness a boat restoration in progress in the museum's working boatyard or climb a lighthouse.

The museum offers scenic 45-minute cruises on the Miles River on a replica buy-boat (May-Oct. Fri.-Mon. at noon, 1pm, 2pm, and 3pm). Buyboats were used to buy catches off watermen's boats and take them directly to market. Cruises depart from the lighthouse (tickets are sold in the Admissions Building, $10).

Both self-guided tours (by map) and guided tours are available with admission to view the museum's many exhibits, including art and maritime displays.

## Recreation

St. Michaels is all about water. Those looking for an upscale sailing adventure can charter the *Selina II,* a vintage catboat, through **Sail Selina** (101 N. Harbor Rd., 410/726-9400, www.sailselina.com, May-Sept.). Passengers are limited to just six per two-hour outing and are offered a personal sailing experience/tour through the harbor and on the Miles River. Guests are invited to help sail the vessel or to just sit back and relax. The boat is docked at the Harbor Inn and Marina. Outings start at $65 per person.

Narrated cruises up the Miles River are also available through **Patriot Cruises** (410/745-3100, www.patriotcruises.com, early spring-late fall, $24.50). This two-level, 49-passenger cruising boat is climate-controlled and offers 60- to 70-minute tours. It leaves from 301 N. Talbot Street.

If you long to sail aboard an authentic skipjack, the **Skipjack *H. M. Krentz*** (800/979-3370, www.oystercatcher.com, Apr.-Oct. daily, $40) offers two-hour narrated cruises aboard a 70-foot working skipjack from the 1950s. Sailing cruises leave from the Chesapeake Bay Maritime Museum.

Kayaks ($30 per hour), stand-up paddle-boards ($30 per hour), and bikes ($10 per hour) can be rented from **Shore Pedal & Paddle** (store: 500 S. Talbot St., dock: 125 Mulberry St., 410/745-2320, www.shorepedalandpaddle.com). They also offer guided two-hour kayak tours in St. Michaels Harbor on weekends and by appointment during the week. Bikes can also be rented from **TriCycle & Run** (929 S. Talbot St., 410/745-2836, www.tricycleand-run.com, Sun. 10am-2pm, Mon. 10am-5pm, Thurs.-Sat. 10am-5pm, $10 for 2 hours).

## Shopping

Talbot Street is the place to start your shopping adventure in St. Michaels. For unique gifts, stop by **The Preppy Redneck** (310 S. Talbot St., 410/829-3635, www.thepreppyred-neck.com), a fun gift shop; **NETime Designs** (404 S. Talbot St., 410/745-8001) for home decor, gifts, and jewelry; and **Ophiuroidea** (609 S. Talbot St., 410/745-8057) for coastal-inspired furnishings and gifts.

## Food
### AMERICAN
Good food with a romantic atmosphere and modern ambience can be found at **Theo's Steaks, Sides, and Spirits** (407 S. Talbot St., 410/745-2106, www.theossteakhouse.com, Wed.-Sun. for dinner at 4:30pm, $15-55) on Talbot Street. This popular eatery offers a small but diverse menu of pub fare and steaks, expertly prepared and presented.

Another good date-night spot is **208 Talbot** (208 N. Talbot St., 410/745-3838, www.208talbot.com, Wed.-Sun for dinner at 5pm, tavern menu $12-23, dining room menu $28-36). They offer delicious steak and seafood dishes such as pan-seared grouper, grilled ribeye, and seared sea scallops in the dining room and a casual menu with items

The Preppy Redneck gift shop

such as pizza, burgers, and shrimp and grits in their tavern. Reservations are recommended.

A good bet for casual American fare any day of the week is **Mike and Eric's Front Street Restaurant & Bar** (200 S. Talbot St., 410/745-8380, www.mikeandericsfrontstreet. com, Mon.-Sat. 11am-10pm, Sun. 9am-10pm, $13-27). They serve sandwiches, flatbread, and an eclectic selection of entrees that includes pasta, lamb, chicken potpie, salmon, and oysters.

### ITALIAN

Theo's sister restaurant, **Ava's Pizzeria and Wine Bar** (409 S. Talbot St., 410/745-3081, www.avaspizzeria.com, daily 11:30am-9:30pm, $8-24) serves exceptional pizza, pasta, and sandwiches. They also have an extensive wine and beer menu. The atmosphere is fun and inviting with an outdoor patio, fireplaces, and even a waterfall. They do not take reservations, although they do have a call-ahead list. They are known for pizza, but the meatballs are out of this world.

### MEXICAN

Feeling funky? Then try **Gina's Cafe** (601 Talbot St., 410/745-6400, Wed.-Mon. noon-10pm, $11-28). This tiny, 1,000-square-foot Southwestern eatery on the corner of Talbot Street and East Chew is barely large enough to be termed a restaurant, but they serve up interesting, south-of-the-border goodness with a nod to fresh seafood. They offer fish tacos, drinks, and house-made tortilla chips, in addition to a host of other unique favorites. This is the place to come when your taste buds need a break from the usual restaurant fare. People either love it for its uniqueness or dislike it for its quirkiness. Try the soft-shell tacos with crab and guacamole or the crab nachos.

### SEAFOOD

A great view and a harbor atmosphere are the calling cards of the **Town Dock Restaurant** (125 Mulberry St., 410/745-5577, www.town-dockrestaurant.com, Sun. 11am-8pm, Thurs. 4pm-9pm, Fri.-Sat. 11:30am-9pm, $15-30). This waterfront restaurant specializes in seafood, but also offers steak, ribs, and seasonal menu items. The atmosphere is casual, but it's best to come on a nice day so you can enjoy the harbor-side porch.

Another waterfront seafood house is the **St. Michaels Crab and Steakhouse** (305 Mulberry St., 410/745-3737, www.stmichaelscrabhouse.com, Thurs.-Mon. at 11am for lunch and dinner, $9-30). They offer a large menu of seafood favorites along with sandwiches, steak, pasta, and salad. All meals are made to order, and they pride themselves on being flexible in accommodating requests. The atmosphere is fun and lively. This is a good place to grab a drink and enjoy the local food and a good view.

## ICE CREAM

Mouthwatering ice cream in a friendly atmosphere can be found at **Justine's Ice Cream Parlour** (106 N. Talbot St., 410/745-0404, www.justinesicecreams.com, Sun.-Thurs. 11am-8pm, Fri.-Sat. 11am-10pm, under $10) on North Talbot Street. They have been a staple in St. Michaels for more than 25 years. They serve ice cream, floats, shakes, and malts.

## Accommodations
### $100-200

There is no shortage of comfortable bed-and-breakfasts and inns in St. Michaels. The **Cherry Street Inn** (103 Cherry St., 410/745-6309, www.cherrystreetinn.com, $155-180) is one good option, with its convenient location, great breakfasts, and friendly, down-to-earth hosts. Just a short walk from the downtown area, this Victorian inn offers two suites with queen beds and private bathrooms. The inn was built in the 1880s by a steamboat captain and has been fully renovated.

### $200-300

Bring your kayak or fishing rod to the **Point Breeze Bed and Breakfast** (704 Riverview Ter., 410/745-9563, www.pointbreezebandb.com, $205, minimum stays may be required). This lovely home has 400 feet of waterfront on the harbor, a pier, and complimentary kayaks, canoes, and bicycles for guest use. There are several guest rooms, all decorated with family heirlooms from five generations. Breakfast is included with each stay.

An additional nice bed-and-breakfast option is the **Snuggery Bed and Breakfast** (203 Cherry St., 410/745-2800, www.snuggery1665.com, $200-250), with two guest rooms in the oldest residence in St. Michaels.

## OVER $300

Also located on Cherry Street is the ★ **Dr. Dodson House Bed and Breakfast** (200 Cherry St., 410/745-3691, www.drdodsonhouse.com, $290-385). This charming bed-and-breakfast is steps from Talbot Street and a stone's throw from the harbor. The inn was built in 1799 for use as a tavern and also served as the first post office in town. The home still has many of its original features, such as the fireplaces, woodwork, doors, and glass. It is considered to be one of the best-preserved examples of federal architecture in St. Michaels. The interior is modern but keeps with the character of its time. There are three guest rooms: two with queen beds and one with a king or two twins. All have fireplaces (either wood-burning or electric) and private bathrooms. There are large sofas on the first floor and a second-floor porch for guests to relax on. A wonderful breakfast is served each morning in the elegant dining area.

The lavish **Inn at Perry Cabin** (308 Watkins Ln., 410/745-2200, www.belmond.com/inn-at-perry-cabin-st-michaels/, $615-1,035) is a grand old resort and spa formerly owned by Sir Bernard and Lady Laura Ashley. It sits on the Miles River and has nice views of the water. The hotel was built around 1816 and is surrounded by antique gardens from the same period. Docking facilities (free for guest use), a fitness center, heated outdoor pool, and complimentary bicycles are part of the property amenities. There are 78 guest rooms and the resort is pet friendly. Ask for a room on an upper floor with a view of the water.

The **St. Michaels Harbour Inn Marina & Spa** (101 N. Harbor Rd., 410/745-9001, www.harbourinn.com, $279-729) is also located on the Miles River and offers 46 guest rooms and a full-service marina. This is a lovely property in a good location.

## Information and Services

For additional information on St. Michaels, visit www.stmichaelsmd.org.

# TILGHMAN ISLAND

Tilghman Island is one of the few remaining working watermen's villages in the mid-Atlantic. It provides an unvarnished look at life on the Chesapeake Bay. Tilghman Island is home to the last commercial sailing fleet in North America. The fleet is known as the Skipjacks in honor of the classic oyster boat (and Maryland's state boat), which visitors can see at **Dogwood Harbor,** on the east side of the island. Tilghman Island is in the middle Chesapeake Bay region and is separated from the Eastern Shore by Napps Narrows, but is easily accessed by driving over a drawbridge. Tilghman Island is three miles long and reachable via Route 33, 11 miles west of St. Michaels. It has a population of less than 800 people.

## Sights

The **Phillips Wharf Environmental Center** (6129 Tilghman Island Rd., 410/886-9200, www.pwec.org, Apr.-mid-Oct. Thurs.-Mon. 10am-4pm, free, donations appreciated) is a wonderful place for children and adults to learn about creatures living in the Chesapeake Bay. The center gives visitors the opportunity to see, touch, and learn about the wildlife such as horseshoe crabs, turtles, and oysters.

The **Tilghman's Watermen's Museum** (6031 Tilghman Island Rd., 410/886-1025, www.tilghmanmuseum.org, Apr.-Dec. Sat.-Sun. 10am-3pm, free) features exhibits on the heritage of the local watermen. It houses a collection of artifacts, boat models, and artwork by local artists.

## Recreation

Boat tours and charters are available on Tilghman Island through **Harrison House Charter Fishing** (21551 Chesapeake House Dr., 410/886-2121, www.chesapeakehouse.com, starting at $125). They have a charter fleet of 14 boats that can carry 6-40 passengers. They tout the "complete charter experience," regardless of the size of your party.

**Lady Patty Classic Yacht Charters** (6176 Tilghman Island Rd., 410/886-1127, www.

ladypatty.com, $42) offers seasonal two-hour charters in the waters surrounding Tilghman Island. Beer, wine, and cocktail service is available on all charters. Private charters can be arranged.

Charters aboard the oldest working skipjack on the Chesapeake Bay can be arranged on the **Skipjack Rebecca T. Ruark** (410/829-3976, www.tilghmanisland.com, $30). This beautiful boat was built in 1886, and the wonderful captain helps make this a great two-hour sail. Sailing charters leave from **Dogwood Harbor** (21308 Phillips Rd.).

Several **Tilghman Island Water Trails** (410/770-8000, www.dnr2.maryland.gov/boating/Pages/eastern_north.aspx) are available for kayaking. The **East Tilghman Island Trail** is 10.2 miles and explores the eastern portion of the island, while the **Tilghman Island Trail** tours the entire island. Maps can be downloaded at the trail website. **Tilghman Island Marina** (6140 Mariners Ct., 410/886-2500, www.tilghmanmarina.com) rents kayaks and canoes.

## Food

**Two If By Sea Restaurant** (5776 Tilghman Island Rd., 410/886-2447, www.twoifbysearestaurant.com, breakfast Mon., Tues., Thurs. 8am-11am, breakfast and lunch, Wed., Fri.-Sun. 8am-2pm, dinner Thurs. and Sun. 6pm-8:30pm, Fri. and Sat. 6pm-9pm, $15-24) is a cozy little restaurant serving breakfast, lunch, and dinner. They have wonderful traditional breakfasts, sandwiches, salads, fresh seafood, and homemade pastries. This is a delightful choice for a casual meal at a reasonable price.

The **Marker Five Restaurant** (6178 Tilghman Island Rd., 410/886-1122, www.markerfive.com, $11-27) offers a casual waterfront dining experience. They serve soup, sandwiches, local seafood, and other items such as barbecue and house-smoked ribs. They have an outdoor bar with more than 30 beers on tap.

If you're looking for a great view, laid-back atmosphere, and an interesting take on casual fare, grab a seat on the deck at the **Characters**

**Bridge Restaurant** (6136 Tilghman Island Rd., 410/886-1060, www.charactersbridgerestaurant.com, daily 11am-10pm, $8-29). The menu offers staples like local seafood, burgers, and steak, but also includes interesting dishes such as oyster pie and Cajun burgers. This is a great place to watch the boats on Knapps Narrows and the activity at the drawbridge.

## Accommodations

For peace and serenity, stay a few nights at the ★ **Black Walnut Point Inn** (4417 Black Walnut Point Rd., Tilghman, 410/886-2452, www.blackwalnutpointinn.com, $150-350). This charming bed-and-breakfast is at the southern point of Tilghman Island and bounded by water on three sides. The main house is meticulously maintained and offers four rooms with private baths. Two nicely appointed cabins right on the Choptank River provide a larger, more private space, and one is wheelchair accessible. The innkeepers are extremely friendly and knowledgeable about the long history of the property. Full breakfast is served each morning in the dining room, and the beautiful grounds offer a swimming pool, hot tub, pier, bird-watching trails, and unrivaled views of the Chesapeake Bay.

The **Knapps Narrows Marina and Inn** (6176 Tilghman Island Rd., 410/886-2720, www.knappsnarrowsmarina.com, $120-260) is a wonderful little waterfront inn, restaurant, and tiki bar that offers 20 guest rooms and great views of the Chesapeake Bay. Each room has a private waterfront patio or balcony. The inn is three stories, and each room is nicely furnished but not overstuffed. The staff is truly accommodating and friendly. The inn is adjacent to the Knapps Narrows Bridge (the entrance to the island). There is an outdoor pool on-site.

**The Lazy Jack Inn on Dogwood Harbor** (5907 Tilghman Island Rd., 410/886-2215, www.lazyjackinn.com, $185-305) has two rooms and two suites with private bathrooms. This charming waterfront inn has watched over Dogwood Harbor for more than 150 years. It is within walking distance of several restaurants and activities in the harbor. Nicely restored, the current owners have owned and run the inn for more than 20 years. A full gourmet breakfast is included. This is a great place for a peaceful getaway with wonderful views.

## Information and Services

For additional information on Tilghman Island, visit www.tilghmanisland.com.

# EASTON

Easton is a wonderful small town on the Eastern Shore that was founded in 1710. It is an hour's drive (42 miles) southeast of Annapolis. Easton is the largest town in Talbot County, with a population of around 16,000. It offers residents and visitors a beautiful downtown area with colonial and Victorian architecture, casual and fine restaurants, shopping, antiques, and galleries, while also providing ample opportunities for recreation such as golf and water sports on the Chesapeake Bay.

## Sights
### ACADEMY ART MUSEUM
The **Academy Art Museum** (106 South St., 410/822-2787, www.academyartmuseum.org, Mon. and Fri.-Sun. 10am-4pm, Tues.-Thurs. 10am-8pm, $3) is a little museum near downtown Easton that has five studios. It is housed in a charming building was built in 1820 and was the location of the first chartered school in Easton. It is now a historic landmark. The museum offers both regional and national exhibits; hosts concerts, lectures, and educational programs; and offers performing arts education for adults and children. More than 70,000 visitors come to the museum each year. Past exhibits have included original works by Ansel Adams, Roy Lichtenstein, and N. C. Wyeth.

### ★ PICKERING CREEK AUDUBON CENTER
The **Pickering Creek Audubon Center** (11450 Audubon Ln., 410/822-4903, www.

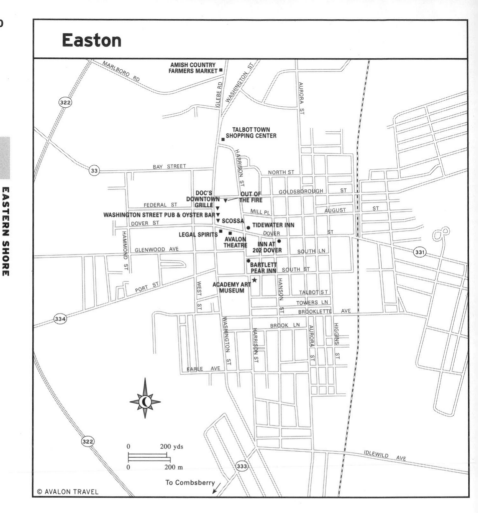

# Easton

pickeringcreek.audubon.org, trails and viewing areas daily dawn-dusk, free) is a 400-acre working farm next to Pickering Creek in Talbot County. The property is a natural habitat of forest, marsh, meadow, a freshwater pond, wetlands, more than a mile of shoreline, and farmland. More than 3.5 miles of walking trails are available as well as gardens, a canoe and kayak launch, and 100 acres of hardwood forest. Trails and viewing areas are open to the public from dawn until dusk every day, and there is no admission fee. The center is great for bird-watching and features viewing

platforms, a bluebird trail, and 90 acres of wetlands. Office hours at Pickering Creek are Monday-Friday 9am-4pm. The center is north of Easton: Take Route 662 north past the airport. Turn left on Sharp Road (west) and go right at the Y. Turn right (north) on Presquille Road and then right again on Audubon Lane.

## THE AMISH COUNTRY FARMERS MARKET

**The Amish Country Farmers Market** (101 Marlboro Ave., 410/822-8989, www.amishcountryfarmersmarket.com, Thurs.

9am-6pm, Fri. 9am-7pm, Sat. 9am-3pm) is a tradition on the Eastern Shore. The market features numerous authentic Amish vendors from Pennsylvania selling a great variety of produce, dairy products, baked goods, meats, candy, furniture, and crafts. Many locals do their regular grocery shopping at the market, but it is a popular stop for tourists wishing to purchase fresh foods and handmade products.

## Recreation and Entertainment

Easton is home to the popular **Hog Neck Golf Course** (10142 Old Cordova Rd., 410/822-6079, www.hogneck.com, $55). The facility offers an 18-hole championship course and a 9-hole executive course.

Visitors can catch a show at the **Avalon Theatre** (40 E. Dover St., 410/822-7299, www. avalontheatre.com). This cozy little theater has a full schedule of entertainment including theatrical performances, symphonies, bluegrass, jazz, comedians, and art festivals.

The largest annual event in Easton, and one of the best known on the Eastern Shore, is the **Waterfowl Festival** (www.waterfowlfestival. org, $15 for all three days). Taking place over three days in November, this event began in the early 1970s and now hosts 17,000 visitors, 300 of the best wildlife artists, craftspeople, and vendors, and 1,500 volunteers. This is a citywide event that closes several streets and prompts businesses to decorate their buildings with natural greens. The festival is a leader in promoting conservation of waterfowl and natural habitat.

## Shopping

Downtown Easton is a shopper's delight, with many gift stores, antiques shops, crafts, clothing, and shops with collectibles. Two of the prime streets to include on your shopping journey are Harrison and Washington, although many lovely stores may be found on various side streets. The **Talbot Town Shopping Center** on North Washington Street offers national retail chains.

## Food

Good Northern Italian food is served at **Scossa** (8 N. Washington St., 410/822-2202, www.scossarestaurant.com, lunch Thurs.-Sun. 11:30am-3pm, dinner Mon.-Thurs. 4pm-9pm, Sun. 4pm-8pm, Fri.-Sat. 4pm-10pm, $15-35) in the heart of the downtown

downtown Easton

area on North Washington Street. The owner/ chef was born in northern Italy and has an impressive culinary résumé. The modern dining room is the perfect place to meet with friends, business associates, and family. The dinner menu is a step above traditional Italian with creative combinations, fresh ingredients, and daily specials that offer something new each visit. They also offer a prix fixe menu for $40. Lunch is a completely different experience and features wonderful salads and sandwiches. The bar area is very inviting and serves top-shelf wine and liquor. They have a large specialty drink menu. Sunday brunch is also served.

Another excellent choice for Italian food is **Out of the Fire** (22 Goldsborough St., 410/770-4777, www.outofthefire.com, lunch Tues.-Sat. 11:30am-2pm, dinner Tues.-Thurs. 5pm-9pm, Fri.-Sat. 5pm-10pm, $14-28) on Goldsborough Street. They serve gourmet pizza and other creative entrées made from high-quality ingredients procured from mostly local farmers and vendors (try the mussels). The wraps and sandwiches are delicious, and they offer organic and gluten-free choices. The atmosphere is very warm and relaxing with tile floors and soft lighting.

Washington Street Pub & Oyster Bar

For a good pub-style meal in Easton, go to the **Washington Street Pub & Oyster Bar** (20 N. Washington St., 410/822-1112, www. washingtonstreetpub.com, Mon.-Thurs. 11am-2am, Fri.-Sat. 11am-2am, Sun. 11am-2am, $10-17). The trendy decor and lively atmosphere rival the food at this cozy pub and raw bar. They also have a good selection of beer on tap. Try the Chesapeake chicken sandwich (crab imperial and cheese on top of chicken); it is decadent to say the least.

The **Bartlett Pear Inn** (28 S. Harrison St., 410/770-3300, www.bartlettpearinn.com, Wed.-Sun. 5:30pm-10pm, $26-44) has a lovely upscale American bistro serving delicious entrées such as Alaskan halibut, New York strip steak, and curry-dusted sea scallops. They also offer a five-course tasting menu for $75 and a seven-course tasting menu for $95. The food is very flavorful, and the presentation is exquisite. The restaurant is part of a working inn with seven guest rooms.

For a fun atmosphere or to watch your favorite sports event, dine at **Doc's Downtown Grille** (14 N. Washington St., 410/822-7700, daily 11am-2am, $11-30). They serve traditional pub food and delicious local seafood (crab cakes, shrimp po'boy, fried oysters, etc.). The restaurant is family owned and operated and their passion for their business is evident in the friendly service.

## Accommodations

The ★ **Bartlett Pear Inn** (28 S. Harrison St., 410/770-3300, www.bartlettpearinn.com, $234-289) is a beautiful property on South Harrison Street in downtown Easton. This lovely inn dates back to the late 1700s and offers seven individually decorated guest rooms named for different types of pears. The handsome brick building with white covered porches is on a quiet street within walking distance to shopping and restaurants. The husband-and-wife owners are very gracious hosts, and they pay attention to the small details that make their guests feel welcome. The inn is pet friendly and can even accommodate large dogs. Ask for a room on the upper floor; this will provide the most quiet and privacy. There is an on-site restaurant that is open Wednesday-Sunday for dinner.

Luxurious accommodations can be found on Dover Street at the ★ **Inn at 202 Dover** (202 E. Dover St., 410/819-8007, www.innat-202dover.com, $289-525). This grand, beautifully renovated home is truly a work of art. From the stately exterior of this historic 1874 mansion to the inviting common areas and the themed rooms and suites, every last detail is attended to. An example of this is the Safari Suite, which has an elephant vanity, exotic lamps, and themed details down to the bath soap. Each of the five rooms is furnished with antique and reproduction items, pillow-top mattresses, and comfortable linens. Air jet tubs, steam showers, high-speed Internet, and cable television are also standard. The upscale

Peacock Restaurant serves delightful cuisine with Eastern Shore influence prepared by a Cordon Bleu-trained executive chef. They also have wonderful martinis.

The gracious **Tidewater Inn** (101 E. Dover St., 410/822-1300, www.tidewaterinn.com, $189-289) is the landmark lodging property in Easton. This elegant downtown hotel opened in 1949 and is known as a romantic getaway. The inn has 89 guest rooms with yesterday's charm and some modern conveniences such as wireless Internet and flat-screen televisions. The hotel does not have some of the amenities many travelers are used to such as a fitness room and on-site pool, although many of the rooms underwent renovations in early 2016. If you are looking for a comfortable manor house atmosphere with good service, this is a lovely choice. There is a good restaurant (the Hunter's Tavern) on-site and many more within walking distance.

## Information and Services

For additional information on Easton, visit www.eastonmd.org or stop by the **Talbot County Visitors' Center** (11 S. Harrison St., 410/770-8000).

Bartlett Pear Inn

## Getting There and Around

Most people arrive in Easton by car. There is a small public airport, the **Easton Airport** (29137 Newnam Rd., 410/770-8055, www.eastonairport.com), two miles north of Easton.

# OXFORD

The small waterfront town of Oxford, 10 miles southwest of Easton, is a fun day-trip destination. Oxford was settled in the mid-1660s on just 30 acres and is one of the oldest towns in Maryland. It was selected shortly after its settlement to be one of only two ports of entry for the Maryland Province (the other was Anne Arundel, which later became Annapolis). What followed was a period of prominence for the little town, and it became known as an international shipping center and home to many thriving tobacco plantations. After the Revolutionary War, when British ships stopped visiting its waters for trade, the town declined. Today, Oxford has a population of less than 1,000 people, but it remains a scenic and inviting place.

## Oxford-Bellevue Ferry

The **Oxford-Bellevue Ferry** (27456 Oxford Rd., 410/745-9023, www.oxfordbellevueferry.com, mid-Apr.-mid-Nov. daily, one-way/round-trip $12/20 car and driver, $6/9 motorcycle, $4/7 bike, $3/5 pedestrian) is one of the oldest privately run ferries in the country, dating back to 1683. It runs between Oxford and Bellevue, Maryland, across the Tred Avon River. The trip is less than a mile and takes approximately 10 minutes. The ferry accommodates cars, motorcycles, bikes, and pedestrians and has a capacity of nine vehicles. This is a popular connection for cyclists biking a circular route from St. Michaels.

## Food and Accommodations

Overnight visitors to Oxford can enjoy a stay at the **Oxford Inn** (504 S. Morris St., 410/226-5220, www.oxfordinn.net, $50-190). This lovely bed-and-breakfast is on a charming street across from a small marina. The exterior of the building is white with a green roof, covered porches, and seven dormer windows. The seven guest rooms are quaintly decorated in a country style, and the inn has a wonderful European bistro, **Pope's Tavern** ($24-34), that offers elegant dinner space for 40 guests. They serve entrées such as chicken, crab cakes, beef tenderloin, and pasta. There is also a cozy teak bar with seating for 12. A note at

the Oxford Inn

the bottom of their menu states "unattended children will be given a double espresso and a puppy."

The ★ **Robert Morris Inn** (314 N. Morris St., 410/226-5111, www.robertmorrisinn.com, $145-240), near the ferry landing, is another wonderful choice for accommodations in Oxford. This historic building with a yellow exterior and large patio dates back to 1710 and was once the home of a prosperous merchant and famous financier of the American Revolution, Robert Morris. A close friend of George Washington's, Morris entertained Washington at his home on multiple occasions. In later years, author James Michener spent time at the inn while working on his novel *Chesapeake*. The rooms offer a choice of cozy period furniture and canopy beds or more modern furnishings.

The inn contains a great restaurant, **Salter's Tavern and Tap Room,** that serves breakfast ($4-12), lunch ($14-21), and dinner ($17-31). The ambience is warm and inviting with slate floors, redbrick walls, and timber beams. The casual menu is centered on the local seafood treasures found in the bay such as crab, oysters, and fresh fish, but also features land-based menu items such as burgers

and salads. The restaurant is overseen by Mark Salter, a well-known British master chef.

## Information and Services

For additional information on Oxford, visit www.oxfordmd.net.

## CAMBRIDGE

Cambridge is 17 miles south of Easton off Route 50. It is the largest town in Dorchester County and one of the oldest colonial cities in Maryland, having been settled in 1684. It sits directly on the Choptank River (which was the setting for James Michener's book *Chesapeake*) near the Chesapeake Bay. The town was originally a trading center for tobacco.

In the late 19th century, Cambridge opened food processing businesses that canned foods such as oysters, tomatoes, and sweet potatoes. At its peak, the primary packing concern, Phillips Packing Company, employed 10,000 people. By the 1960s the decline in the canning industry had led to the closure of the company and left behind a struggling city that is still fighting to prosper.

Today Cambridge offers a pretty downtown area with historic 18th- and 19th-century

the Cambridge waterfront

homes and scenic waterfront parks and marinas.

## Sights

### HARRIET TUBMAN MUSEUM & EDUCATIONAL CENTER

The **Harriet Tubman Museum & Educational Center** (424 Race St., 410/228-0401, www.visitdorchester.org/harriet-tub-man-museum-educational-center, Tues.-Fri. noon-3pm, Sat. noon-4pm, tours by appointment only, free) is a tribute to Harriet Ross Tubman (1822-1913), a freedom fighter and former slave who was known for leading many slaves to freedom through the Underground Railroad. This small museum is dedicated to telling stories of this heroine's life and features exhibits on her work helping dozens of slaves. Tubman was a Dorchester County native.

### J. M. CLAYTON COMPANY

Pay a visit to the market at the world's oldest working crab house, **J. M. Clayton Company** (108 Commerce St., 410/228-1661, www.jmclayton.com, Mon.-Fri. 8am-5pm) on Commerce Street. This historic crab house is still operated by the same family that started it back in 1890. They even have an 80-year old canning machine. Their market is open daily where visitors can purchase local crabmeat and crab-related items.

### RICHARDSON MARITIME MUSEUM

Visitors can learn about the lost tradition of wooden boatbuilding at the **Richardson Maritime Museum** (401 High St., 410/221-1871, www.richardsonmuseum.org, Sat. 10am-4pm, Sun. 1pm-4pm, $3). This historic brick building on the corner of High and Locust Streets housed a bank for almost a hundred years. One step into the museum takes visitors into the world of wooden sailing vessels and their role on the Chesapeake Bay. Boat models, building tools, and original artifacts are just some of the items on display. The rich wooden boat history includes everything from crabbing skiffs to dovetails to clipper ships and even schooners.

### ★ BLACKWATER NATIONAL WILDLIFE REFUGE

**Blackwater National Wildlife Refuge** (2145 Key Wallace Dr., 410/228-2677, www.friendsofblackwater.org, daily dawn-dusk, vehicles $3, pedestrians $1, cyclists $1) was established in 1933 as a sanctuary for waterfowl migrating along the **Atlantic Flyway** (a migration route along the Atlantic coast). The refuge 12 miles south of Cambridge encompasses 27,000 acres including freshwater, brackish tidal wetlands, meadows, and forest. It is open year-round.

More than 250 species of birds live in the refuge, and it is home to the largest breeding population of bald eagles on the East Coast north of Florida. The eagle population swells in the winter months, when many birds migrate here from northern areas. During the winter, the refuge is also home to more than 35,000 geese and 15,000 ducks. Fall (Sept.-Nov.) is the best time to see migrating waterfowl and songbirds.

A wide variety of mammals also live in the refuge. Delmarva fox squirrels, southern flying squirrels, voles, shrews, nutria, gray foxes, red foxes, river otters, mink, skunks, deer, and beavers all call the refuge home.

There is a wonderful visitors center on Key Wallace Drive (year-round Mon.-Fri. 8am-4pm, Sat.-Sun. 9am-5pm) with wildlife exhibits, nature books, birding guides, a butterfly garden, maps, restrooms, and a gift shop. The prime attraction in the refuge is the Wildlife Drive, a four-mile paved road where visitors can drive, bike, and walk through the refuge to view wildlife. There is also a great viewing platform over the marsh. In addition to the Wildlife Drive, the refuge has four land trails and three paddling trails. Visitors can also hunt, fish, and crab. Environmental education programs are also offered for young people.

## Recreation and Events

One-hour **Historic High Street Walking Tours** (410/901-1000, $8) are offered by the West End Citizens Association. Reservations are not required but they are recommended. Tours meet at 11am on Saturday April-October at Long Wharf (High Street and Water Street).

One- or two-hour cruises on the skipjack *Nathan of Dorchester* (Long Wharf on High St., 410/228-7141, www.skipjack-nathan.org, most Saturdays May-Oct., two-hour sails $30, call for reservations) offer an authentic Chesapeake Bay experience. Tours go out on the Choptank River and teach the history of oystering.

There are two lovely parks in Cambridge that offer nice views of the Choptank River. **Great Marsh Park** (at the end of Somerset Ave. on the Choptank River, www.choosecambridge.com) has a boat launch, fishing pier, playground, and picnic tables. **Sailwinds Park East** (2 Rose Hill Pl., 410/228-1000, www.tourdorchester.org) is next to the Dorchester County visitors center. There is a playground, and the park is known as a good spot to fly kites.

Cambridge is the site of many endurance events including the **Ironman 70.3 Eagleman Triathlon** (www.ironman.com) in June, **Ironman Maryland** (www.ironman.com) in early October, and the **Six Pillars Century** bike ride (www.6pillarscentury.org) in early May.

**Blackwater Paddle & Pedal** (2524 Key Wallace Dr., 410/901-9255, www.blackwaterpaddleandpedal.com) offers guided three-hour bike tours and two-hour kayak tours. Bike tours depart from the Hyatt Regency, and kayak tours leave from the Hyatt Beach. They also offer rentals for bikes, kayaks, and paddleboards (call for pricing).

## Food

★ **The High Spot** (305 High St., 410/228-7420, www.thehighspotgastropub.com, Mon.-Thurs. 11am-11pm, Fri.-Sat. 11am-midnight, Sun. 11am-10pm, $7-25) is a trendy gastropub serving lunch and dinner. Their food is innovative and tasty, and they have a great beer list and full bar. They also offer special events such as beer pairing dinners. This is a fun

place to eat, with delicious food, a hip atmosphere, and cute little terrariums with cacti on the tables. The only drawback is that it is sometimes very loud inside, but that is due in part to its popularity.

An unexpected French treat in Cambridge is the ★ **Bistro Poplar** (535 Poplar St., 410/228-4884, www.bistropoplar.com, Thurs.-Sun. starting at 5pm, $24-30). They serve traditional French cuisine infused with local seafood flavors such as scallops and flounder. The restaurant is housed in a historic building constructed in 1895. The interior is unmistakably French with ornate floor tiles, dim lighting, a dark-framed bar, and red velvet cushions. The food is artfully presented by servers well versed in the menu. This is a special find in Cambridge and has won many awards.

The **Blue Point Provision Company** (100 Heron Blvd. at Rte. 50, 410/901-6410, www.chesapeakebay.hyatt.com, Wed.-Sun. 5pm-9pm, $20-45) at the Hyatt Regency is a waterfront restaurant with a great seafood menu and a wonderful deck overlooking the

The High Spot

Choptank River. The restaurant is at the far end of the resort, a short walk down the beach from the main complex. The interior is inviting with nautical touches and soaring ceilings, beautiful ceiling fans, parquet floors, and wooden furniture. There is also a large bar area. The menu offers goodies such as Maryland crab dip, Asian barbecued salmon, fried oysters, and the famous Drunkin' Dancin' Jumbo Shrimp. They also have fresh fish selections daily based on the local catch at area fish markets. For landlubbers, they offer steak and chicken.

For good beer and pub fare, stop in **RaR Brewing** (504 Poplar St., 443/225-5664, www.rarbrewing.com, Mon.-Thurs. 2pm-midnight, Fri. 2pm-2am, Sat.-Sun. noon-midnight, under $15). Located inside a former billiards hall, this friendly brewery is a local favorite. They serve a casual menu with pizza, crab dip, hummus, hot dogs, sandwiches, and more than a dozen delicious beers.

Good diner food at a reasonable price can be found at the **Cambridge Diner and Restaurant** (2924 Old Rte. 50, 410/228-8898, daily 6am-10pm, $10-15). They serve traditional comfort food in large portions.

## Accommodations

At first glance, ★ **The Hyatt Regency Chesapeake Bay Golf Resort, Spa & Marina** (100 Heron Blvd. at Rte. 50, 410/901-1234, www.chesapeakebay.hyatt.com, $399-469 per night) seems a bit "glam" for the quiet town of Cambridge, but it does quite well in providing a self-contained oasis of luxury for both golfing and non-golfing visitors. One of the premier hotels on the Eastern Shore, it sits on 400 acres along the Choptank River and has beautiful views of the water and surrounding marsh. The resort offers elegant rooms and enough activities that visitors can easily park their car and never leave the compound during their stay. The resort is known for its golf course, the River Marsh Golf Club, but is also family friendly, with planned children's activities and many amenities (two pools, hot tub, mini golf, game room, fitness center, spa, water sports, etc.). It is also dog friendly on the first floor.

Guests can grab a drink or a bottle of wine and relax in one of the big rocking chairs that line the patio. The centerpiece is a large open fireplace where guests can toast marshmallows or gather for happy hour. There

The Hyatt Regency Chesapeake Bay Golf Resort, Spa & Marina

are several dining options at the hotel that are nice but not as exquisite as might be expected. Book a room with a view and/or balcony; it costs more but makes a big difference. Opening your curtains in the morning to look out at the water is worth the added expense. Rooms are clean and spacious, and the beds are comfortable. The staff does a good job of making guests feel welcome, and the hotel can also make arrangements for activities both on and off the property.

A wonderful waterfront bed-and-breakfast is the **Lodgecliffe on the Choptank Bed and Breakfast** (103 Choptank Ter., 866/273-3830, www.lodgecliffe.com, $180-200). This gorgeous mansion was built in 1898 and sits on a bluff with wonderful views of the lower Choptank River. The establishment was the first bed-and-breakfast in Dorchester County when it opened in 1986 and has remained a family business. There are four guest rooms, each with an individual personality. A glorious three-course breakfast is served each morning. This is a relaxing retreat with wonderful water views and matching service.

Another lovely inn in the historic area of Cambridge is the **Mill Street Inn** (114 Mill St., 410/901-9144, www.millstinn.com, $179-229). This beautiful Victorian-style home was built in 1894 and offers three individually decorated guest rooms. Each features high-quality linens and towels, specialty soaps, fresh flowers, cable television, DVD players, and free wireless Internet. It is a half block from the Choptank River and within walking distance to restaurants. The innkeepers,

who are retired organic growers and bakers, pride themselves in serving delicious breakfasts, complete with locally grown produce and some unusual items from their yard such as figs and pecans.

Additional accommodations in Cambridge include large chain hotels such as the **Holiday Inn Express Cambridge** (2715 Ocean Gtwy., 877/859-5095, www.ihg.com, $117-135), which is clean, quiet, and well-located on Route 50. This hotel has 85 guest rooms, an indoor pool, wireless Internet, and a fitness room. Each room comes with a refrigerator. Another similar option is the **Comfort Inn and Suites** (2936 Ocean Gtwy., 410/901-0926, www. choice hotels.com, $190-210). This hotel is also on Route 50 and has 65 guest rooms. It also offers an indoor pool, fitness room, free breakfast, and free wireless Internet.

## Information and Services

Additional information on Cambridge can be found at the **Visitors Center at Sailwinds Park East** (2 Rose Hill Pl., daily 8:30am-5pm) or online at www.visitdorchester.org/about-dorchester/visitor-center/.

## Getting There

Most travelers arrive in Cambridge on U.S. Route 50. This east-west route runs from Ocean City, Maryland, to Sacramento, California. The road is known locally as the Ocean Gateway. The **Cambridge-Dorchester Airport** (5263 Bucktown Rd.) is southeast of Cambridge. It is a general aviation airport with one runway.

# Assateague Island

Assateague Island sits opposite Ocean City across the Ocean City Inlet. It is considered part of both Virginia and Maryland. The inlet didn't always exist: It was formed during the Chesapeake-Potomac Hurricane in 1933, which created a nice inlet at the south end of Ocean City, and the Army Corps of Engineers decided to make it permanent.

In its southern reaches, Assateague Island borders Chincoteague Island. Both Assateague and Chincoteague are known for their resident herds of wild ponies and the famous **Wild Pony Swim** (www.chincoteaguechamber.com) that takes place each year in late July, when the herd is taken for a swim from Assateague Island across the channel to Chincoteague Island.

## SIGHTS
### ★ Assateague Island National Seashore

Assateague Island National Seashore (www.nps.gov, year-round in Maryland, 24 hours, $5) was established in 1962. It is managed by three agencies: the National Park Service, U.S Fish & Wildlife Service, and the Maryland Department of Natural Resources. The island includes a beautiful 37-mile beach, dunes, wetlands, and marsh. The island is protected as a natural environment, and many opportunities exist for wildlife viewing. Assateague Island is a stopover for migrating shorebirds and provides important areas for feeding and resting. More than 320 bird species can be viewed here during the year, including the piping plovers, great egrets, and northern harriers.

Assateague Island is also known for its wild ponies. It is widely believed that the ponies originally came to the island years ago when a Spanish cargo ship loaded with horses sank off the coast and the ponies swam to shore. In 1997, a Spanish shipwreck was discovered off the island, which supports this theory.

Other mammals in Assateague include rodents as small as the meadow jumping mouse,

wild ponies on Assateague Island

along with red fox, river otters, and deer. Several species of whales feed off the island's shore, along with bottlenose dolphins.

There are two entrances to the national seashore. One is eight miles south of Ocean City at the end of Route 611. The second is at the southern end of the island at the end of Route 175, two miles from Chincoteague, Virginia. Visitors to Assateague Island mostly stay in Chincoteague or Ocean City since there are no hotel accommodations on the island, but camping is allowed and quite popular.

Park hours and fees are different in Virginia and Maryland and also vary by month in Virginia. Consult www.assateagueisland.com for specific information for the time of year and location you wish to visit.

The **Assateague Island Visitor Center** (Maryland District of Assateague Island, on the southern side of Route 611, 410/641-1441, Jan.-Feb. Thurs.-Mon. 9am-5pm, rest of the year daily 9am-5pm) offers a film on the wild ponies, brochures, aquariums, a touch tank, maps, and other exhibits.

## Assateague Island Lighthouse

The red-and-white-striped **Assateague Island Lighthouse** (www.assateagueisland. com, 0.25 mile from Chincoteague Island and accessible from Chincoteague by car in approximately five minutes and from Maryland in an hour, 757/336-3696, Apr.-Nov. weekends 9am-3pm, free but donations encouraged) is on the Virginia side of Assateague Island. There is a trail that connects Chincoteague with Assateague Island that can be walked or accessed by bicycle. The original lighthouse was built in 1833 but was replaced by a taller, more powerful lighthouse in 1867. The lighthouse is still in operation and features twin rotating lights that sit 154 feet above sea level. The U.S. Coast Guard maintains the light as a working navigational aid, but the Chincoteague National Wildlife Refuge is responsible for the lighthouse preservation efforts. The top of the lighthouse can be visited by the public.

# RECREATION

Due in part to its relative isolation, Assateague Island has one of the nicest beaches on the East Coast. Visitors can enjoy the area by kayaking, beach walking, swimming, fishing, biking, and bird-watching.

The **Maryland Coastal Bays Program** (www.mdcoastalbays.org/rentals) operates a kayak ($15 per hour), canoe ($22 per hour), paddleboard ($25 per hour), and bike rental ($6 per hour) stand at Assateague Island National Seashore (13002 Bayside Dr., Berlin, 410/726-3217, mid-Apr.-Memorial Day weekends 10am-4pm, Memorial Day-Labor Day daily 9am-6pm, Labor Day-mid-Oct. weekends only 10am-4pm). To find the stand, take the second right after the park tollbooth. A 3.5-mile paved bike path leads from Route 611 through the parks.

# CAMPING

Camping is allowed on the Maryland side of the national seashore through the **National Park Service** (410/641-2120, $30). Oceanside and bayside campsites are available all year. Sites do not have hookups but can accommodate tents, trailers, and RVs. There are also horse sites ($50) and group tent sites ($50). Cold showers and chemical toilets are available on-site. Camping is also permitted in **Assateague State Park** (7307 Stephen Decatur Hwy., 410/641-2918, late Apr.-Oct., $30), also on the Maryland side of the island. There are 300 campsites here. Each site has a picnic table, fire ring, room for one car, and access to a bathhouse with warm showers. Backpackers and kayakers can also take advantage of backcountry camping. Camping information can be found at www. assateagueisland.com.

# GETTING THERE

There are two entrances to Assateague Island National Seashore. One is eight miles south of Ocean City at the end of Route 611. From Ocean City, cross the bridge on Route 50 heading west. Turn left at the third traffic light onto Route 611. Follow the brown signs to the park. The second is at the southern end of the island at the end of Route 175, two miles from Chincoteague, Virginia. There are no hotel accommodations on the island; visitors to Assateague Island can stay in Chincoteague or Ocean City.

# Ocean City

For many people, the quintessential summer vacation is a trip to the beach. Ocean City, the most popular destination in Worcester County, stretches for 10 miles along the Atlantic Ocean between Delaware and the Ocean City Inlet. It offers enough stimulation to keep kids of all ages entertained for days. The three-mile wooden boardwalk is packed with shopping, restaurants, games, and amusements and is open all year. Seemingly every inch of real estate is claimed along the strip, and more than 9,500 hotel rooms and 21,000 condominiums provide endless choices for accommodations.

Ocean City's history dates back to the 1500s, when Giovanni da Verrazano came through the area while surveying the East Coast in service of the King of France. By the 17th century, British colonists had settled the area, after moving north out of Virginia. Ocean City took off as a beach community in 1900 when the first boardwalk was built. Back then, the boardwalk was a seasonal amenity that was taken apart each winter, plank by plank, and stored until the following season.

Today, Ocean City is bustling, to say the least. It is a major East Coast destination for people who enjoy the beach, company, entertainment, and a lot of activity. Visitors can get a good taste for the town in a weekend, but many people stay for a week or more. Approximately eight million people visit Ocean City each year.

Ocean City is a family town but also a party town. Unlike its northern neighbor, Atlantic City, it lacks casinos and has limited development options and, as such, is able to keep the beach as its main focus. Although the city refers to itself as "The East Coast's Number One Family Resort," it is also a popular area for high school seniors letting off steam after graduation at what is traditionally known as

Ocean City Boardwalk

# Ocean City

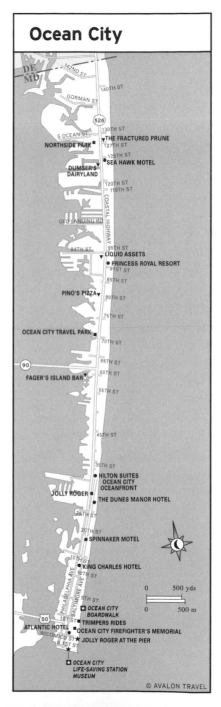

THE FRACTURED PRUNE
NORTHSIDE PARK
SEA HAWK MOTEL
DUMSER'S DAIRYLAND
LIQUID ASSETS
PRINCESS ROYAL RESORT
PINO'S PIZZA
OCEAN CITY TRAVEL PARK
FAGER'S ISLAND BAR
HILTON SUITES OCEAN CITY OCEANFRONT
JOLLY ROGER
THE DUNES MANOR HOTEL
SPINNAKER MOTEL
KING CHARLES HOTEL
OCEAN CITY BOARDWALK
TRIMPERS RIDES
ATLANTIC HOTEL
OCEAN CITY FIREFIGHTER'S MEMORIAL
JOLLY ROGER AT THE PIER
OCEAN CITY LIFE-SAVING STATION MUSEUM

0    500 yds
0    500 m

© AVALON TRAVEL

"Senior Week" or "Beach Week." Keep this in mind if you plan to visit in June. You will have a lot of young, unchaperoned company (the average number of graduating seniors visiting in June is 100,000). Some rental complexes even cater specifically to high school and college groups.

## SIGHTS

### ★ Ocean City Boardwalk

The primary attraction in Ocean City is the three-mile-long boardwalk. It begins at the south end of the beach at the Ocean City Inlet. The boardwalk is lined with dozens of hotels, motels, condos, shops, restaurants, and entertainment venues. There is 24-hour activity on the boardwalk and many attractions and establishments orient visitors by their proximity to this popular landmark. During the summer season the boardwalk is very crowded, so if you like hearing the ocean, smelling french fries, and listening to the sounds of vacationers enjoying themselves, then this is the place to go.

### Ocean City Beach

The beach in Ocean City is wide and sandy. Brightly colored umbrellas are lined up like soldiers in the sand in front of most hotels and are available for rent. Lifeguards are on duty throughout the season and go through a vigorous training program. The beach is swept every night so it remains in fairly clean condition. It is also patrolled regularly by the local police force. In peak season, the beach and water can get very crowded, so visitors should be prepared for a lot of company.

### ★ Ocean City Life-Saving Station Museum

The **Ocean City Life-Saving Station Museum** (813 S. Atlantic Ave., 410/289-4991, www.ocmuseum.org, May and Oct. daily 10am-4pm, June-Sep. daily 10am-6pm, Apr. and Nov. Wed.-Sun. 10am-4pm, Dec.-Mar. weekends 10am-4pm, $3) preserves the history of Ocean City and the U.S. Life-Saving Service (a predecessor of

Ocean City Life-Saving Station Museum

the coast guard that conducted marine rescues). Several fascinating historical exhibits, including one on rescue equipment used to save people who were shipwrecked, and aquariums housing local marine life are on display in a beautifully renovated historic building at the extreme southern end of the Ocean City Boardwalk. Visitors can learn about the history of the boardwalk and its lifeguards, how sailors were rescued at sea, and see examples of old-fashioned bathing suits. This well-maintained, one-of-a-kind museum offers an inexpensive learning experience, powerful exhibits, and great views of the beach. There is a gift store on-site and parking in the municipal lot next door.

## Northside Park

**Northside Park** (125th-127th Sts. on the Bay, 410/250-0125, www.ococean.com) is a beautiful 58-acre park at the end of 125th Street. It has ball fields, a fishing lagoon, paths for walking or biking, a playground, a pier, a picnic shelter, an indoor gym, conference facilities, and a 21,000-square-foot sports arena. Regular events such as Sundaes in the Park (entertainment and make-your-own sundaes) are held regularly.

## Amusement Parks

There are two famous amusement parks on the boardwalk in Ocean City. **Trimpers Rides** (S. 1st St. and the Boardwalk, 410/289-8617, www.trimpersrides.com, outdoor rides: summer starting in June, weekdays 3pm-midnight, weekends noon-midnight; indoor rides: year-round daily noon-midnight, unlimited rides during the day $26) is a historical icon in Ocean City. This amusement park was built in 1893 at the southern point of the boardwalk near the inlet. There are three outdoor amusement lots and a year-round indoor facility. A historic carousel, the Herschel-Spellman merry-go-round, dating back to 1902, is also at Trimpers Rides.

The **Jolly Roger at the Pier** (at the pier at the south end of the Boardwalk, 410/289-3031, www.jollyrogerpieroc.com) is home to the tallest Ferris wheel in town, a double-decker carousel, a coaster called Crazy Dance, and many other amusements. The view from the Ferris wheel is phenomenal. A second Jolly Roger Park is at 30th Street. There is no admission fee to the parks; the rides are "pay-as-you-go," and costs vary between rides.

There are several other amusement parks in Ocean City including the **Frontier Town**

Western Theme Park (Rte. 611, www. frontiertown.com, Apr.-Nov.), and **Baja Amusements** (12639 Ocean Gtwy./Rte. 50, www.bajaoc.com, June-Aug. 9am-midnight, shorter hours Apr.-May and Sept.).

## Ocean City Firefighter's Memorial

The **Ocean City Firefighter's Memorial** (Boardwalk and N. Division St., www.ocvfc. com) is a six-foot-tall bronze statue of a firefighter that stands on a black granite base. The memorial honors "firefighters of the world, the Ocean City firefighters of the past, present, and future, as well as the 343 FDNY firefighters lost on 9/11." The memorial stands in a 2,500-square-foot plaza, surrounded by engraved brick pavers. A recovered piece of twisted steel from the World Trade Center also stands as a memorial to the firefighters who lost their lives on 9/11. A memorial event is held at the site each year on September 11.

## ENTERTAINMENT
### Nightlife

There's no shortage of nightlife in Ocean City. One of the premier hot spots is **Seacrets** (117 W. 49th St., 410/524-4900, www.seacrets. com), a Jamaican-themed entertainment complex featuring 14 bars and a dance club with nightly music (DJ and live). It is open all year and has an artificial beach and real palm trees. It is one place where people of different ages can mingle together. There is a dress code, so consult the website if you think your attire might be questionable.

**The Purple Moose Saloon** (on the Boardwalk between Talbot and Caroline Sts., 410/289-6953, www.purplemoose.com) is a nightclub on the boardwalk that offers nightly live rock and roll mid-May-August. It is one of the few places to walk into and have a drink on the boardwalk.

**Fager's Island Bar** (201 60th St. on the Bay, 410/524-5500, www.fagers.com) is a good place to have a drink on the bay. They offer nightly entertainment with dancing and DJs. Jazz and bluegrass music is featured early with

pop and dance music taking over after 9pm. The establishment has a bit of a split personality. The restaurant side has an upscale feel to it, while the nightclub side caters to the younger dance crowd.

## SPORTS AND RECREATION
### Fishing

Ocean City is known as the "White Marlin Capital of the World." A large fishing tournament called the **White Marlin Open** (www. whitemarlinopen.com) is held there each year at the beginning of August. Anglers of all abilities will find plenty of places to cast a line, whether it be off a boat, pier, or in the surf. For starters, try the public fishing piers at **Inlet Park** (S. 2nd St.), the **Third Street Pier** (bayside), **Ninth Street Pier** (bayside), and **Northside Park** (125th Street, bayside). Fishing charter companies include **Fin Chaser Sportfishing Charters** (12806 Sunset Ave., 443/397-0315, www.finchasersportfishing.com, $800-2,550) and **Ocean City Girl** (302/448-4184, www.oc-girl.com, starting at $266).

### Boating

There are several public boat ramps in Ocean City including ones at **Assateague State Park** (Rte. 611 at the Assateague Island Bridge), **Gum Point Road** (off Rte. 589), and **Ocean City Commercial Harbor** (Sunset Ave. in West Ocean City).

### Kayaking, Paddleboarding, and Windsurfing

For some hands-on action on the water, rent a kayak or paddleboard from **48th Street Watersports** (4701 Coastal Hwy., 410/524-9150, www.48thstreetwatersports.com, starting at $15). This bayfront facility has a wonderful beach and is a great location to try out a number of water sports. Learn to sail, try out sailboarding—they have just about every type of water toy you can dream of. They will even deliver kayaks to your location and pick them up at no extra charge. Kayak rentals and tours are also available from **Ayers Creek**

**Adventures** (8628 Grey Fox Ln., Berlin, 443/513-0889, www.ayerscreekadventures.com, starting at $15) in nearby Berlin.

## Boat Tours

Take a dolphin and nature excursion with **The Angler** (312 Talbot St. bayside, 410/289-7424, www.angleroc.net) aboard a 65-foot boat to explore the shores of Assateague Island and catch a glimpse of the resident ponies on land and dolphins at sea. Tours originate at the Ocean City Inlet. The Angler also offers deep-sea fishing ($65) and 45-minute scenic evening cruises.

## Surfing

If surfing like a local is more your style, rent a board from **Chauncey's Surf Shop** (2908 Coastal Hwy., 410/289-7405, www.chaunceyssurfshop.com, $25). They also rent paddleboards.

## Biking

Bike rentals are available from **Dandy Don's Bike Rentals** (1109 Atlantic Ave., 410/289-2289, www.dandydonsbikerentals.com, starting at $7). They rent beach cruisers, "Boardwalk Cars," banana bikes, and surreys. **Bike World** (6 Caroline St., 410/289-2587, www.bikeworldoc.com) also rents bikes and surreys near the boardwalk.

## Miniature Golf

Ocean City boasts a wide selection of mini golf courses. Try one or two or a new one every day. **Old Pro Golf** (outdoor locations 23rd St. and 28th St., indoor locations 68th St. and 136th St., 410/524-2645, www.oldprogolf.com, $8.50) has four locations in Ocean City. The indoor golf course and arcades on 68th Street and 136th Street are open all year. **Lost Treasure Golf** (13903 Coastal Hwy., 410/250-5678, www.losttreasuregolf.com, open Mar.-Nov.) offers 18 holes dedicated to noted explorer Professor Duffer A. Hacker.

# FOOD
## American

**Liquid Assets** (9301 Coastal Hwy., 410/524-7037, www.la94.com, Sun.-Thurs. 11:30am-11pm, Fri.-Sat. 11:30am-midnight, $13-34) is a surprisingly trendy little restaurant hidden within a strip mall, inside a liquor store. Guests pick their wine right off the shelf with or without the help of the staff and pay a corking fee to drink it with dinner. The menu is wide-ranging, the food is delicious, and the presentation is appealing. This unusual little gem is geared toward adults and does not serve a children's menu. The bar area is rustic with oak barrels, and the bistro has couches and tables that are well spaced so you aren't sitting on top of your neighbor. There's normally a long wait for seating, but they do not take reservations.

## Italian

For good pizza, try **Pino's Pizza** (8101 Coastal Hwy., 410/723-3278, open daily in summer season, hours vary by month, $8-37). This joint has terrific pizza with a zesty sauce and is open until 4am. They offer pick-up and delivery only—no dining in. They are very generous with their cheese (both mozzarella and white cheddar) and toppings, and the slices are delicious and filling. They have reliable, friendly service and often offer coupons on their website. Be aware when ordering the really large pizzas that sometimes the price of two smaller ones is much cheaper.

## Seafood

★ **The Shark on the Harbor** (12924 Sunset Ave., 410/213-0924, www.ocshark.com, Sunday brunch 10:30am-3pm, lunch daily 11:30am-4:30pm, dinner daily 4:30pm-10pm, $12-35) offers an ever-changing menu of fresh seafood, dictated by what is available and fresh on that day. They serve lunch and dinner daily and have a happy hour and a kid's menu. The restaurant is on a commercial fishing harbor and is known for having great views of the harbor and Assateague Island. The owners describe the style of food offered as "globally influenced seasonal cuisine," which allows them to be creative in their daily menu offerings. Local seafood is prominently featured on the menu, and they also serve organic produce and natural dairy and meat products. Don't let the plain exterior fool you; the inside of this restaurant is hip and comfortable and has large windows. The large bar is the primary internal feature, with seating on three sides. The full menu can be ordered at the bar, at pub-style tables, or at regular dining tables. The clientele is good mix of vacationers and locals, and the owners are extremely friendly.

The **Captain's Galley Restaurant and Lounge** (12817 Harbor Rd., 410/213-2525, www.captainsgalleyoc.com, daily 11:30am-10pm, upstairs $6-14, downstairs $14-33) is on the waterfront in the harbor and offers free boat docking for customers. They specialize in seafood and are known for having some of the best crab cakes in Ocean City, which is a steep claim given the overwhelming competition. They also have a variety of steaks on the menu. The restaurant has two levels and two menus. The downstairs menu is a dinner menu (starting at 4:30pm), and the upstairs menu is casual (starting at 11:30am) with sandwiches, seafood baskets, steamed

seafood, and individual sides. You can't mix menus, so choose which floor to dine on based on what you want to eat. Enjoy a great view of the harbor from the inside or dine outside on the large deck, which is a great place for digging into a pile of freshly steamed crabs. The interior is a bit dated, but the food and view compensate.

For great local crab cakes visit the **Crabcake Factory** (12000 Coastal Hwy., 410/250-4900, www.crabcakefactoryonline. com, Mon.-Thurs. 11am-9pm, Fri.-Sat. 9am-11pm, Sun. 9am-9pm). They specialize in local seafood, including their signature crab cakes, peel-and-eat shrimp, and crab pizza. They are also known for their breakfasts and Bloody Marys. Breakfast is served Friday-Sunday at the Ocean City location, and the second location in Fenwick Island (37314 Lighthouse Road, 302/988-5000) serves breakfast daily and has great views of the bay.

## Doughnuts
**The Fractured Prune** (127th St. and Coastal Hwy., 410/250-4400, www.fracturedprune. com) is a well-known doughnut shop that was featured on the Food Network's *Unwrapped*.

The Shark on the Harbor

It is hidden in the North Bay Shopping Center near Ledo Pizza. The specialty is "hot-dipped, made to order" doughnuts, and they're home to the "create your own donut." Guests can select from 15 doughnut glazes and multiple toppings to create their dream doughnut. Standard Fractured Prune flavors include interesting names such as "Black Forest" and "Sand." This small shop turns out 840 yummy cake doughnuts each hour and has become an icon at the beach. The shop doesn't offer prune toppings; it was named after an iconic lady named Prunella, who lived in Ocean City in the early 1900s and traveled around competing against men in different sports. She was always on crutches from getting hurt, so the shop is named the Fractured Prune after her. There are five additional locations in West Ocean City (9636 Stephen Decatur Hwy.), on the boardwalk (Boardwalk and 14th Street), on 81st Street (81st and Coastal Hwy) at 28th Street (2808 Philadelphia Ave.) and 56th Street (5601 Coastal Hwy.).

### Classic Beach Food

The beach and ice cream go hand in hand. **Dumser's Dairyland** (124th St. and Coastal Hwy., 410/250-5543, www.beach-net. com, Memorial Day-Labor Day daily 7am-11:30pm), which was established in 1939, offers beachgoers an ice-cream parlor and restaurant that is open late in the summer (hours are shorter in the off-season). They also have locations at 49th Street and Coastal Highway plus three stands on the boardwalk.

Another longtime favorite is **Thrasher's French Fries** (www.thrashersfrenchfries. com, under $5). They've been making french fries on the boardwalk since 1929. With three locations in Ocean City—at the Pier, 2nd Street and Boardwalk, and 8th Street and Boardwalk—the aroma of Thrasher's is one of the defining smells of the boardwalk.

**Dolle's** (500 S. Boardwalk at Wicomico St., 410/289-6000, www.dolles.com, daily 10am-6pm, Fri.-Sat. 10am-8pm) has been a staple on the boardwalk since 1910. They make

mouthwatering saltwater taffy, fudge, popcorn, and other candy.

**Fisher's Popcorn** (200 S. Boardwalk, www.fisherspopcorn.com, 410/289-5638) is another Ocean City icon. This family-owned and operated business opened in 1937 and offers many flavors of mouthwatering popcorn. They are especially known for their caramel popcorn.

## ACCOMMODATIONS
### $100-200

A good value is the **Sea Hawk Motel** (12410 Coastal Hwy., 410/250-3191, www. seahawkmotel.com, $178-210). This older motel is a half block from the beach and offers 60 motel rooms and efficiencies with kitchens. Sleeping areas are separated from living areas. The rooms are spacious and clean, and there's an outdoor pool.

The **King Charles Hotel** (1209 N. Baltimore Ave., 410/289-6141, www. kingcharleshotel.com, $114-189) is a small hotel a block from the boardwalk. The 22 rooms are modest but competitively priced and clean. They are available with one queen bed or two double beds. There are small refrigerators and microwaves in the rooms. The hotel owners are very friendly and make it feel more like a bed-and-breakfast (minus the breakfast) than a hotel.

The **Atlantic Hotel** (oceanfront on the Boardwalk and Wicomico St., 410/289-9111, www.atlantichotelocmd.com, $160-250) was the first boardwalk hotel in Ocean City. It was built in 1875 and was considered one of the finest hotels on the East Coast. It burned down in a devastating fire in 1925 but was rebuilt the following year. Today, the hotel is still going strong and offers guests a central location on the boardwalk and a rooftop deck overlooking all the action and the ocean. They offer 100 rooms with one or two queen beds, and there are also two apartments for rent on a weekly basis. The rooms are small and cozy but clean. They feature dark wood furniture and small private bathrooms. There is an outdoor pool for guests. The staff is very friendly, and the location is ideal for those wanting to stay on the boardwalk.

## $200-300

### The ★ Atlantic House Bed and Breakfast

(501 N. Baltimore Ave., 410/289-2333, www. atlantichouse.com, $200-250) is a diamond in the rough in a town packed with imposing hotels and motels. This little Victorian-style treasure built in the 1920s sits right on North Baltimore Street and is conspicuously different from the surrounding accommodations. The nine guest rooms (seven with private baths and two with semiprivate) are small since the home was originally a boardinghouse, but they are immaculate and tidy. Second-story room decor is mostly floral and wicker, while the third-floor rooms have paneling. The grounds are nicely maintained, and there is a wonderful front porch where guests can watch the bustle of activity on the busy street. The location is central to the Ocean City attractions, just one street back from the boardwalk. The innkeepers are extremely warm and helpful and are a great asset to the establishment. Breakfast is delicious and plentiful with egg dishes, meats, fruit, and waffles. Snacks are also offered each afternoon. This bed-and-breakfast gets a lot of repeat business.

The **Dunes Motel** (2700 Baltimore Ave., 410/289-4414, www.ocdunes.com, $269-309) is an older motel at the end of the boardwalk offering 49 oceanfront rooms and 62 poolside rooms. The decor is older, but the motel is a good value for budget-minded travelers and the rooms are clean. There's an outdoor pool and direct beach access. The motel's sister property, **The Dunes Manor Hotel** (2800 Baltimore Ave., 410/289-1100, www.dunes-manor.com, $449-469), is next door. It offers 174 rooms and an indoor pool that can be used by guests of both establishments.

The **Spinnaker Motel** (18th St. and Baltimore Ave., 410/289-5444, www.ocmotels.com, $242-346) offers 100 clean guest units within a short walk to the boardwalk (about a half block). Although not fancy, the rooms are reasonably priced and many have good views of the ocean. There is parking on-site, an outdoor pool, and free wireless Internet. This hotel is a good value for families on a budget.

## Over $300

The **Hilton Suites Ocean City Oceanfront** (3200 N. Baltimore Ave., 410/289-6444, www. oceancityhilton.com, $579-659) is one of the nicest hotels in Ocean City. All 225 modern rooms are oversize, luxurious suites on the oceanfront and offer nicely sized balconies. Each suite has a kitchen. There are both an indoor pool and a lovely outdoor pool overlooking the ocean that has a swim-up bar. There is also a children's pool with a waterslide and a lazy river. The hotel is about five blocks from the boardwalk (10-minute walk). The hotel offers live music, movie nights, and children's activities. It is very family-oriented. Parking right at the hotel is limited, but there is additional parking across the street. This is a beautiful hotel with nice amenities, as it should be for the price.

The **Princess Royal Resort** (91st St. Oceanfront, www.princessroyale.com, $299-399) is an oceanfront hotel with 310 two-room suites and 30 condos. They offer pleasant rooms with kitchenettes, comfortable beds, and great views. Ask for a room with a good view; the staff will often do their best to accommodate the request. The hotel has a large indoor pool and scheduled activities such as movie night on the beach and live music by the outdoor bar. The furniture is a bit dated, but otherwise this is good choice for oceanfront accommodations. Their prime rib and seafood buffet is a tasty option for dinner.

## Condos

There are many condos for rent in Ocean City. **Summer Beach Condominium** (410/289-0727, www.summerbeachoc.com) and **Holiday Real Estate** (800/638-2102, www. holidayoc.com) are management companies that offer weekly rentals.

the Princess Royal Resort

## Camping

**Frontier Town** (Rte. 611 and Stephen Decatur Hwy., Berlin, 410/641-0880, www.frontiertown.com, Apr.-Nov., starting at $32) in nearby Berlin offers tent and RV facilities. They are open seasonally and only five minutes from Ocean City.

## INFORMATION AND SERVICES

For additional information on Ocean City, visit www.ococean.com or stop by the **Ocean City Visitor Information Center** (12320 Ocean Gateway, 410/213-0552).

## GETTING THERE

Ocean City is a 2.5-hour drive from Annapolis (109 miles). Most people arrive by car via Route 50 or Route 113 (the two primary routes to the area). **Greyhound** (12848 Ocean Gtwy., 410/289-9307, www.greyhound.com) bus service is also available to Ocean City.

## GETTING AROUND

Route 528 is the only major road running north-south in Ocean City. It is called Philadelphia Avenue at the southern end and the Coastal Highway everywhere else. Streets running east-west in Ocean City are numbered beginning in the south, and run up to 146th before the Delaware border. Locations are normally explained by the terms "oceanside" (east of the Coastal Highway) or "bayside" (west of the Coastal Highway).

The **Boardwalk Tram** (410/289-5311, June-Aug. daily 11am-midnight, shorter hours spring and fall, $3 per ride or $6 unlimited daily pass) is a seasonal tram that runs the entire length of the boardwalk from the inlet to 27th Street. The tram stops at most locations along the boardwalk. It takes 30 minutes to ride the entire length of the boardwalk.

The Coastal Highway **Beach Bus** (410/723-2174, www.oceancitymd.gov, $3 all-day pass) is a municipal bus service that runs 24/7 along the Coastal Highway. Free parking is available at the two bus transit centers at South Division Street and at the West Ocean City Park and Ride.

# Delaware Beaches

Just north of Ocean City, along the Coastal Highway, is the Delaware state line and some of the nicest beach resort areas in the mid-Atlantic. Three main areas—Bethany Beach, Rehoboth Beach, and Lewes—attract visitors year-round. They offer first-class restaurants, historic beach charm, and lovely accommodations in all price ranges. Although not as busy as their southern neighbor, they each offer their own attractions and have sights of historical interest.

## GETTING THERE

**DART First State and the Delaware Transit Corporation** (www.dartfirststate. com) offers public bus transportation between Ocean City and the Delaware beaches. A parking lot ($8) is north of Rehoboth Avenue on Shuttle Road. With the price of parking, you receive four free unlimited-ride daily bus passes. Stops are located throughout the resort areas.

## BETHANY BEACH

Bethany Beach is located in southeastern Delaware, 15 miles north of Ocean City, Maryland. It is part of a seven-mile stretch of beach referred to as the "Quiet Resorts," along with South Bethany Beach and Fenwick Island. Bethany Beach is small and much lower-key than nearby Ocean City and Rehoboth Beach. It is mostly residential, and there is a small shopping area at its heart.

Since 1976, visitors to Bethany Beach have been greeted by **Chief Little Owl,** a 24-foot totem pole that was donated to the town as part of a project by sculptor Peter Wolf Toth, who carved more than 50 wooden works of art in honor of famous Native Americans and gave one to every state. The current totem is actually the third version of the sculpture to stand in Bethany Beach. The first two were destroyed by decay. The current version was created in 2002 of red cedar and is expected to last 50-150 years.

**EASTERN SHORE**
DELAWARE BEACHES

downtown Bethany Beach

## Sights

### BETHANY BEACH

The beach at **Bethany Beach** is wide, sandy, and family-oriented. Although it would be a stretch to say it's empty during the season, it is mostly quiet at night and offers a relaxing atmosphere during the day. Visitors will need to pay to park (there are meters near the beach entrance on Garfield Street).

### BETHANY BEACH BOARDWALK

The **Bethany Beach Boardwalk** is a pleasant family area with less fanfare than the boardwalk in nearby Ocean City. It is basically a nice walkway made of wooden planks. The boardwalk entrance is at the end of Garfield Street, and the boardwalk itself stretches between 2nd and Parkwood Streets. There is plenty to do and see with shops, restaurants, and free concerts at the bandstand on weekends during the summer.

### BETHANY BEACH NATURE CENTER

The **Bethany Beach Nature Center** (807 Garfield Pkwy., Rte. 26, 302/537-7680, www.inlandbays.org, mid-June-Oct. Tues.-Fri. 10am-3pm, Sat. 10am-2pm, donations appreciated) offers interactive exhibits that enable visitors to explore the Inland Bays watershed and learn about local flora and fauna. It is housed in a beautiful cottage built around 1901. Nature trails on the 26-acre grounds take visitors through wetlands and forest. There is also a play area for children.

### THE FENWICK ISLAND LIGHTHOUSE

The **Fenwick Island Lighthouse** (146th St. and Lighthouse Ave., http://fenwickislandlighthouse.org, end of May-June weekends 9am-noon, July-Aug. Fri.-Mon. 9am-noon, Sept. weekends 9am-noon, free) stands 87 feet above Fenwick Island. It was built in 1859 after an increase in shipwrecks near the Fenwick Shoals (a shallow area 6 miles offshore). The operational lighthouse tower is closed to visitors, but there is a small museum at its entrance that is run by the New

Friends of the Fenwick Island Lighthouse. Visiting hours are Friday-Monday 10am-2pm during the summer. Admission is free but donations are appreciated.

### DISCOVERSEA SHIPWRECK MUSEUM

The **DiscoverSea Shipwreck Museum** (708 Coastal Hwy., Fenwick Island, 302/539-9366, www.discoversea.com, June-Aug. daily 11am-8pm, free) is a dynamic museum that recovers and preserves the area's maritime history. Exhibits are centered on shipwreck artifacts dating back to the colonial era (gold, coins, cannons, personal items, even old rum). The museum is run by public donations and owner contributions. Exhibits change with the discovery and acquisition of new artifacts, but the average number of items on display is 10,000. Many additional items are rotated through exhibits around the world. Check the website for hours during the off-season.

## Recreation and Entertainment

**Delaware Seashore State Park** (Rte. 1 between Bethany Beach and Dewey Beach, 302/227-2800, www.destateparks.com, daily 8am-sunset, $10) is to the north of Bethany Beach along the coast. The park of more than 2,800 acres covers a thin strip of land between the Atlantic and Rehoboth Bay. The primary attraction in the park is the beach itself—a six-mile-long beach lover's paradise—where visitors can swim and relax along the shore. There are modern bathhouses with showers and changing rooms, and lifeguards are on duty during the day in the summer. There are also snack vendors and beach equipment rentals such as chairs, rafts, and umbrellas. Fishing is popular in the park and can be done in the surf in designated locations or from the banks of the Indian River Inlet. There is also a special-access pier for the elderly or people with disabilities.

Just north of the inlet on the beach in Delaware Seashore State Park is a designated surfing and sailboarding area. The shallow bays are also good areas for sailboarding and sailing. A boat ramp for nonmotorized craft is also available.

**Holt's Landing State Park** (302/227-2800, www.destateparks.com, daily 8am-sunset, $10) is on the southern shore of the Indian River Bay (take Route 26 West from Bethany Beach and turn right on County Road 346 to the park entrance). Clamming, fishing, and crabbing are possible in the park, along with facilities such as a picnic pavilion, playground, horseshoe pit, and ball fields. Two great kayaking trails start in the park. The first is a 10-mile paddle to the **Assawoman Wildlife Area** (allow five hours), and the second is to Millsboro, which is just under 10 miles.

Mini golf is a staple at the beach, and **Captain Jack's Pirate Golf** (21 N. Pennsylvania Ave., 302/539-1122, www.captainjackspirategolf.com, seasonal daily 9am-11:30pm, $8.50) is the place to go in Bethany Beach. It has eye-catching features such as a large skeleton pirate and pirate's ship, rock and water features, and palm trees. The course is well maintained and a fun place for the entire family. There's a small gift shop on-site.

If you're visiting in early September, check out the one-day **Annual Bethany Beach Boardwalk Arts Festival** (Bethany Beach Boardwalk, 302/539-2100, www.bethanybeachartsfestival.com). More than 100 artists exhibit their work on the boardwalk and surrounding streets. Local and national artists partake in this anticipated event that draws more than 7,500 visitors. Admission is free.

## Food

★ **Off The Hook** (769 Garfield Pkwy., 302/829-1424, www.offthehookbethany.com, Sun.-Thurs. 11:30am-9pm, Fri.-Sat. 11:30am-10pm, $8-27) offers excellent seafood in an off-the-beaten-path location. The seafood and the atmosphere are both fresh, with creative dishes and specials. They are known for the cioppino (a fish stew with shellfish, finfish, garlic confit, chorizo, and pesto in a tomato broth). The restaurant prides itself in supporting local farmers and anglers. They do not take reservations, so there can be a long wait time.

A local favorite is the **Cottage Café Restaurant** (33034 Coastal Hwy., 302/539-8710, www.cottagecafe.com, daily 11am-1am, $10-29). This is a good family restaurant serving local seafood. The staff is kind and patient,

Off The Hook

and the menu is wide enough to satisfy most tastes. Menu selections include crab cakes, fried oysters, stuffed flounder, pot roast, pasta, and meat loaf. The food is not fancy, but it is consistent and reasonably priced.

For fresh crepes, visit **Sunshine Crepes** (100 Garfield Pkwy., 302/537-1765, summer daily 8am-2pm, under $10). This casual and affordable breakfast stop in downtown Bethany Beach by the boardwalk makes fresh savory and sweet crepes with a nice selection of fillings. You can even watch the kitchen staff at work. The atmosphere is not fancy, but the portions are large and the food is tasty. This is a nice alternative to regular bacon and eggs. If you like bananas, try the banana crepe. This is a wonderful local business offering something a little different coupled with friendly service.

## Accommodations

**Meris Gardens Bed & Breakfast** (33309 Kent Ave., 302/752-4962, www. merisgardensbethany.com, $139-169) is a small, affordable bed-and-breakfast that used to be the Westward Pines Motel. They offer 14 comfortable rooms and are located in a quiet area of Bethany Beach. All rooms have private bathrooms and they are dog friendly ($20 charge). It is convenient to the beach (four blocks), and downtown Bethany Beach is within walking distance. Breakfast is included. This property offers simple, friendly accommodations with personal service.

The **Addy Sea** (99 Ocean View Pkwy., 302/539-3707, www.addysea.com, $175-375) is a renovated oceanfront Victorian home and guesthouse that is now an adults-only bed-and-breakfast. The home offers 13 guest rooms and is furnished with antiques, tin ceilings, and original woodwork. The rooms are comfortable, the staff is friendly, and the location is wonderful. The breakfasts are also plentiful with good choices. Book a room with an ocean view for the best experience. Not all rooms have private baths, and Room 12 is the only one with a television.

The **Sea Colony Resort** (Rte. 1,

888/500-4261, www.wyndhamvacation rentals.com) is a large and well-known condominium resort in Bethany Beach with 2,200 units. Condo rentals are available through a number of management companies. Amenities include tennis courts, a fitness center, a small shopping area, and pools. The beaches around Sea Colony are some of the busiest in Bethany Beach due to the large number of condos in the complex; however, the half-mile stretch of beach is for guests and visitors of the resort only, which does make it somewhat private. Units of different sizes are available for rent. Additional information can be obtained at www.resortquestdelaware.com.

## Information and Services

For additional information on Bethany Beach, visit www.bethanybeachde.com or stop by the **Bethany-Fenwick area visitor information center** (daily Mon.-Fri. 9am-5pm, Sat. 9am-3pm) on the Coastal Highway between Fenwick Island State Park and Lewes Street.

# REHOBOTH BEACH

Rehoboth Beach is 14 miles north of Bethany Beach. It is the happy medium among the Maryland and Delaware beaches. It is larger and more commercial than Bethany Beach, yet smaller and less commercial than Ocean City.

Rehoboth Beach was founded in 1873 as a Methodist Episcopal Church beach camp. Today, the town is known as "the Nation's Summer Capital," since so many visitors come from Washington DC each year. The town is also noted for its eclectic shops, wonderful eateries, artistic appeal, and the large number of gay-owned businesses. Downtown Rehoboth Beach is one square mile and has more than 200 shops, galleries, and spas, 40 hotels and bed-and-breakfasts, and more than 100 restaurants.

Just south of Rehoboth is **Dewey Beach,** which is known as a party town for young adults during the summer months. The two towns share a beautiful strand of sandy white

# Rehoboth Beach

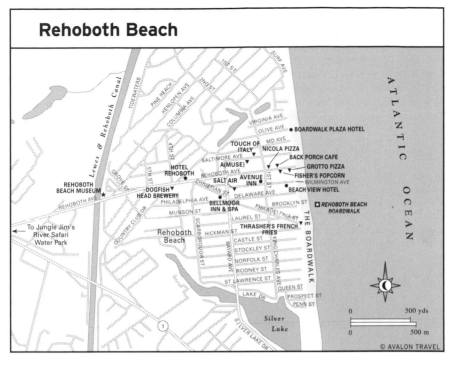

beach that continues to be the main attraction despite all the built-up distractions.

Dogs are not permitted to run loose on the beach in Rehoboth. They are prohibited from the beach and boardwalk 24 hours a day between May 1 and September 30, but they are allowed on the beach in Dewey prior to 9:30am and after 5:30pm (although they still must be leashed and have a Dewey Beach license). There is a strict leash law, and owners must pick up after their dogs.

## Sights
### ★ REHOBOTH BEACH BOARDWALK

The easiest public access to the mile-long boardwalk in Rehoboth Beach is from Rehoboth Avenue. Less crowded than Ocean City, yet more lively than Bethany Beach, the boardwalk offers all the action you could want at the beach including terrific views of the ocean, french fries, T-shirt shops, games, candy stores, and entertainment. The boardwalk is wide and clean and stretches from Penn Street at the south end to Virginia Avenue at the north end. Parking is available on Rehoboth Avenue, and parking meters are enforced during the summer months 10am-midnight. The meters take quarters and credit cards. Change machines are available at the Bandstand on Rehoboth Avenue.

### REHOBOTH BEACH MUSEUM

The **Rehoboth Beach Museum** (511 Rehoboth Ave., 302/227-7310, www.rehobothbeachmuseum.org, Labor Day-Memorial Day Mon.-Fri. 10am-4pm, Sat.-Sun. 11am-3pm, free but donations appreciated) is a small museum with displays portraying the history of Rehoboth Beach. Visitors can see vintage bathing suits, postcards, and classic boardwalk rides and games, and learn about the early beach hotels in town.

## Entertainment and Events

The **Clear Space Theatre Company**

(www.clearspacetheatre.org) is a year-round professional theatrical company that presents musical and dramatic productions. Performances are held in the **Rehoboth Theatre of the Arts** (20 Baltimore Ave.).

The **Rehoboth Beach Jazz Festival** (www.rehobothjazz.com) is an annual event that takes place for four days in October. There are three stages throughout the town for performances as well as additional venues in local establishments.

## Shopping

The first thing shoppers should know is that there is no sales tax in Delaware. The second thing is that every outlet store you can think of may be found in a large shopping area on Route 1 between Rehoboth and Lewes, at **Tanger Outlets** (36470 Seaside Outlet Dr., 302/226-9223, www.tangeroutlet.com, Mon.-Sat. 9am-9pm, Sun. 10am-7pm).

## Recreation

**Jungle Jim's River Safari Water Park** (36944 Country Club Rd., 302/227-8444, www.funatjunglejims.com, daily in summer 10am-8pm, $38) is Delaware's largest water park and also offers go-karts, mini golf, batting cages, and bumper boats. **Funland at**

**Rehoboth Beach** (6 Delaware Ave., 302/227-1921, www.funlandrehoboth.com, mid-June-mid-Aug. daily, games starting at 10am, rides starting at 1pm, park closes at 11pm, shorter hours on weekends in mid-late May and daily in early-mid-June) is a tradition on the boardwalk dating back to the early 1960s. It offers 19 rides and operates on a ticketed basis ($0.35 per ticket).

## Food
### AMERICAN

**Salt Air** (50 Wilmington Ave., 302/227-3744, www.saltairrestaurant.com, Sun., Wed. and Thurs. 5pm-9pm, Fri.-Sat. 5pm-10pm, $16-46) is a busy, upscale farm-to-fork restaurant with a good vibe. Patrons can watch the skilled kitchen at work and get a text message when their table is ready. The cuisine is American, and there are a lot of creative seafood dishes. Start with the crab deviled eggs; a plate of four can be a bite each for a small group. The menu is full of little surprises (but changes often) such as boardwalk fries, oven-roasted honey sriracha wings, and seafood stew. They also serve incredible salads, such as the kale caesar salad. The kids' menu is worth mentioning, because it strays from the usual chicken tenders to provide small portions of real

Rehoboth Beach Boardwalk

food, like filet mignon and grilled fish. This is a wonderful place for dinner and cocktails and their creativity includes a long list of delightful martinis.

**a(MUSE.)** (44 Baltimore Ave., 302/227-7107, www.amuse-rehoboth.com, Tues.-Sun. 5pm-9pm, Fri.-Sat. 5pm-10pm, small plates $5-18, main $22-31) is a one-of-a-kind restaurant that takes guests through a culinary amusement park of fresh, small plates made of local ingredients. If this doesn't sound like your cup of tea, they also offer full-size entrées that are just as delectable as the small plates. A sample of their menu includes potted chicken, yellow perch, north Atlantic halibut, and strip steak. Their menu changes according to what is available from mid-Atlantic farmers, fisherman, ranchers, and foragers. A five-course tasting menu is available for $69 and a seven-course tasting menu is available for $89.

The original **Dogfish Head Brewery** (320 Rehoboth Ave., 302/226-2739, www.dogfish.com, Sun.-Thurs. noon-11pm, Fri.-Sat. noon-1am, $6-26) is on the main strip of Rehoboth Avenue. They serve a nice variety of fish, burgers, sandwiches, and pizza along with many varieties of their delicious beer. Seasonal beers are always rotating with a few staples available all year. The Indian Brown Ale is a personal favorite, along with the salmon sandwich.

## FRENCH

For several decades, the ★ **Back Porch Café** (59 Rehoboth Ave., 302/227-3674, www.backporchcafe.com, June-Sept. daily, May and Oct. weekends, lunch 11am-3pm, après-surf menu 3pm-5:30pm, dinner 6pm-10pm, $34-42) has delighted visitors with upscale creations from its award-winning chef and owner. The cuisine is unmistakably French, with many wonderful sauces, root veggies, and some entrées such as rabbit, but they also look to seasonal ingredients for inspiration. Start with the crab ravioli, a sure crowd-pleaser, and then choose carefully from the interesting array of main courses. If the wild king salmon is on the

menu, it is one good choice; it is served with a savory butternut squash bisque. The interior is cozy with a bar and some outdoor seating. This restaurant is open for lunch, brunch, and dinner in the summer but is closed in the off-season. Reservations are encouraged. There is no kid's menu.

## ITALIAN

**Lupo Italian Kitchen** (247 Rehoboth Ave., 302/226-2240, www.lupodimarerehoboth.com, Sun.-Thurs. 5pm-9pm, Fri.-Sat. 5pm-10pm, $10-29) is a beautiful little restaurant (formerly called Lupo di Mare) on the first floor of the Hotel Rehoboth on Rehoboth Avenue. It is light and airy inside and offers a menu of flatbread, salad, homemade pasta, and other delightful Italian choices. Their fried calamari is perhaps the best in the area. Their salads offer delicious combinations such as roasted beet and citrus with goat gouda, pickled shallot, beet chips, and candied pistachios. Entrees include lobster bucatini, crab and casarecce, and classics such as chicken parmesan and lasagna. They have shorter hours in the off-season and different off-season specials each night of the week (such as 25 percent off your check on Mondays).

**Touch of Italy** (19724 Coastal Hwy, 302/227-3900, www.touchofitaly.com, Sun.-Thurs. 10:30am-9pm, Fri.-Sat. 10:30am-10pm, $10-45) is a dine-in and carryout Italian deli focused on specialty meats, cheeses, and Italian pastries. They have a huge menu and all sandwiches are made to order.

It would be almost negligent to not mention the classic Rehoboth Beach pizza joint, **Nicola Pizza** (8 N. 1st St., 302/227-6211, www.nicolapizza.com, daily 11am-midnight, $5-27). This pizzeria has been a staple in town since 1971, and for many it is *the* beachy place to bring the family. The wood floors and booths are a reminder of the restaurant's long history. Wait times in the summer can easily be an hour or more. The most popular dish is the "Nic-o-Boli," which is their name for stromboli (they can sell up to 2,000 in one night). This is worth a try if you've never had one, although the regular pizza is also a good choice. There's a second location at 71 Rehoboth Avenue.

Another classic pizza place in Rehoboth is **Grotto Pizza** (36 Rehoboth Ave., 302/227-3278, www.grottopizza.com, Sun.-Thurs. 11am-10pm, Fri.-Sat. 11am-11pm, under $15). This well-recognized restaurant has been around since 1960 and has three locations in Rehoboth Beach. The other two locations are on the boardwalk at 15 Boardwalk and Baltimore Avenue and 17 Surf Avenue. They offer dine-in, carryout, and walk-up pizza.

## SNACKS

**Fisher's Popcorn** (48 Rehoboth Ave., 302/227-2691, www.fishers-popcorn.com, daily Memorial Day-Labor Day, weekends year-round) is a staple on the Maryland and Delaware beaches. You can buy the addicting little morsels by the bucket (0.5-6.5 gallons). They are known for the caramel popcorn but offer several other flavors. Please note: It is easy to eat this until you feel sick. Stopping is hard to do. You've been warned.

Perhaps no beach trip is complete without at least one stop at **Thrasher's French Fries** (26 Rehoboth Ave., 302/227-7366, daily from 11am). This local icon serves up buckets of fresh boardwalk fries from the walk-up window on the boardwalk. Even die-hard ketchup lovers will want to try them with salt and vinegar.

A fun place to stop is **Kaisy's Delights** (70 Rehoboth Ave., 302/212-5360, www.kaisysdelights.com, Sun.-Thurs. 7:30am-5pm, Fri.-Sat. 7:30am-7pm, under $10) for an Austrian Kaisy (a treat made of sweet custardy dough with your choice of toppings such as ice cream or fruit sauce). Their delicious samples may lure you into a sweet Kaisy or even a breakfast Kaisy (they are available with eggs, sausage, and bacon). The coffee is also good. They're open all year.

## Accommodations

The **Avenue Inn & Spa** (33 Wilmington Ave., 800/433-5870, www.avenueinn.com, $269-419) is an independently owned hotel one block from the beach. There are 60 guest rooms with many amenities such as full breakfast, complimentary wine and cheese, evening cookies, a day spa, indoor heated pool, fitness room, sauna, beach chairs, beach shuttle, and free parking.

The **Bellmoor Inn and Spa** (6 Christian St., 302/227-5800, www.thebellmoor.com, $379-639) is a comfortable inn about three blocks from the beach. They offer 22 guest rooms and suites. There are two pools on-site and an enclosed hot tub. Breakfast is served daily (with omelets on the weekends), and the staff is friendly and helpful.

The ★ **Boardwalk Plaza Hotel** (2 Olive Ave., 302/227-7169, www.boardwalkplaza.com, $324-679) is an elegant, Victorian-style oceanfront hotel right on the boardwalk. The hotel is furnished with antiques and antique-style furniture and offers oceanfront rooms with deluxe amenities. The hotel is friendly to children (and even offers special events for them such as craft time) but also has special amenities and areas for adults only (including a rooftop hot tub). The 84 guest rooms are comfortable, clean, and warmly decorated. The staff is friendly and goes out of its way to make visitors feel at home. There's also a restaurant on-site that offers water-view dining, a cozy bar, and a boardwalk patio.

A great choice for a clean, affordable, welcoming stay near the boardwalk is the **Beach View Hotel** (6 Wilmington Ave., 302/227-2999, www.beachviewmotel.com, $234-304). This small hotel offers ocean-view rooms with private balconies and poolside rooms with no balconies. Continental breakfast is included. This hotel is a good value in a convenient location.

## Information and Services

For additional information on Rehoboth Beach, visit www.cityofrehoboth.com, www.rehobothboardwalk.com, and www.downtownrehoboth.com or stop by the **Rehoboth Beach-Dewey Beach Chamber**

**of Commerce and Visitors Center** (501 Rehoboth Ave., 302/227-2233, year-round Mon.-Fri. 9am-5pm, Sat.-Sun. 9am-1pm).

# LEWES

Lewes is seven miles north of Rehoboth and can be summed up in one word: charming. This quaint little town near the beach is a relaxing alternative to the busier beaches along the Delaware and Maryland shore. Lewes is also known as the "first town in the first state," since it was the site of the first European settlement in Delaware, founded in 1631. The town has an upscale beach feel to it and draws visitors of many age groups who come to relax, drink wine, eat good food, and shop.

## Sights
### ★ HISTORIC LEWES

The historic downtown area of Lewes is on the harbor, just a short distance from the Atlantic. Second Street is the main street in town and offers wonderful dining and shopping and a cozy, friendly feel. The downtown area is lovely all year round. It truly is one of the prettiest spots on the mid-Atlantic coast with its historic homes (some dating back to the 17th century), friendly atmosphere, and tidy, well-kept streets. Boutique stores and independently owned restaurants line the sidewalks, and the local residents are friendly and welcoming to tourists.

**Shipcarpenter Square** (www. shipcarpentersquare.com) is a community of delicately and accurately preserved and restored 18th- and 19th-century homes in the historic district. The homes in Shipcarpenter Square are mostly colonial farmhouses built in the late 1700s-late 1800s in other parts of Sussex County and moved to the site in the early 1980s. Other relocated buildings include three barns, a schoolhouse, an inn, a log home, a lifesaving station, a lighthouse, a market, and two Victorian houses.

The Shipcarpenter Square community stretches from 3rd and 4th Street on the east and west side to Burton Street and Park Streets on the north and south sides. Parking and walking access are provided to homeowners in this area. Pedestrians can enter a foot traffic-only area from Park Street and two areas on the north and south edges of the common greens that are located in the heart of the community.

harbor in Lewes

## ZWAANENDAEL MUSEUM

The **Zwaanendael Museum** (102 Kings Hwy., 302/645-1148, http://history.delaware. gov, Apr.-Oct. Tues.-Sat. 10am-4:30pm, Sun. 1:30pm-4:30pm, Nov.-Mar. Wed.-Sat. 10am-4:30pm, free, donations appreciated) is an interesting-looking building (a replica of the Town Hall of Hoorn in the Netherlands) that features Dutch elements from the 17th century such as terra-cotta roof tiles, decorated shutters, a stepped facade gable, and stonework. The museum takes visitors through the history of Lewes as the state's first European settlement (by the Dutch) in 1631 and offers exhibits on the attack on Lewes by the British during the War of 1812, the Delaware coastline, and the Cape Henlopen Lighthouse. The museum also includes a maritime and military history of the town.

## CAPE MAY-LEWES FERRY

The **Cape May-Lewes Ferry** (43 Cape Henlopen Dr., 800/643-3779, www. capemaylewesferry.com, Apr.-Sept. 8am-6pm, Oct.-Mar. 8:30am-4:30pm, car and driver one-way $27-45, extra passenger or pedestrian one-way $10) docks on Cape Henelopen Drive and makes daily 70-minute trips across Delaware Bay to Cape May, New Jersey. Auto and foot passengers are allowed on board, and there is no fee for bicycles. Ferry schedules vary throughout the season. Check the website for current departure times.

## Shopping

The primary shopping district in historic Lewes is on 2nd Street, off Savannah Street. Upscale boutiques, houseware shops, and even a wonderful store for dogs line the manicured street. Ice-cream shops and other snack shops offer a nice break from sightseeing or shopping.

## Sports and Recreation

**Cape Henlopen State Park** (15099 Cape Henlopen Dr., 302/645-8983, www. destateparks.com, daily 8am-sunset year-round, $10) covers five miles of shoreline at the mouth of Delaware Bay where it meets the Atlantic. It has a long military and shipping history. A storm in 1920 took out the lighthouse that used to guide ships through the bay, but breakwater barriers still provide a safe harbor during storms and rough water.

A military base was established at the cape in 1941, and bunkers were hidden among the dunes for protection. Observation towers built of cement, which are still standing, were also put in place along the shore to search for enemy ships. The park was created in 1964. Today the park provides many acres of seaside habitat. There's a nature center, hiking, fishing, swimming, a picnic pavilion, fishing pier, and camping in the park. The two swimming beaches are watched over by lifeguards in the summer.

There are several companies offering fishing supplies and charters in Lewes including **Katydid Charters** (Anglers Rd., 302/858-7783 or 302/645-8688, www. katydidsportfishing.com, starting at $375 for 10 people), **Angler's Fishing Center** (213 Anglers Rd., 302/644-4533, www. anglersfishingcenter.com, starting at $50), and **First Light Charters** (907 Pilottown Rd, 302/853-5717, www.firstlightcharters.net, starting at $275).

Sightseeing cruises are also available at the **Fisherman's Wharf** (107 Anglers Rd., 302/645-8862, www.fishlewes.com, $29-35). They offer two- and three-hour dolphin-watching cruises and a sunset cruise that leaves each evening during the summer at 6:30pm from the wharf docks. The trip goes down the canal and out to the ocean and then turns around near the ferry terminal.

**Dogfish Head Brewery** (302/745-2925, www.dogfish.com, $65) offers a "Pints and Paddles" tour May-October. This kayaking outing for beer enthusiasts is a unique out-and-back paddle on the Broadkill River in the McCabe Nature Preserve (a Nature Conservancy area), followed by a tour of the Dogfish Head Brewery (including samples for those over 21). Trips leave at noon on Wednesday, Friday, and Saturday from the

Beacon Motel parking lot (514 E. Savannah Rd.). A souvenir pint glass is included in the outing.

Golfers can enjoy a round at the **Marsh Island Golf Club** (21383 Camp Arrowhead, 302/945-4653, $55). This 18-hole course has a course rating of 65 and a slope rating of 96. It was designed by Herman John Schneider.

## Food

The ★ **Agave Mexican Grill and Tequila Bar** (137 2nd St., 302/645-1232, www.agave-mexicanrestaurant.net, Mon.-Sat. noon-9pm, Sun. 3pm-9pm, $7-24) is a funky, upscale, sought-after Mexican dining spot that Laura Bush even stopped in one evening unannounced to sample the authentic cuisine. All the food is delicious, but they do a particularly good job with their mole, shrimp and garlic guacamole, and fish tacos. For something a little different, try the apple and moon cheese guacamole. Brightly painted glasses adorn patrons' tables and hold three sizes of margaritas (they have more than 70 types of tequila). The atmosphere is great, the service is attentive and friendly, and the clientele is lively. The only downside to this fabulous little gem is the long wait times for a table (sometimes as much as two hours or more). Plan a late lunch or early dinner to get a jump on the competition. Another option is to put your name on the list and stroll around the town while you wait.

**The Buttery** (102 2nd St., 302/645-7755, www.butteryrestaurant.com, daily lunch and dinner and Sun. brunch, hours vary by season, $26-36) is a local favorite right on 2nd Street. This beautiful Victorian restaurant specializes in upscale seafood entrées and appealing food presentation. The service is professional yet personal, and they can even accommodate diet restrictions. The menu is not large, but everything is done top-notch. They also offer a casual pub menu in the evenings and a daily three course pre fixe menu from 5pm to 6:45pm for $33. There have a lovely year-round veranda and beautiful plantings around the house. Reservations are a must.

For good seafood in a lively pub atmosphere, dine at **Striper Bites** (107 Savannah Rd., 302/645-4657, www.striperbites.com, lunch and dinner daily from 11:30am, $10-28). They offer casual dining indoors or on a patio. The seafood choices are excellent, and the service is friendly and usually prompt. The decor is wood furnishings and things from the sea. This is a go-to place for many locals. They don't take reservations, and on a busy night it can be quite loud indoors, but for the most part it offers a pleasant dining experience and delicious food.

**Crooked Hammock Brewery** (36707 Crooked Hammock Way, 302/644-7837, www.crookedhammockbrewery.com, daily 11am-1am, $8-22) is a fun brewery that offers an energetic atmosphere and a large outdoor space. They have a good selection of craft beers and a menu of casual appetizers, salads, sandwiches, and main dishes such as chicken fried chicken, beef short rib, clam bake, and salmon.

The Buttery

## Accommodations

### INNS AND HOTELS

★ **The Inn at Canal Square** (122 Market St., 302/644-3377, www.theinnatcanalsquare. com, $245-625) is a pretty canal-front inn in the heart of Lewes. The inn has 22 rooms and three VIP suites and can accommodate short- or long-term stays. Most of the rooms have water views and balconies, and the suites offer two bedrooms, full kitchens, washers and dryers, fireplaces, screened porches, and decks. The grounds are adorned with lavish plantings, and fresh flowers are brought into the common areas weekly. Special packages such as golf package and a Dogfish Head Brewery package are available. Breakfast is included with your stay, and the friendly staff can assist with recommending the perfect restaurant for lunch and dinner. The inn is convenient to all the shops and dining options on 2nd Street, and it provides free parking and wireless Internet.

The **Hotel Blue** (110 Anglers Rd., 302/645-4880, www.hotelblue.info, $299-349) is a comfortable boutique hotel with some nice little touches such as mirrored televisions and glowing ice buckets. The lobby is inviting, and the 16 guest rooms are modern and spacious. Each room has a fireplace, private balcony, and pillow-top mattresses. There are also a beautiful rooftop pool and lounge area and a fitness room.

### BED-AND-BREAKFASTS

There are several wonderful bed-and-breakfasts in Lewes near the historic district. Most have minimum night stays during the season, some do not allow small children, and some do not take credit cards, so be sure to ask about these things when you make your reservation if they are important to you.

The **Savannah Inn** (330 Savannah Rd., 302/645-0330, www.savannahinnlewes.com, $190-295) is a lovely turn-of-the-20th-century brick home that was remodeled and now offers six contemporary guest rooms with modern bathrooms. The owners are very personable and take pride in their establishment, which goes a long way in making guests feel welcome. The inn is very clean, and the decor is airy and inviting. It is an easy walk to the historic downtown area and the waterfront. The inn is a family-run business, from the reservations to the kitchen. There is an adorable yellow Labrador who lives here, but the owners are careful about not allowing him in guest areas.

The **John Penrose Virden House** (217 2nd St., 302/644-0217, www.virdenhouse.com, $175-245) is a charming green-colored 19th-century Victorian bed-and-breakfast centrally located on 2nd Street. The three guest rooms are well appointed with antiques and offer beach equipment such as towels and chairs. The hosts do a lovely job of making visitors feel welcome and greet guests with fresh fruit and flowers in their rooms. They also serve a scrumptious homemade breakfast to remember and hold a cocktail hour with snacks and beverages. Bicycles are also available for guests. They do not accept credit cards, only cash or checks.

The **Blue Water House** (407 E. Market St., 302/645-7832, www.lewes-beach.com, $200-235) is a bed-and-breakfast a short walk from the beach and geared toward sandy fun. It offers a slightly funky decor with bright colors. There are nine guest rooms, each with private bathrooms. The owner pays attention to every last detail and goes above and beyond to make guests feel welcome and to keep the house immaculate. Guests are offered many beach amenities such as towels, beach chairs, sunscreen, umbrellas, cold water, and bicycles. Children are welcome, and the house is equipped with games and books.

## Information and Services

For additional information on Lewes, visit www.lewes.com or stop by the **Lewes Visitors Center** (120 Kings Hwy., 302/645-8073, www.leweschamber.com, Mon.-Fri. 10am-4pm).

# Coastal Virginia

Look for ★ to find recommended sights, activities, dining, and lodging.

# Highlights

★ **Colonial Williamsburg:** A living museum that is unmatched nationwide, Colonial Williamsburg takes visitors back in time. It's one of America's most popular family destinations (page 155).

★ **Jamestown National Historic Site:** The original site of the Jamestown settlement spans centuries of history. Founded in 1607, it was the first permanent English settlement in the New World (page 165).

★ **NAUTICUS National Maritime Center:** This nautical-themed science and technology center in Norfolk is also home to the battleship USS *Wisconsin* (page 185).

★ **Virginia Beach Boardwalk:** The most popular beach resort in the state offers enough activity to keep visitors busy for days—and provides access to miles of wonderful sand and surf (page 190).

★ **Virginia Aquarium & Marine Science Center:** Hundreds of exhibits, live animals, and hands-on learning make this amazing aquarium one of the most popular attractions in the state (page 192).

★ **Tangier Island:** This remote island in the middle of the Chesapeake Bay feels like another country. The residents even have their own language (page 203).

★ **Chincoteague National Wildlife Refuge:** This 14,000-acre wildlife refuge protects thousands of birds and a herd of wild ponies. Visitors can enjoy miles of natural beaches and hike or bike through the marsh (page 207).

C oastal Virginia sounds like a simple concept: the place where the Atlantic Ocean meets the land. It's actually much more complicated than that. The Chesapeake Bay is a defining feature along the coast, and the area where it opens into the Atlantic Ocean has developed into one of the world's largest and busiest natural ports. Several large rivers empty into the Chesapeake Bay as well, including the Potomac, Rappahannock, James, and York Rivers.

The coastal region can be divided into five main areas. The first is the Northern Neck, which sits between the Potomac and Rappahannock Rivers, both of which flow into the bay. The Northern Neck is quiet and flat, and farms line the riverbanks. The area is home to several notable historic sites including George Washington's birthplace. The second area is known as the Historic Triangle, which includes the colonial cities of Williamsburg, Jamestown, and Yorktown. These cities sit along the James and York Rivers, which also flow into the Chesapeake Bay. Next is the huge area of Hampton Roads. This is where everything converges. The rivers flow into the bay just to the north, and the Chesapeake Bay flows into the Atlantic Ocean just to the east. The main cities in this area are Newport News, Hampton, and Norfolk. Then we have Virginia Beach. The Virginia Beach resort area is truly on the Atlantic coast. Our final region, Virginia's Eastern Shore, is sandwiched between the Chesapeake Bay on the west and the Atlantic Ocean on the east. It is sparsely populated compared to its mainland neighbors and offers charming historic towns and ample bird-watching and fishing.

## PLANNING YOUR TIME

Visiting Coastal Virginia requires some planning, a love of water, and no fear of bridges. Although there is some public transportation between specific cities, the easiest way to get around is by car. I-64 runs from Richmond down to the Historic Triangle and Hampton Roads areas, while Routes 17 and 3 traverse the Northern Neck. Route 13 runs the length of the Eastern Shore.

---

**Previous:** the Public Hospital of 1733 in Colonial Williamsburg; docks on Tangier Island. **Above:** Assateague Island Lighthouse in Chincoteague National Wildlife Refuge.

# Coastal Virginia

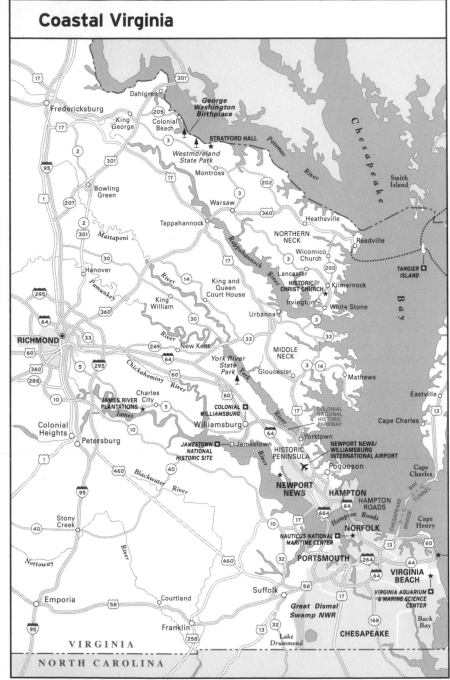

Dahlgren
Fredericksburg
King George
Colonial Beach
205
301
17
17
2
95
301
**George Washington Birthplace**
3
**STRATFORD HALL**
**Westmoreland State Park**
Montross
17
*Potomac River*
*Chesapeake*
Smith Island
1
207
Bowling Green
301
Mattaponi
202
Warsaw
3
360
Tappahannock
Heathsville
NORTHERN NECK
Reedville
2
301
30
Hanover
Pamunkey
River
14
King and Queen Court House
17
Wicomico Church
Lancaster
3
200
*Rappahannock River*
**HISTORIC CHRIST CHURCH**
Kilmarnock
**TANGIER ISLAND**
295
King William
360
30
River
Urbanna
Irvington
White Stone
3
*Bay*
64
RICHMOND
33
New Kent
249
64
60
York River State Park
33
MIDDLE NECK
33
360
295
5
288
Chickahominy River
60
*York River*
Gloucester
3
14
Mathews
10
Charles City
James
5
Eastville
13
**JAMES RIVER PLANTATIONS**
60
**COLONIAL WILLIAMSBURG**
Cape Charles
COLONIAL NATIONAL HISTORIC PARKWAY
Colonial Heights
Williamsburg
10
**JAMESTOWN NATIONAL HISTORIC SITE**
Jamestown
64
Yorktown
HISTORIC PENINSULA
17
Petersburg
1
460
*Blackwater River*
40
*James River*
NEWPORT NEWS/ WILLIAMSBURG INTERNATIONAL AIRPORT
Cape Charles
**NEWPORT NEWS**
Poquoson
95
**HAMPTON**
HAMPTON ROADS
CHESAPEAKE BAY BRIDGE TUNNEL
Stony Creek
40
10
17
564
64
*Hampton Roads*
Cape Henry
*Nottoway River*
460
32
**NORFOLK**
13
60
**NAUTICUS NATIONAL MARITIME CENTER**
**PORTSMOUTH**
264
44
Emporia
58
Courtland
Suffolk
58
17
**VIRGINIA BEACH**
**VIRGINIA AQUARIUM & MARINE SCIENCE CENTER**
Franklin
258
Great Dismal Swamp NWR
13
32
Lake Drummond
168
**CHESAPEAKE**
Back Bay
95

**VIRGINIA**

**NORTH CAROLINA**

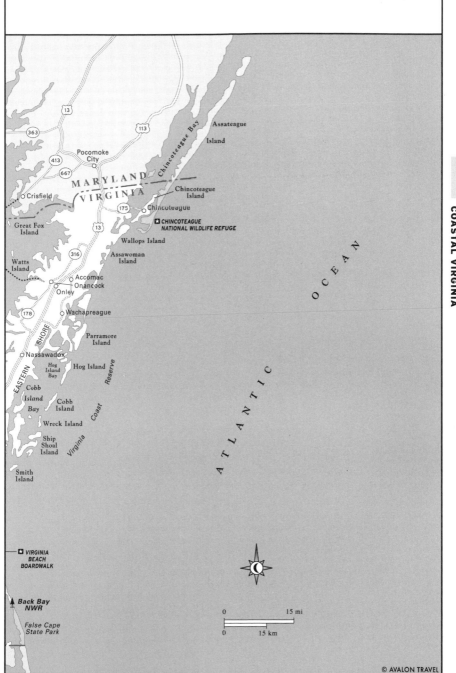

© AVALON TRAVEL

Coastal Virginia is a beautiful region but one that takes days, not hours to explore. If you are limited on time, select one or two key destinations such as Williamsburg and Virginia Beach, or maybe spend a day or two on the Eastern Shore. Wherever you decide to go, keep in mind that the area is heavily visited in the summer months, so you will likely have a few thousand close friends to share the experience with, especially in the historic towns and the beachfront areas.

If you are looking for a one-of-a-kind experience, spend a day visiting Tangier Island. This isolated sandbar of a town is 12 miles out in the Chesapeake Bay and almost feels like a different country.

# Northern Neck

The Northern Neck is a peninsula bordered by the Potomac and Rappahannock Rivers, not far from the Chesapeake Bay and approximately 75 miles from Washington DC. The Northern Neck is laden with history and was explored as early as 1608 by the famed Captain John Smith. George Washington, who was born here, called the region the "Garden of Virginia" for the tidewater landscape and the many forests and creeks that shape this area of the state.

During the steamboat era between 1813 and 1937, the Northern Neck supported a network of approximately 600 steamboats. These mechanical works of art were used to transport both people and goods throughout the Chesapeake Bay area.

In modern times, the Northern Neck is still rural and supports a thriving, generations-old fishing industry. It is also a popular area for recreational boating and water sports. It offers small-town charm, historical sites, colonial architecture, and marinas. Many establishments are only open seasonally, so if you are traveling during the colder months, a quick call ahead could pay off.

## SIGHTS
### George Washington Birthplace
Although the father of our country only lived in the Northern Neck until he was three years old, his birthplace on **Pope's Creek Plantation** (1732 Popes Creek Rd., Colonial Beach, 804/224-1732, www.nps.gov/gewa, daily 9am-5pm, free) on the banks of the Potomac River is a lovely place to visit. The National Park Service maintains a visitors center with a film, exhibits, and bookstore. The actual house Washington was born in no longer exists (it burned down in 1779), but ranger talks about the historic area are offered on the hour between 10am and 4pm. There is a reconstructed colonial farm, with animals and tobacco, operated by costumed interpreters. A one-mile nature trail can be accessed from the picnic area. There is also a beach along the river, but no swimming is permitted. Relatives spanning five generations of Washington's family are buried on the site in the Washington Family Burial Ground, including George's father, grandfather, and great-grandfather.

### Stratford Hall
**Stratford Hall** (483 Great House Rd., Stratford, 804/493-8038, www.stratfordhall. org, daily 9:30am-4pm, $12) is the birthplace of General Robert E. Lee. The beautiful brick mansion, which sits on 1,900 acres next to the Potomac River, was built in the late 1730s. It is furnished with 18th-century American and English pieces (including Lee's crib). The home has 16 fireplaces. Visitors can take a 45-minute house tour (given on the hour), walk six nature trails, enjoy the beach overlook, examine exhibits in a visitors center, and browse a gift shop. There site maintains two great mobile apps, one for the house tour and one for the landscape. The house tour includes a fun historical education component geared

for kids called the SquirrelLee University. The on-site dining room can be reserved for groups of 15 or more for a special buffet.

## Reedville

**Reedville** is a little gem of a town founded in 1867 and a jumping-off point to **Tangier Island** in the Chesapeake Bay. It is known for its thriving Atlantic menhaden fishing industry (menhaden are small, oily fish found in the mid-Atlantic) and in the early 20th century was the wealthiest city per capita in the country. (Millionaire's Row, a string of Victorian mansions along the water, attests to this affluence.) Reedville remains a major commercial fishing port in terms of weight of catch, second behind Kodiak, Alaska.

Don't miss the **Reedville Fishermen's Museum** (504 Main St., 804/453-6529, www.rfmuseum.org, hours change often, call ahead for information, $5) on Cockrell's Creek. There are several parts to the museum: the **William Walker House,** a restored home built in 1875 that represents a watermen's home; the **Covington Building,** which houses temporary exhibits and a permanent collection; and the **Pendleton Building,** which contains a boatbuilding and model shop. In addition, there are two historic boats

at the museum, a skipjack and deck boat. Both are in the National Register of Historic Places.

## Irvington

The historic village of **Irvington** (www. irvingtonva.org) was established in 1891 during the steamboat era. A busy port on the well-traveled Norfolk-Baltimore route, the town thrived during the early 1900s. The Great Fire of Irvington destroyed many businesses in June of 1917, coinciding with the decline of the steamboat era. In 1947, the town was put back on the map with the opening of the **Tides Inn Resort,** and today Irvington is a hip little town with boutique shopping, friendly dining, and several key attractions. It's easy to feel the fun vibe in Irvington. Stroll down Irvington Road and read some of the fun sayings that are posted on signs in the gardens of shops and restaurants. Keep in mind that many establishments are closed on Monday.

The **Steamboat Era Museum** (156 King Carter Dr., 804/438-6888, www. steamboateramuseum.org, Fri.-Sat. 10am-4pm, $5) is a delightful little museum in Irvington that preserves artifacts and information from the steamboat era of the Chesapeake Bay (1813-1937). Steamboats were

the Historic Christ Church

a vital mode of transportation along the bay for both goods and people and the lifeline of the economy connecting the region to cities such as Norfolk, Virginia, and Baltimore, Maryland. This is the only museum fully dedicated to the steamboats of the Chesapeake Bay, and the docents are very entertaining and knowledgeable.

The most treasured historic structure in the Northern Neck is arguably the **Historic Christ Church** (420 Christ Church Rd., Weems, 804/438-6855, www. christchurch1735.org, year-round Mon.-Fri. 10am-4pm, Apr.-Nov. Sat. 10am-4pm, Sun. 1pm-4pm, weekends by appointment the rest of the year, $5). Less than two miles north of Irvington, the church was finished in 1735 and remains one of the few unaltered colonial churches in the United States. It was a center of social and political activity during colonial times, and Sunday service was a big event. In addition to being a place or worship, it was a place to exchange news and the cornerstone of the community. The detailed brickwork in the tall walls and a vaulted ceiling help make it one of the best-crafted Anglican parish churches of its time. Services are still held there, and the interior boasts a triple-decker pulpit, walnut altar, and high-backed pews. **The Carter Reception Center** houses a museum dedicated to the church and its founder, Robert Carter. Guided tours are available from the center, and there is also a gift shop.

## ENTERTAINMENT AND EVENTS

Many of the events in the Northern Neck revolve around water and nature. The **Blessing of the Fleet** is an annual event in Reedville that opens the fishing season on the first weekend of May. There is a parade of boats and the official blessing service. The **Reedville Bluefish Derby** is a large fishing tournament held annually in mid-June that features substantial cash prizes.

Mid-September brings the **Reedville Antique and Classic Boat Show** (www.

acbs.org), featuring an antique boat parade. And mid-November is the time for the much-anticipated **Reedville Fishermen's Museum Oyster Roast** (www.rfmuseum. org). Tickets go on sale in October and sell out quickly for this mouthwatering event.

Wine enthusiasts will enjoy the **Kilmarnock Wine Festival** (www. northernneckwinefestival.com) held annually at the end of June. It offers tastings and sales from local wineries along the **Chesapeake Bay Wine Trail** (www. chesapeakebaywinetrail.com), including more than a dozen wineries in Virginia in the Chesapeake Bay area that can be visited year-round. Each offers wine tastings, sales, gift shops, and tours.

## SPORTS AND RECREATION
### Westmoreland State Park

**Westmoreland State Park** (1650 State Park Rd., Montross, 804/493-8821, www. dcr.virginia.gov, open 24 hours, $5) along the Potomac River offers riverfront beaches, hiking trails, a public pool, kayak and paddleboat rentals, a pond, and cliffs housing fossils. It became one of Virginia's first state parks in 1936. This 1,300-acre park also provides camping cabins for rent year-round and 133 seasonal campsites. The Potomac River Retreat is a lodge that is available for rent; it holds 15 overnight guests and up to 40 people for meetings. There is a small camp store, but it's best to bring your own food because they stock only limited drinks and snacks. Dogs and cats are allowed in the park and cabins for an additional fee. Take in the great view of the Potomac from **Horsehead Cliffs,** and don't miss a stroll down fossil beach where you might even find some ancient shark's teeth. There is a visitors center that is open daily 8am-4:30pm.

### Westmoreland Berry Farm

If picking berries makes you feel connected to colonial times, stop by the **Westmoreland Berry Farm** (1235 Berry Farm Ln., Colonial

# The Steamboat Era

the Steamboat Era Museum

Steamboats came on the scene in the Chesapeake Bay in the early 1800s. As their popularity rose, they quickly became as important to the cities along the bay as the railroad was to the rest of the country. By the mid-1800s, steamboats were used to transport passengers, mail, and goods.

By the turn of the 20th century, nearly 600 steamboats cruised the bay, carrying thousands of passengers to the cities of Norfolk, Virginia, and Baltimore, Maryland, and every place in between. Steamboat excursions became extremely popular, and commerce flourished. Farms grew as their potential for distributing goods expanded, and many canneries were built near the shore. At one time, 85 percent of the world's oyster trade came from the Chesapeake Bay, and these little delicacies were shipped via steamboat.

The 20th century brought the development of the automobile and the slow demise of the steamboat. As cars became affordable and more common, passenger traffic on the steamboats began to dwindle. Still, the boats were used for commerce until the 1930s, when a hurricane in 1933 wiped out many of the Chesapeake Bay wharfs.

The final excursion of a popular steamboat named the *Anne Arundel* was made on September 14, 1937. That day is still celebrated in Virginia as "Steamboat Era Day."

Visit the **Steamboat Era Museum** (156 King Carter Dr., 804/438-6888, www.steamboat-eramuseum.org, Fri.-Sat. 10am-4pm, $5) in Irvington to learn more about the steamboat era of the Chesapeake Bay. Additional information on the era can be found on the museum's website.

Beach, 804/224-9171, www.westmorelandber-ryfarm.com, May-Nov. daily 10am-5pm). This farm on the banks of the Rappahannock River offers visitors the opportunity to pick their own fruit and berries (depending on what's in season). Or you can browse their country store for fresh produce or have lunch at the country kitchen.

## Canoeing and Kayaking

The country's first national water trail, the **Captain John Smith Chesapeake National Historic Trail** (www.smithtrail.net) includes 3,000 miles of routes through the Chesapeake Bay, Northern Neck, Middle Neck, and their tributaries in Virginia and Maryland. The route was inspired by the

regions explored in the 17th century by Captain John Smith.

Two-hour interpretive kayak trips are offered at **Westmoreland State Park** (800/933-7275, $19 solo kayak, $25 tandem) and include basic instruction and a guided trip along the shoreline.

### Fishing

**Captain Billy's Charters** (545 Harveys Neck Rd., Heathsville, 804/580-7292, www.captbillyscharters.com) runs boat charters for both fishing and cruising from the **Ingram Bay Marina** into the Chesapeake Bay. **Crabbe Charter Fishing** (51 Railway Dr., Heathsville, 804/761-0908, www.crabbescharterfishing.com, $600 for up to six people) is another charter fishing company in the Northern Neck. They offer outings year-round.

### Bird-Watching

Bird-watchers have many opportunities to view songbirds, waterfowl, eagles, and wading birds along the **Northern Neck Loop** birding trail (www.dgif.virginia.gov). This driving trail passes by historical sites and through an area known to have the largest population of bald eagles on the Eastern Seaboard.

## FOOD

### Reedville

**The Crazy Crab Restaurant** (902 Main St., 804/453-6789, www.reedvillemarina.com, $11-24), at the Reedville Marina, is a casual joint offering an abundance of local seafood choices and a few land-based choices. The waterfront view from the restaurant is nice, the atmosphere is fun, and outdoor seating is available. Hours vary greatly each season.

**Cockrell's Seafood** (567 Seaboard Dr., 804/453-6326, www.smithpointseafood.com, Mon.-Thurs. 11am-3pm, Fri.-Sat. 11am-4pm, $8-10) is a seafood deli on the waterfront. The atmosphere is very casual, with diners sitting at picnic tables. They serve delicious crab dishes.

Satisfy your sweet tooth at **Chitterchats**

Nate's Trick Dog Café

**Ice Cream** (846 Main St., 804/453-3335, www.chitterchatsicecream.com, $5-10). This family-oriented ice cream shop offers delicious homemade ice cream in roughly 20 flavors.

### Irvington

**Nate's Trick Dog Café** (4357 Irvington Rd., 804/438-6363, www.trickdogcafe.com, Tues.-Sat. 5pm-close, $21-35) is a trendy little find in a town full of fun surprises. A statue of the "Trick Dog" guards the entrance and brings good luck to those who pet it. The statue, which depicts a terrier, was found in the basement of the local opera house after a devastating fire in 1917 that destroyed many local businesses. The statue was sooty and dirty, and was called the Trick Dog since it didn't need food or water. It is an institution at this fine little spot and, judging by the good times and laughter flowing out of the restaurant's doors, seems to be working its magic. The menu offers tasty entrées such as jumbo crab cakes, fillet of yellowfin tuna, and shrimp and grits. There's also a bar menu of interesting finger food, burgers, and sandwiches. This place is worth a stop.

★ **The Local** (4337 Irvington Rd., 804/438-9356, www.thelocalblend.com, daily 7:30am-3pm, under $10) is a good choice for a grabbing a sandwich at lunchtime. This friendly little restaurant has cute decor and a good selection of sandwiches and salads, including a unique menu of panini and wraps. A personal recommendation is the "Tom" wrap, which has turkey, brie, apples, and honey mustard. It goes well with a Northern Neck soda. They also serve ice cream, great coffee, and beer and wine.

## ACCOMMODATIONS

### $100-200

**Ma Margaret's House** (249 Greenfield Rd., Reedville, 804/453-9110, www.mamargaretshouse.com, $110-210) is a cozy, recently renovated 4,000-square-foot home built in 1914 that belonged to the owner's grandparents. It offers several guest suites, a lot of privacy, and a wonderful staff.

### $200-300

★ **The Hope and Glory Inn** (65 Tavern Rd., Irvington, 804/438-6053, www.hopeandglory. com, $240-395) is a boutique inn with 6 rooms and 10 cottages. Lavish and romantic, with a little sense of humor, the inn was originally a schoolhouse built in 1890. The school had two front doors, one for girls and one for boys. The building now boasts beautifully appointed rooms, lush gardens, and even a moon garden with flowers that only bloom in the evening. There's a spa, meeting facilities, and a dock for boating, kayaking, or canoeing on-site as well as an outdoor pool and an outdoor bath (that is not a typo, there really is a claw-foot tub in an enclosed area outside). Tennis and three golf courses are a short distance away. The town of Irvington, which sits on the Chesapeake Bay, offers trendy shopping and a fun atmosphere.

Wine lovers won't want to miss visiting **The Dog and Oyster,** the Hope and Glory Inn's vineyard. It's named for the establishment's rescue dogs who guard the grapes from area wildlife and also in honor of the local oysters, which pair well with the wines. If the weather is nice, enjoy a bottle of wine on the porch.

The **Tides Inn** (480 King Carter Dr., Irvington, 804/438-5000, www.tidesinn.com, $265-575) is a well-known resort bordered by the Potomac and Rappahannock Rivers and

The Local

the Chesapeake Bay. This romantic waterfront inn hangs on the banks of Carters Creek as a little oasis of red-roofed buildings offering peace and relaxation to visitors of all ages. It features luxurious waterfront accommodations, golf, a marina, and a spa. There is also a sailing school with many options for lessons and family sailing activities. Packages include some geared toward golf, family vacations, and romance. There are also several good restaurants on-site and the inn is dog friendly.

## CAMPING

**Westmoreland State Park** (1650 State Park Rd., Montross, 804/493-8821, www. dcr.virginia.gov, open 24 hours) offers 133 campsites and a handful of camping cabins.

Camping sites feature a fire ring grill or box grills. Forty-two sites offer electric and water hookups for $30 per night; sites without these amenities are $20 per night. There is also one group tent site that can accommodate up to 40 people ($122). Camping cabins have a maximum capacity of four and require a two-night minimum stay. Cabins do not have bathrooms, kitchens, heat, air-conditioning, or linens. Bathhouses are available on-site for all campers.

## INFORMATION AND SERVICES

For additional information on the Northern Neck, visit www.northernneck.org.

# Williamsburg and the Historic Triangle

The "Historic Triangle," as it is known, consists of Williamsburg, Jamestown, and Yorktown. These three historic towns are just minutes apart and are the sites of some of our country's most important Revolutionary War history.

The **Colonial Parkway,** a scenic, 23-mile-long, three-lane road, connects the points of the Historic Triangle. Millions of travelers drive the road between Williamsburg, Jamestown, and Yorktown each year. The parkway is maintained by the National Park Service and was designed to unify the three culturally distinct sites while preserving the scenery and wildlife along the way. The construction of the parkway took more than 26 years and stretched through the Depression and World War II. It was completed in 1957. The parkway enables motorists to enjoy the surrounding landscape and has a speed limit of 45 miles per hour.

The National Park Service also maintains the **Colonial National Historical Park,** which contains two of the most historically significant sites in the country, the **Jamestown National Historic Site** (which

is jointly administered by Preservation Virginia) and **Yorktown National Battlefield.** These sites are connected by the Colonial Parkway.

## WILLIAMSBURG

The original capital of the Virginia Colony, Jamestown, was founded in 1607. It was located on the banks of the James River with a deepwater anchorage on a peninsula between the York and James Rivers. By 1638, an area called Middle Plantation (named for its location halfway across the peninsula) was settled about 12 miles away on higher ground. In 1676, Jamestown burned down and the government seat was temporarily moved to Middle Plantation. The statehouse was rebuilt, but burned down again in 1698. Once again, the capital was relocated to Middle Plantation. Finding the temporary location to be safer and less humid than Jamestown, the House of Burgesses permanently moved the colonial capital there in 1699. A village was planned in the new location and the name Middle Plantation was changed to Williamsburg in honor of King William III of England.

# Colonial Williamsburg

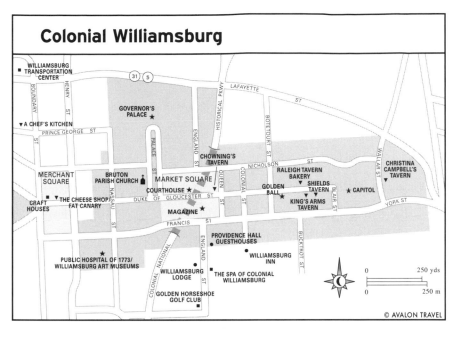

© AVALON TRAVEL

Williamsburg is one of America's earliest planned cities. It was designed as the capital of the Virginia Colony, which was the most populous of the British colonies in America in 1699. As such, Williamsburg had the oldest legislative assembly in the New World, and a series of elaborate capitol buildings were erected as the city developed into the thriving center of Virginia. Williamsburg remained the capital of Virginia until 1780, when the seat of government was moved to its current location in Richmond.

Today, when people speak of Williamsburg, they most often are referring to the area known now as **Colonial Williamsburg.** This original capital city is the country's prime example of not only the preservation of American colonial history but also its interpretation. However, although Colonial Williamsburg is the best-known attraction in the Williamsburg area, there are many other attractions nearby including the historic **College of William & Mary** and a number of popular theme parks.

## Sights
### ★ COLONIAL WILLIAMSBURG

**Colonial Williamsburg** (888/965-7254, www.colonialwilliamsburg.com, one-day ticket $40.99, three-day ticket $50.99) is the largest living museum in the country, and it is truly a historical marvel. It is open 365 days a year and run by the private, not-for-profit **Colonial Williamsburg Foundation.** The museum encompasses the restored 18th-century colonial Virginia capital city, which was the center of politics in Virginia for 80 years, and includes the real city streets and buildings that were erected during that time. There are historical exhibits, taverns, shops featuring original trades, and many other sites within the museum area. Ticketholders gain access to the historical buildings, theatrical performances, 15 site tours, 35 exhibitions, and museums. It is free to wander the streets themselves.

Although Colonial Williamsburg is open all year, if you are flexible in choosing when to visit, spring and fall can be the most rewarding. This is when crowds are less dense and the temperatures are the most moderate (plan to do a lot of walking around the city). Summer is the busiest tourist season because school is out of session, and it can also be very hot and humid, especially in August.

It is best to begin your visit at the **Colonial Williamsburg Regional Visitor Center** (101 Visitor Center Dr., 888/965-7254, daily 9:15am-5pm). The staff can help you put together an itinerary for your stay that will allow you to hit the highlights and choose additional sites you are interested in. You can also purchase tickets and learn about events and activities taking place during your time here. The highlights in Colonial Williamsburg can be seen over a weekend, but to really soak in the atmosphere, it can be fun to spend an extra day or two, or to make it your base for exploring other nearby attractions.

Everything within the museum area is neat, clean, well-maintained, and historically correct. The staff is dressed in period clothing and plays their roles very seriously. Conversations between staff members and the public are always in character. Visitors become "Residents of the City" and are immersed in history—and can enjoy authentic colonial-era dining and shopping while staying in hotels with all the modern conveniences.

There's a large pedestrian area through the center of the historical enclave along **Duke of Gloucester Street.** President Franklin D. Roosevelt called this road the "most historic avenue in all of America." Horses and horse-drawn carriages are allowed on the street if they are part of the museum.

**Market Square,** the center of activity in Colonial Williamsburg, straddles Duke of Gloucester Street. Residents went there on a regular basis (if not daily) to purchase goods and socialize. Visitors can experience the same atmosphere along Duke of Gloucester Street, where the official Williamsburg-brand shops are located.

Ticket-holding visitors can explore a variety of historical buildings such as the reconstructed **Capitol,** which sits at the east end of Duke of Gloucester Street (daily 9am-5pm). The current building is the third capitol to stand on the site, but it is very much

a shop in Colonial Williamsburg

the same as the original completed in 1705. A trip through this tall brick building is like a history lesson on the government in colonial Virginia and the contributions the colony made to the American Revolution. Evening programs in the Capitol include reenactments of political and social events that actually occurred here in the 18th century. One day a year, a naturalization ceremony is carried out at the Capitol for immigrants becoming Americans, carrying on a tradition that began nearly 300 years ago.

The impressive **Governors Palace,** built between 1706 and 1722 at the end of Palace Green Street off of West Duke of Gloucester Street, was home to seven royal governors, as well as Thomas Jefferson and Patrick Henry. After many decades as a symbol of the power of royal England, the home served as a military headquarters and twice as a wartime hospital (156 soldiers and 2 women are buried in the garden, casualties of the Battle of Yorktown). The original structure burned to the ground in 1781, but the building was reconstructed to its current grandeur in the 1930s. Since then, the home has been furnished with American and British antiques in the colonial revival style. This is perhaps the most popular site in Colonial Williamsburg, so make it first on your list, early in the day, before the crowds set in.

The **Courthouse** (Duke of Gloucester Street) is a focal point of Market Square and one that no doubt put fear in the hearts of many criminals in its day. Built in 1770, it is one of Williamsburg's original 18th-century buildings, and it housed the municipal and county courts until 1932. The building's T-shaped design is common to many Virginia courthouses, but an octagonal cupola and several other formal design elements (such as a weather vane, arched windows, and a cantilevered pediment) make it distinct in appearance. The signing of the Treaty of Paris (ending the Revolutionary War) was announced at the Courthouse.

A small but fascinating building is the **Magazine** (Duke of Gloucester Street). It was constructed in 1715 at the request of Governor Alexander Spotswood, who wanted a solid-brick house in which to store and protect weapons and ammunition. The

the Courthouse in Colonial Williamsburg

Magazine is well known for its role in the **Gunpowder Incident** on April 20, 1775, an episode that occurred in the opening days of the Revolutionary War between the royal governor, Lord Dunmore, and the militia (led by Patrick Henry). Lord Dunmore gave orders to remove all the gunpowder from the Magazine and move it to a Royal Navy ship. This led to unrest in Virginia and the movement of Patrick Henry's militia toward Williamsburg to secure the gunpowder for the colonial troops. The matter was resolved peacefully, but Dunmore retreated to a naval ship, thus ending royal governance of the colony. The incident helped move Virginia toward revolution.

Many craftspeople, some who have spent years learning the trade, create colonial-era crafts in dozens of shops throughout Colonial Williamsburg. Visitors can watch blacksmiths and armorers shape tools, weapons, and hardware out of iron and steel at **Anderson's Blacksmith Shop & Public Armoury** (E. Duke of Gloucester Street) or visit the **Wigmaker** (E. Duke of Gloucester Street) to learn the importance of 18th-century wigmakers and barbers and how these trades were essential to the social structure of the day. Other crafters include the **Shoemaker** (W. Duke of Gloucester Street), the **Weaver** (W. Duke of Gloucester Street), and the **Bindery** (E. Duke of Gloucester Street).

A number of historic taverns and restaurants are also located in Colonial Williamsburg and serve authentic colonial-style food. Look for the colonial flags out in front of the buildings. If a flag is out, it means the establishment is open.

More than 20 tours, both guided and self-led, are included in a Colonial Williamsburg admission ticket. The visitors center is the best place to find out what tours are offered on the day(s) you are there and what time they leave. Some popular tours include the **Freshest Advices for Travelers, Archaeology Walking Tours,** and the **Tavern Ghost Walk.** Dates and times change daily.

## WILLIAMSBURG ART MUSEUMS

Two top-notch art museums, the **DeWitt Wallace Decorative Arts Museum** (326 Francis St. W, 888/965-7254, daily 10am-7pm) and the **Abby Aldrich Rockefeller Folk Art Museum** (326 Francis St. W, 888/965-7254, daily 10am-7pm) are located in the same building and can be reached by walking through the **Public Hospital of 1773** (326 Francis St. W, admission is included with the Colonial Williamsburg ticket). The DeWitt Wallace Decorative Arts Museum opened in 1985, funded by a generous donation from DeWitt and Lila Wallace, the founders of *Readers Digest*. It houses a large collection of American and British art and antiques, including the world's most extensive collection of southern furniture. The Abby Aldrich Rockefeller Folk Art Museum features a colorful variety of paintings, sculptures, and other art forms. Each work created by self-taught artists and shows an imaginative array of details and color selections. There is also a kid-friendly animal-themed exhibit called Down on the Farm. While you're there, take in the exhibits at the Public Hospital. It was the first facility in North America dedicated to caring for the mentally ill. In this day and age, the hospital is seen as part jail, part infirmary, and the treatments used in the 18th and 19th centuries are thankfully just part of history.

## THE COLLEGE OF WILLIAM & MARY

Early on, Williamsburg developed into a hub for learning. **The College of William & Mary** (200 Stadium Dr., www.wm.edu), which is the second-oldest college in the country, was founded in 1693. It is just west of Colonial Williamsburg and an easy walk from the colonial city. William & Mary turned out many famous early political leaders including Thomas Jefferson, John Tyler, and James Monroe. Today, the 1,200-acre campus is bustling with students. Visitors can enjoy a handful of historical attractions right on campus, including the **Sir Christopher Wren Building,** which was built 1695 and is known for being the oldest college building in the country. It was named for a royal architect, although concrete evidence has not been found that Wren actually designed it.

## WILLIAMSBURG WINERY

Wine lovers will want to stop in for a tour and tasting at the **Williamsburg Winery** (5800 Wessex Hundred, 757/229-0999, www. williamsburgwinery.com, Jan.-Feb. Mon.-Fri. 11:30am-4:30pm, Sat.-Sun. 10:30am-5:30pm, Mar.-Dec. daily 10:30am-5:30pm, $8), about a 10-minute drive from the Colonial Williamsburg visitors center. The winery is Virginia's largest and accounts for one-quarter of all the wine produced in the state. Tours are available daily on the half hour.

## BUSCH GARDENS WILLIAMSBURG

**Busch Gardens Williamsburg** (1 Busch Gardens Blvd., 800/343-7946, www. seaworldparks.com, mid-May-Labor Day Mon.-Thurs. 10am-6pm, Fri. 10am-9pm, Sat. 10am-10pm, Sun. 10am-9pm, reduced schedule the rest of the year, $77) is a theme park with rides, re-created European villages, shows, exhibits, and exclusive tours. The park is less than five miles southeast of Williamsburg and is owned by SeaWorld. Hair-raising roller coasters, water rides, authentic food, and special attractions for little kids are just part of the fun at this beautiful park. Test your nerves on the Griffon, a 205-foot dive coaster (the tallest in the world), where brave riders free-fall at 75 miles per hour. Thrill seekers will also enjoy the Verbolten, one of the park's newest additions, an indoor/outdoor multi-launch coaster set in Germany's Black Forest. This coaster winds through the dark and ends with a heart-pounding plunge toward the Rhine River. The park's classic ride is the Loch Ness Monster, a 13-story, double-loop roller coaster that made Busch Gardens famous 30 years ago. This popular park also offers an Oktoberfest Village, a high-tech simulator that takes passengers over Europe, and animal attractions such as Jack Hanna's Wild Reserve, where visitors can see and learn about endangered and exotic animals. A combined Busch Gardens Williamsburg and Water Country USA ticket can be purchased for $87.

## WATER COUNTRY USA

Busch Gardens Williamsburg's sister park **Water Country USA** (176 Water Country Pkwy., 800/343-7946, www.watercountryusa. com, Memorial Day-Labor Day daily 10am-close, $52) is the largest water theme park in the mid-Atlantic. It is approximately three miles southeast of Williamsburg, just north of Busch Gardens. The park offers waterslides, pools, and more than 30 rides for kids of all ages as well as restaurants and live entertainment. A combined Busch Gardens Williamsburg and Water Country USA ticket can be purchased for $87.

## Entertainment and Events

Colonial Williamsburg doesn't shut down after dark. A variety of tours are available, including the "Original Ghost Tour" given by **The Original Ghosts of Williamsburg Candlelight Tour** (345 W. Duke of Gloucester St., 877/624-4678, www.theghosttour.com, Apr.-Aug. daily 8pm, reduced schedule the rest of the year, $12). This is a family-friendly candlelit walking ghost tour of the town and taverns that offers a relaxing end to a day of sightseeing. The **Kimball Theatre** (428 W. Duke of Gloucester St., 757/565-8588, www. colonialwilliambsburg.com) is a film and stage venue right in the middle of Colonial Williamsburg in Merchants Square. It offers programming in alliance with the College of William & Mary, including foreign, classic, and documentary films along with live concerts.

Outside of the historic center—but only minutes away—visitors can play pool and enjoy live music on some nights at **The Corner Pocket** (4805 Courthouse St., 757/220-0808, www.thecornerpocket.us, Mon.-Tues. 11:30am-1am, Wed.-Sat. 11:30am-2am, Sun. 3pm-1am), an upscale pool hall.

Many festivals are held throughout

the year in Williamsburg. The **Colonial Williamsburg Early Music Festival** (Historic Area, www.colonialwilliamsburg. com) happens over four days at the end of September and showcases musical instruments that were popular in colonial Virginia. The fifes and drums play daily in the historic area, but during the festival many other instruments are featured and lectures explain their origins.

Busch Gardens Williamsburg hosts an annual **Howl-O-Scream** (1 Busch Gardens Blvd., www.seaworldparks.com) event starting at 6pm daily in mid-September and running all through October. During Howl-O-Scream the park becomes a horrorfest for brave souls, featuring scary shows, creepy creatures lurking about the park, and fun characters. It is not advisable to take young children.

The holiday season is a very popular time to visit Colonial Williamsburg. The **Grand Illumination,** held on the Sunday of the first full weekend in December, is an eagerly awaited street festival where the entire historic area is decorated with traditional natural adornments for the season such as pinecones, evergreen branches, and candles. The area flickers at night by candlelight as carols are sung, concerts are held, and fireworks light up the night. Holiday festivities continue until the **First Night** celebration on New Year's Eve.

## Shopping

Williamsburg offers endless shops. Strip malls and outlet stores can be found in much of the area surrounding Colonial Williamsburg. For unique souvenirs, try stopping in the **Williamsburg Craft House** (420 W. Duke of Gloucester St., 757/220-7747) run by the Colonial Williamsburg Foundation. Pewter and ceramic gifts, jewelry, and folk art are for sale. Other favorite shops in the historic district include **The Prentis Store** (214 E. Duke of Gloucester St., 757/229-1000), which sells handcrafted leather pieces, pottery, furniture, ironware, and baskets; the

**Market House,** an open-air market on Duke of Gloucester Street that sells hats, toys, and other handmade items; and the **Golden Ball** (406 E. Duke of Gloucester St., 757/229-1000), which sells one-of-a-kind jewelry.

## Sports and Recreation
### GOLF
The **Golden Horseshoe Golf Club** (401 S. England St., 757/220-7696, www. colonialwilliamsburg.com, $52-79) is part of Colonial Williamsburg and offers 45 walkable holes. This scenic course is well maintained and has received accolades from publications such as *Golf Magazine* and *Golfweek.*

The **Kingsmill Resort** (1010 Kingsmill Rd., 757/253-1703. www.kingsmill.com, $60-165) offers three championship 18-hole courses that are open to the public (one of which was ranked in the top 10 for women by *Golf Digest*).

The award-winning **Williamsburg National Golf Club** (3700 Centerville Rd., 757/258-9642, www.wngc.com, $69-89) has two 18-hole courses.

### SPAS
The **Spa of Colonial Williamsburg** (307 South England St., 757/220-7720, www. colonialwilliamsburg.com) is behind the Williamsburg Inn. Enjoy treatments made from botanicals used by the early settlers or a variety of soaks and massages. Packages are available.

### HORSEBACK RIDING
If horseback riding seems appropriate while visiting Williamsburg, contact **Lakewood Trails** (575/566-9633, www. lakewoodtrailrides.com, $75) for one-hour guided trail rides.

### GO APE TREETOP ADVENTURE
For something completely different, try a **Go Ape** (5537 Centerville Rd., 800/971-8271, www.goape.com, $58) Treetop Adventure. This adventure course is appropriate for ages 10 and up (who are taller than 4'7") and

includes high wires, ladders, tunnels, zip lines, and a lot of treetop excitement. A junior course is available for children under 10 who are 3'3" or taller.

## Food
### AMERICAN
If you just need to grab a quick sandwich or you'd like to enjoy a gourmet cheese platter and a glass of wine, stop in **The Cheese Shop** (410 Duke of Gloucester St., 757/220-0298, www.cheeseshopwilliamsburg.com, Mon.-Sat. 10am-6pm, Sun. 11am-6pm, under $15) in Merchants Square. They make custom cheese plates (from 200 varieties of imported and domestic cheese) at their cheese counter (to the left) and deli sandwiches at the back of the store (try their chicken salad; it has just enough bacon to taste wonderful but not enough to feel guilty). The store also carries fresh-baked bread and a variety of snacks and drinks. Their wine cellar has more than 4,000 bottles of wine. There's seating outside (pay before you exit).

The ★ **Fat Canary** (410 Duke of Gloucester St., 757/220-3333, www.fatcanary williamsburg.com, daily 5pm-10pm, $28-39) in Merchants Square is named for the wine brought to the New World by ships that stopped in the Canary Islands for supplies. The wine was called a "canary," and this wonderful restaurant knows its wine. Widely considered one of the top dining spots in Williamsburg, The Fat Canary is an upscale restaurant that delivers an interesting menu of mouthwatering entrées such as quail, scallops, lamb, and beef tenderloin. They also have delicious desserts. The restaurant has a romantic ambience with soft pendant lighting and friendly service. This is a great place for a date or to relax after a day touring Colonial Williamsburg. Reservations are strongly suggested.

For a unique dining experience, make reservations at **A Chef's Kitchen** (501 Prince George St., 757/564-8500, www.achefskitchen. biz, Tues.-Sat. seating 6:30pm, $85) in the heart of Williamsburg. This food destination allows guests to learn about the fare they are eating and how it's prepared while being entertained by a talented chef. The fixed-price menu is for a multicourse meal in which recipes are prepared, served, and paired with great wines. Diners sit at elegant long tables in tiered rows. The menu changes monthly, but sample dishes include asparagus and sweet pea soup, scallion and lime Gulf shrimp cake, roast rack of lamb, and strawberries sabayon in lace cup cookie. This small restaurant only seats 26 people, and it only offers one seating per night, so reservations are a must. Plan for 2-3 hours of dining time.

### TREATS
To satisfy a craving or pick up an afternoon snack, stop in the **Raleigh Tavern Bakery** (Duke of Gloucester Street, behind the Raleigh Tavern, under $10). They offer a selection of fresh cookies, muffins, rolls, sandwiches, drinks, and other treats. Try the sweet potato muffins and the gingerbread cookies, which are done to perfection and are much better than the peanut butter and chocolate chip cookies. Casual seating is available in the courtyard outside. Alcohol must be consumed in the courtyard and cannot be taken out on Duke of Gloucester Street. A cookbook with the recipes is available for purchase, and this writer knows firsthand that almost nothing has changed in this historical little bakery in the past 30 years—but then again, that's the idea here.

The **Jamestown Pie Company** (1804 Jamestown Rd., 757/229-7775, www.buyapie. com, Sun. 10am-9pm, Mon.-Sat. 9am-9pm, $5-23) sells everything round including pizza, potpie, and dessert pie. They also offer a small selection of sandwiches. Pies are also available to go.

### COLONIAL TAVERNS
There are four taverns in the historic area of Williamsburg, and dining in one is a great way to get into the spirit of the town. Costumed servers bring authentic dishes from two centuries ago to wooden tables in flickering candlelight. Don't be hesitant to

try some 18th-century staples such as spoon bread and peanut soup. There are a few featured items available in all four taverns, but aside from that, each specializes in its own dishes. Make reservations when you book your hotel. The same phone number (757/229-2141) can be used for all four taverns (www.colonialwilliamsburg.com). These restaurants are very popular.

**Christiana Campbell's Tavern** (101 S. Waller St., Tues.-Sat. 5pm-close, $24-37) is noted as George Washington's favorite tavern. It specializes in seafood dishes. The tavern was re-created from artifacts excavated on-site and from a sketch of the building found on an original insurance policy. George and other famous colonial figureheads often met here for business and pleasure, and private rooms could be reserved alongside public chambers where travelers sometimes shared beds with complete strangers when the tavern was full. The crab cakes are a signature dish.

**Chowning's Tavern** (109 E. Duke of Gloucester St., lunch daily 11:30am-2pm, dinner daily 5pm-9pm, lunch $7-13, dinner $24-33) is a casual alehouse where lively singing and other reenactments of 18th-century life are common. Light fare is served at Chowning's for lunch, including soups and sandwiches, and more substantial entrées are available for dinner (such as pork and Brunswick stew). Outdoor seating is available behind the tavern in the garden where light meals and pints are served.

**The King's Arms Tavern** (416 E. Duke of Gloucester St., lunch Thurs.-Mon. 11:30am-2:30pm, dinner Thurs.-Mon. 5pm-close, $33-37) is a genteel tavern serving southern food and decadent desserts. This chophouse-style tavern offers entrées such as chicken, pork chops, venison, and prime rib. The peanut soup is a signature dish.

**Shields Tavern** (422 E. Duke of Gloucester St., daily 11:30am-9pm, $7-30) is the largest of the taverns, and it specializes in comfort food such as bangers and mash and barbecue ribs. Try the potato leek pie or a sample plate. The ale-potted beef is also a favorite.

## Accommodations

If Colonial Williamsburg is the focus of your Williamsburg trip, and you'd like to be immersed in the Revolutionary City, book a room in one of the Colonial Williamsburg Foundation hotels or guesthouses. These are conveniently located near the museum sites and have a historic feel to them. Reservations, especially during the peak summer months, should be made in advance.

### COLONIAL WILLIAMSBURG FOUNDATION

The **Colonial Williamsburg Foundation** maintains 5 hotels/lodges and 26 guesthouses. Each offers a different atmosphere and price range. Hotel guests have access to a terrific fitness facility located behind the Williamsburg Inn that includes a spa, state-of-art fitness room, indoor lap pool, and two gorgeous outdoor pools. Hotel guests also receive the best rate on general admission passes and discounts on special events. Reservations are handled through the foundation (www.colonialwilliamsburg.com).

The **Colonial Houses** (888/965-7254, $199-459) are individual colonial homes and rooms, each with a unique history. The number of rooms per house varies, but all are decorated with authentic reproductions of period pieces such as canopy beds and all have modern amenities. Look out over Duke of Gloucester Street, or sleep in the home where Thomas Jefferson lived while attending The College of William & Mary. Some homes are original historic buildings and others are replicas.

The luxurious ★ **Williamsburg Inn** (136 E. Francis St., 757/220-7978, www.colonialwilliamsburg.com $449-669) was built in 1937 by John D. Rockefeller Jr., and the decor and furnishings in the lobby are still arranged exactly the way his wife, Abby Aldrich Rockefeller, designed it. This stately, upscale hotel has hosted many heads of state including President Dwight D. Eisenhower, Queen Elizabeth II, and Sir Winston Churchill. In 1983, the inn welcomed the

Economic Summit of Industrialized Nations, hosted by President Ronald Reagan. It is listed in the National Register of Historic Places, but offers modern first-class accommodations in its 62 guest rooms. The hotel was the first in the United States to have central air-conditioning. Each elegant and spacious room is furnished similar to an English country estate. The setting and decor are charming, and the service is excellent. Mrs. Rockefeller wished for guests to feel at home in the inn and as such instilled a warmth throughout the staff that still radiates today. Every last detail is attended to in the luxurious rooms, from beautifully tiled temperature-controlled showers to a fresh white rose in the bathroom (the rose is the official inn flower) and little comforts like vanity mirrors and nightlights. The hotel is centrally located adjacent to Colonial Williamsburg. The Golden Horseshoe Golf Club is behind the inn, and daily participatory events such as lawn bowling are offered to guests. There are two restaurants on-site (one formal dining room and a more casual lounge), and the hotel is very family friendly.

The **Williamsburg Lodge** (310 S. England St., 757/220-7976, www.colonialwilliamsburg.com $199-289) is decorated in the classic Virginia style. Colorful fabric, leather, and warm woods give this hotel a lodge feel. This 300-room hotel hosts many conferences, and its unique garden gives it a relaxing focal point. The rooms are spacious, the lodge is conveniently located near Colonial Williamsburg, and it's an easy walk to the attractions.

The **Providence Hall Guesthouses** (305 S. England St., 757/220-7978, www.colonialwilliamsburg.com, $229-279) is in a quiet area near the Williamsburg Inn. It offers 43 large, bright rooms in a quiet, parklike setting with a more modern look to it. The hotel is pet friendly.

The **Williamsburg Woodlands Hotel and Suites** (105 Visitor Center Dr., 757/220-7978, www.colonialwilliamsburg.com, $139-209) is next to the visitors center for Colonial

Williamsburg. This 300-room hotel offers contemporary rooms in a wooded setting. It is one of the least expensive options of the Colonial Williamsburg Foundation hotels.

The **Governor's Inn** (506 N. Henry St., 757/253-2277, www.colonialwilliamsburg.com, $85-100) is a short walk from historic Colonial Williamsburg and the visitors center. This 200-room hotel offers economy accommodations and a seasonal outdoor pool.

## OUTSIDE COLONIAL WILLIAMSBURG

There are quite a few choices for accommodations outside Colonial Williamsburg. Many are within an easy drive of the historical area.

The **Marriott's Manor Club at Ford's Colony** (101 St. Andrews Dr., 757/258-1120, www.marriott.com, $129-305) is in the private community of Ford's Colony and offers colonial architecture, deluxe guest rooms, and one- and two-bedroom villas. Each villa has a kitchen, living/dining area, washers and dryers, a balcony or patio, and a fireplace. This is a great place for families or groups who need a bit more space or plan an extended stay. Colonial Williamsburg and the College of William & Mary are about a 15-minute drive away, and Busch Gardens is about 20 minutes. There's a spa and golf course in the community, a fitness center, indoor and outdoor pools, and a sport court. Rooms are nicely appointed, and the buildings are spread out on a well-manicured property.

The **Wedmore Place** (5810 Wessex Hundred, 757/941-0310, www.wedmoreplace.com, $195-575) offers 28 individually decorated rooms in a variety of price ranges. Each room is designed after a European province and a different time in history, including all the furnishings and wall hangings. The 300-acre farm is also the site of the Williamsburg Winery and is about a 10-minute drive to the Colonial Williamsburg visitors center.

If you're looking for a kid-oriented hotel, the **Great Wolf Lodge** (549 E. Rochambeau Dr., 757/229-9700, www.greatwolf.com,

$239-410) provides endless amusement for the little ones. This Northwoods-themed lodge offers 405 guest rooms and a huge indoor water park complete with waterslides, a wave pool, and a tree house. It is a four-season resort.

The **Kingsmill Resort and Spa** (1010 Kingsmill Rd., 757/253-1703, www.kingsmill. com, $179-399) offers 425 luxurious rooms and suites (with up to three bedrooms) as well as breathtaking views of the James River. It also has golf, a spa, an indoor pool, and summer children's programs. This is a great place for a romantic getaway or to spend time with friends playing golf or taking a spa day.

## Camping

There are several good options for camping in Williamsburg. The **Anvil Campground** (5243 Mooretown Rd., 757/565-2300, www. anvilcampground.com, $40-155) is open year-round and offers 77 campsites and two cottages. It has been in operation since 1954 and is close to Colonial Williamsburg with shuttle service available to attractions, restaurants, and shopping. The **Williamsburg KOA Campground** (4000 Newman Rd., 757/565-2907, www. williamsburgkoa.com, starting at $46) is another good option close to Colonial Williamsburg and the theme parks. They offer 180 acres of wooded sites and patio sites (with more than 100 sites total). They also offer bus service to attractions in the peak season. Two additional campgrounds in Williamsburg are the **Williamsburg RV Resort and Campground** (4301 Rochambeau Dr., 757/566-3021, $49), with 158 sites, and the **American Heritage R.V. Park** (146 Maxton Ln., 757/566-2133, www. americanheritagervpark.com, $38), with 103 sites.

## Information and Services

The best information on Colonial Williamsburg can be obtained from the **Colonial Williamsburg Foundation** (800/447-8679, www.history.org) and at the **Colonial Williamsburg Regional Visitor Center** (101 Visitor Center Dr., 757/220-7645, daily 8:45am-5pm). For additional information on Williamsburg, contact the **Greater Williamsburg Chamber and Tourism Alliance** (www.williamsburgcc. com) or visit www.visitwilliamsburg.com.

## Getting There

Most people arrive in Williamsburg by car. The city is off I-64 and approximately 1 hour from Richmond, 1 hour from Norfolk, and 2.5 hours from Washington DC.

The **Newport News/Williamsburg International Airport** (PHF, 900 Bland Blvd., Newport News, www.flyphf.com) is off I-64 at exit 255B. Williamsburg is a 20-minute drive from the airport.

**Amtrak** (468 N Boundary St., 800/872-7245, www.amtrak.com) offers train service into Williamsburg.

## Getting Around

Getting around Colonial Williamsburg requires a lot of walking. The pedestrian area where you'll find many of the attractions is preserved as it was during Revolutionary times when there were no cars. If you are not staying at one of the Colonial Williamsburg hotels, you will want to arrive early during peak season to park outside the pedestrian area. Parking spaces can be difficult to come by, but designated areas are clearly marked. The important thing to remember is not to park in private lots or at the College of William & Mary (even in the summer). Parking restrictions are strictly enforced.

Williamsburg has a reliable bus system called the **Williamsburg Area Transit (WATA)** (www.gowata.org), which offers bus service seven days a week and stops at many of the local hotels. An all-day pass is $2.

Shuttle service between the Colonial Williamsburg Regional Visitor Center and select hotels is available for free to those who have a Colonial Williamsburg ticket. Shuttle tickets can also be obtained at the visitors center.

From mid-March through October, the **Historic Triangle Shuttle** (www.nps.gov/colo, daily every 30 minutes, 9am-3:30pm) provides transportation service between the Colonial Williamsburg Regional Visitor Center and Jamestown via the scenic Colonial Parkway. There is no charge if you have purchased a ticket to either historical area. Boarding passes can be obtained from the Colonial Williamsburg Regional Visitor Center.

# JAMESTOWN

Jamestown was the first permanent English settlement in America. It was founded in 1607, more than a decade prior to the Pilgrims' arrival at Plymouth. Three small ships carrying 104 men made landfall at Jamestown (which is actually an island) on May 13, 1607. They moored the ships to trees, came ashore the following day, and never left. The newly formed town served as the capital of Virginia during the 17th century.

## ★ Jamestown National Historic Site

The **Jamestown National Historic Site** (1368 Colonial Pkwy., 757/856-1200, www.nps.gov/jame, daily 8:30am-4:30pm, $14) occupies the site of the original Jamestown settlement on the banks of the James River. It is run by the National Park Service and Preservation Virginia. The site was also the location of a military post during the American Revolution where prisoners were exchanged from both sides.

Purchase your admission ticket at the visitors center (your ticket also grants access to Yorktown National Battlefield), which shows an informative 18-minute video that is a good start to orienting yourself with the site. From there, continue to "Old Towne," the original settlement site, and explore it on foot. Highlights include the original Memorial Church tower (the oldest structure still standing in the park, dating to 1639), a burial ground (many of the first colonists died here), a reconstructed sample of a "mud-and-stud"

cottage, and the foundations of several buildings. Another don't-miss sight is the Jamestown Rediscovery excavation, where remains of the original James Fort built in 1607 are being uncovered at an archaeological dig site open to visitors. History programs and children's events are held in the summer months.

Continue on to "New Towne," where you can explore the part of Jamestown that was developed after 1620. The foundations of many homes were excavated in the 1930s and 1950s and replicas can be seen throughout the site. Next, take a cruise along the Loop Drive, a five-mile wilderness road. Be sure to stop to read the interpretive signs and view the paintings along the route to learn how inhabitants used the island's natural resources, or visit the **Glasshouse** to see artisans creating glass products as glassblowers did back in the early 1600s.

## Jamestown Settlement

The **Jamestown Settlement** (2110 Jamestown Rd., 757/253-4838, www.historyisfun.org, daily 9am-5pm, $17) is one of the most popular museums in Coastal Virginia. It is a living museum that re-creates and honors the first permanent English-speaking settlement in the country and takes visitors back to the 1600s. Costumed guides share facts about a Powhatan Village, and there are replicas of the three ships that sailed from England under the command of Captain Christopher Newport and eventually landed at Jamestown. The ships are a highlight of the museum, and the costumed crew does an excellent job of answering questions and showing off every nook and cranny of the ships. The **James Fort** is another main attraction. There, visitors can see authentic meals being prepared, witness arms demonstrations, and even try on armor. Ninety-minute tours of the outdoor interpretive areas are available several times a day. Thanksgiving is a great time to visit because special events are held in the museum. Combined-entry tickets to Colonial Williamsburg and the Yorktown

historical building and artifacts at Jamestown Settlement

Victory Center can be purchased, and bus service between the sites is offered during the summer season.

## Getting There

Jamestown is nine miles southwest of Colonial Williamsburg along the Colonial Parkway.

From mid-March through October, the **Historic Triangle Shuttle** (www.nps.gov/colo, daily every 30 minutes 9am-3:30pm) provides transportation service between the Colonial Williamsburg Regional Visitor Center and Jamestown via the Colonial Parkway. There is no charge if you have purchased a ticket to either historical area. Boarding passes can be obtained from the **Colonial Williamsburg Regional Visitor Center** (101 Visitor Center Dr., Williamsburg, 757/220-7645, daily 8:45am-5pm).

## YORKTOWN

The quaint waterfront village of Yorktown was established in 1691 and is most famous as the site of the historic victory in the American Revolutionary War. It was also an important tobacco port on the York River where crops were exported from local plantations. During its peak in the mid-1700s, it had nearly 2,000 residents and several hundred buildings. It

was a thriving city of primarily merchants, planters, shopkeepers, and indentured servants.

There are many earthworks surrounding Yorktown. These were first built by British troops in 1781, when nearly 80 percent of the town was damaged or destroyed during the Siege of Yorktown. These earthworks were built over with new fortifications by Confederate troops during the Civil War. During the **Siege of 1862,** the Union army was held back by the Confederates for more than a month in this area. After the Confederates left town, Union troops settled in for the rest of the war.

In addition to learning about history, visitors can enjoy art, shopping, special events, and water sports.

### Sights

#### YORKTOWN NATIONAL BATTLEFIELD AND VISITOR CENTER

The **Yorktown National Battlefield** (757/898-2410, www.nps.gov/york) is a national park that marks where, on October 19, 1781, the British army, led by General Charles Lord Cornwallis, surrendered to General George Washington, ending the

Yorktown

Revolutionary War. Visitors can see the battlefield, Washington's Headquarters and tent, and the actual surrender field.

The **Yorktown National Battlefield Visitor Center** (1000 Colonial Pkwy., 757/898-2410, reservations 757/898-2411, daily 9am-5pm, $7) is a great place to begin your exploration of the battlefield and town. It is a living-history museum where re-creations are staged by historical interpreters in costume. Two self-guided driving tours allow visitors to learn about the Siege of Yorktown at a relaxed pace. Guided group tours are also available for a fee (rates vary depending on the number of participants), and reservations should be made two months in advance.

The entrance fee is paid at the visitor centers, where maps are available as well as an informative orientation film that should be your first order of business if you're a first-timer to the site. The admission fee at Yorktown includes entrance into historic houses, entrance to the battlefield, and access to a variety of interpretive programs and is good for seven days. Your pass can be upgraded to visit Jamestown Settlement at the Historic Jamestown Visitor Center for an additional $7.

The 84-foot-tall **Yorktown Victory Monument** and the **Moore House,** where the surrender terms were negotiated, are fascinating sites at the battlefield. The Victory Monument was not erected until 100 years after the end of the war. Its purpose was to "keep fresh in memory the all decisive successes that had been achieved." The four-sided base has an inscription on each side: one for victory, one for a succinct narrative of the siege, one for the treaty of alliance with France, and one for the resulting peace treaty with England. The pediments over the inscriptions feature emblems of nationality, war, alliance, and peace. The monument's podium is a "symbol of the birth of freedom." The column (coming out of the podium) symbolizes the greatness and prosperity of the United States after a century. On top of the monument's shaft is a sculpture of Liberty, which attests to the existence of a nation governed by the people, for the people.

### YORKTOWN VICTORY CENTER

Next to the battlefield is the **Yorktown Victory Center** (Rte. 1020 near Colonial Pkwy., 757/253-4838, www.historyisfun.org, daily 9am-5pm with extended summer hours, $9.75), an informative museum dedicated to

Yorktown National Battlefield

the American Revolution that chronicles the entire era beginning with unrest in the colonies and ending with the creation of a new nation. Visitors can view 1,300 artifacts, enjoy artillery demonstrations, explore a re-created Continental Army encampment featuring live historical interpreters, and join seasonal celebrations such as the Yorktown Victory Celebration in October honoring the anniversary of the end of the Revolutionary War.

Summer is the best time to visit since there are outdoor living-history exhibits (you might even be asked to help load a cannon). Indoor exhibits are also offered year-round. A free shuttle runs between the Victory Center and historic Yorktown as well as other Williamsburg-area attractions. A combination admission ticket for the Yorktown Victory Center and the Jamestown Settlement can be purchased for $21.25.

If you're lucky enough to be here on the Fourth of July, you can experience the **Liberty Celebration** firsthand. What better location to celebrate American's independence than where it all began? The celebration includes a plethora of reenactments, military drills, and food demonstrations. This event complements the **Yorktown Fourth of July**

**Celebration** that takes place in the evening on July 4.

## HISTORIC YORKTOWN

Yorktown still has a sparse population of full-time residents. Its streets are lined with historic homes, some more than two centuries old. There's Yorktown Beach, a pleasant sandy beach along the York River, and overall, Yorktown offers a relaxing place to explore history, shop, and dine.

**Riverwalk Landing** (425 Water St., 757/890-3370, www.riverwalklanding.com) is a pedestrian walkway along the York River. This quaint area includes retail shops and dining. Take a stroll on the mile-long River View path that runs along the York River from the Yorktown Battlefield to the Yorktown Victory Center. Riverwalk Landing is a great place to take a walk, go shopping, or grab an ice cream cone on a hot day.

The **Watermen's Museum** (309 Water St., 757/887-2641, www.watermens.org, Apr.-Dec. 23 Tues.-Sat. 10am-5pm, Sun. 1pm-5pm, closed the rest of the year, $5) highlights the role that watermen on the Chesapeake Bay's rivers and tributaries had in the formation of our country. This is done through

Riverwalk Landing

displays illustrating the methods of their trade and craft. Visitors learn what it means to earn a living harvesting seafood from the Chesapeake Bay watershed. The museum offers educational programs and a waterfront facility that can be rented for events.

The **Nelson House** (Main St., 757/898-2410, www.nps.gov/york, open as staffing permits, $10) is a prominent 18th-century structure on Main Street. It was built in the Georgian manor style by the grandfather of Thomas Nelson Jr., one of Yorktown's most famous residents. The younger Nelson was the governor of Virginia in 1781 and the commander of the Virginia militia during the siege. He was also a signer of the Declaration of Independence. Damage from the siege is still evident at the Nelson House. Informal tours are available throughout the year. It's best to call for hours because the house is not open continuously.

## Entertainment and Events

The **Lighted Boat Parade** (Yorktown Beach) kicks off the holiday season in early December with a festive procession featuring power- and sailboats adorned with holiday lights. Musical performances and caroling are held on the beach by the light of a bonfire, and hot cider is served. The event is free to the public.

The **Yorktown Wine Festival** (425 Water St. at Riverwalk Landing, tastings $30) is held in October and features wines from throughout Virginia. Art and food vendors also share their wares at the festival.

## Shopping

Yorktown's Main Street in the Historic Village is lined with unique shops and galleries. There are antiques stores, galleries, and jewelry and glass shops to name a few. Down by the water at Riverwalk Landing are additional shops featuring colonial architecture and offering art, home items, jewelry, quilts, and clothing.

## Sports and Recreation

Yorktown is a waterfront town and outdoor recreation haven. The mile-long **Riverwalk** is a great place for a power walk or to stretch your legs after travel. The two-acre beach near the Riverwalk offers a great location for launching a kayak, swimming, and beachcombing.

There are also kayak and canoe launches at nearby **Wormley Creek Landing** (1110 Old Wormley Creek Rd.) with access to Wormley

the Watermen's Museum

Creek and the York River, **Rodgers A. Smith Landing** (707 Tide Mill Rd.) with access to the Poquoson River and the lower Chesapeake Bay, and **New Quarter Park** (1000 Lakeshead Dr., Williamsburg, 757/890-5840, www.yorkcounty.gov) with access to Queens Creek and the York River.

The **Riverwalk Landing Pier** is a pleasant place to enjoy a day of fishing, and visitors can dock their boats there.

For bicycle rentals ($7.50 per hour or $25 for four hours), kayak and paddleboard rentals ($30 for two hours), or guided Segway tours ($39 for one hour or $65 for two hours), contact **Patriot Tours & Provisions** (757/969-5400, www.patriottoursva.com).

If sailing on a romantic schooner sounds appealing, **Yorktown Sailing Charter** (757/639-1233, www.sailyorktown.com, $37 for two hours) docks its beautiful sailing vessel, the schooner *Alliance,* at the pier at Riverwalk Landing April-October. They offer daily sailing trips during the day and at sunset. Daytime trips leave at either 11am or 2pm. Sunset cruise times vary by month. Its sister schooner, *Serenity,* offers pirate cruises (Sun., Mon., Wed., Fri., and Sat. 11:30am-1pm,

$37), educational trips, and charters for those looking for a bit of adventure.

## Food

The ★ **Carrot Tree Kitchen** (323 Water St., Suite A-2, 757/988-1999, www.carrottreekitchens.com, Mon.-Thurs. 10am-5pm, Fri.-Sat. 8am-5pm, $8-20) is a small, casual lunch spot on the waterfront with delightful food. Don't be turned off by the paper plates and plastic utensils; the Carrot Tree offers delicious lunches of sandwiches and comfort food. Save room for the carrot cake—it's their signature dessert.

The **Riverwalk Restaurant** (323 Water St., Suite A-1, 757/875-1522, www.riverwalkrestaurant.net, daily 11am-9pm, $12-32) provides diners with a scenic view of the York River through large glass windows and a cozy fireplace for cool evenings. The fare is primarily seafood, but they offer selections from the land as well. This is a great place to relax after a day of sightseeing.

If fresh seafood and cold beer right on the beach sound like a good ending to a day of exploration in Yorktown, stop in at the **Yorktown Pub** (540 Water St., 757/886-9964, www.yorktownpub.com, Sun.-Thurs. 11am-midnight, Fri.-Sat. 11am-2am, $7-16). The atmosphere is very casual, but the food and service are good. The pub burger, local oysters, and hush puppies are among the best choices. The place is crowded on the weekends, so plan ahead.

For a quick sandwich, pizza, or burger, stop in the **Beach Delly** (524 Water St., 757/886-5890, www.beachdellyandpizzaria.com, daily 11am-9pm, $7-20). This little restaurant is across from the beach and offers good food and friendly service.

## Accommodations

The **Duke of York Hotel** (508 Water St., 757/898-3232, www.dukeofyorkmotel.com, $149-199) is an older hotel with a great location right on the water. This family-run establishment has all river-view rooms (some have balconies and some open to landscaped grounds), an outdoor pool, and an on-site café and restaurant. The Yorktown Trolley stops in front of the hotel.

The **York River Inn Bed & Breakfast** (209 Ambler St., 757/887-8800, www.yorkriverinn.com, $135-165) sits on a bluff overlooking the York River and offers two rooms, a suite with private bathrooms, and all the hospitality you can imagine from its friendly owner (who is also a knockout breakfast chef). This is a wonderful colonial-style inn with elegant rooms.

The ★ **Hornsby House Inn** (702 Main St., 757/369-0200, www.hornsbyhouseinn. com, $149-285) offers five beautiful guest rooms with private modern bathrooms in an exquisite colonial home. The inn is in the heart of Yorktown and offers a great view of the York River. It is also just a short walk from the Yorktown Battlefield. The inn is run by two friendly brothers who grew up in the house and provide exemplary service, wine and cheese, and a delicious fresh breakfast each morning. The owners take the time to eat breakfast with and get to know their guests as well as share the history of their home. They also make recommendations for attractions

in the area and the best strategy for enjoying them. The house is beautifully appointed and is a warm and inviting home away from home. Book the Monument Grand Suite and enjoy a private outdoor terrace overlooking the York River and Yorktown Victory Monument.

The **Marl Inn Bed & Breakfast** (220 Church St., 301/807-0386, www.marlinnbandb.com, $99-139) is two blocks from the Riverwalk. This colonial-style home is a private residence and inn offering four guest rooms; rates can be booked with no breakfast or with full breakfast. The owner is a great-grandson of Thomas Nelson Jr.

## Information and Services

For additional information on Yorktown, visit www.visityorktown.org and www.yorkcounty. gov.

## Getting There and Around

Yorktown is 13 miles southeast of Williamsburg along the Colonial Parkway. The **Yorktown Trolley** (757/890-3500, www.yorkcounty.gov, daily 11am-5pm, extended service hours June-Aug., free) is a free seasonal trolley service with stops in nine locations around Yorktown. It runs every 20-25 minutes from the end of March until November.

# JAMES RIVER PLANTATIONS

Between Richmond and Williamsburg (in Charles City County) along Route 5 are four stunning plantations that survived the Revolutionary War, War of 1812, and Civil War. These treasures, which span three centuries, are all privately owned National Register properties that are open to the public. For additional information on all four plantations, visit www.jamesriverplantations.org.

## Sherwood Forest

**Sherwood Forest** (Rte. 5, 14501 John Tyler Hwy., Charles City, 804/829-5377, www.sherwoodforest.org, grounds open daily 9am-5pm) sounds like a place out of a fairy tale, and it

# James River Plantations

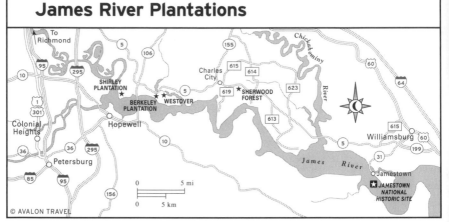

kind of is. This beautiful plantation was the home of President John Tyler for 20 years. The home has been the residence of the Tyler family continuously since he purchased it in 1842.

At more than 300 feet in length—longer than a football field—Sherwood Forest is the longest frame house in the country. The home evolved from a modest 17th-century English-style home (circa 1660) into a substantial 19th-century "Big House" that features a ballroom designed specifically for dancers to engage in the Virginia reel. There is also a resident ghost.

Self-guided walking tours of the grounds are available for $10 per person. The tour features 21 numbered stations on 25 acres with information on the 19th-century plantation. The grounds include terraced gardens, quiet woodlands, and lush lawn. A printed guide is available at a kiosk at the main entrance and features descriptions and history information for each station. House tours are only available by appointment and cost $35.

## Westover

Speaking of fairy tales, **Westover** (off Rte. 5, 7000 Westover Rd., 804/829-2882, www. jamesriverplantations.org, grounds open daily 9am-6pm, $5) could have come straight off the pages of one. William Byrd II, who founded the city of Richmond, built the home in 1730.

Westover is known for its architectural details, but kids of all ages will love it for its secret passages and enchanting gardens. The mansion is widely considered to be one of the top examples of Georgian architecture in the country. The house itself is not open to the public, but there are still many interesting things to see on the grounds, which offer wide views of the James River. The icehouse and another small structure to the east of the mansion contain a dry well and passageways leading under the house and down to the river. These were created as an escape route from the house during attacks.

## Shirley Plantation

**Shirley Plantation** (501 Shirley Plantation Rd., 804/829-5121, www.shirleyplantation. com, Dec.-Mar. daily 10:30am-4pm, longer summer hours, $11) was the first plantation built in Virginia. It was established in 1613, just six years after Jamestown, and construction was completed in 1738. This property has a legacy of 11 generations of one family (descendants of Edward Hill I) who still own and operate the colonial estate. It has survived attacks, war, and the Great Depression and remains the oldest family-owned business in the United States.

Admission includes a guided house tour that showcases original furnishings, artwork, silver, and hand-carved woodwork. Special architectural features include a "flying staircase" and a Queen Anne forecourt. A self-guided grounds tour features gardens and original outbuildings. Allow at least one hour for your visit.

## Berkeley Plantation

**Berkeley Plantation** (12602 Harrison Landing Rd., 888/466-6018, www.berkeley-plantation.com, daily Jan.-mid-Mar. 10:30am-3:30pm, mid-Mar.-Dec. 9:30am-4:30pm, $11) is famous for being the site of the first official Thanksgiving in 1619, although substantiated claims for the first Thanksgiving also belong to locations in Florida, Texas, Maine, and Massachusetts. It is also the birthplace and

home of Declaration of Independence signer Benjamin Harrison and President William Henry Harrison. The beautiful Georgian mansion, which was erected in 1726, sits on a hilltop overlooking the James River. The brick used to build the home was fired on the plantation.

Guided tours are conducted in the mansion and feature a nice collection of 18th-century antiques. An audiovisual presentation is included in the tour as is access to a museum collection of Civil War artifacts and unique paintings by artist Sydney King. Visitors can then tour the grounds on their own and explore five terraces of boxwood and flower gardens. Allow approximately 1.5 hours for the house tour and to roam the gardens.

# Hampton Roads

The Hampton Roads region is all about water. In sailors' terms, "Roadstead" means a safe anchorage or sheltered harbor. The word "Hampton" came from an English aristocrat, Henry Wriothesley, who was the third earl of Southampton. Hence, Hampton Roads.

Hampton Roads, which used to be known as Tidewater Virginia, contains one of the largest natural deepwater harbors in the world. The harbor is where the James, Elizabeth, and Nansemond Rivers meet the Chesapeake Bay. Pioneers first settled the area in 1610, after disease struck nearby Jamestown. The area was a throughway for goods from both the colonies and England and, as such, drew merchants and pirates. One of history's most famous pirates, Blackbeard (Edward Teach), plundered the port and waters of Hampton Roads, which was just a short distance from his base in North Carolina.

The port in Hampton Roads is the country's second largest to New York City, and is notable for remaining ice-free year-round. It is also the birthplace of the modern U.S. Navy.

Defining the Hampton Roads area can be a bit confusing. Technically, the Historic

Triangle is considered part of Hampton Roads, but the coastal cities from Newport News to Virginia Beach are more commonly thought of as the Hampton Roads area.

## NEWPORT NEWS

Newport News is a short drive from Williamsburg, Virginia Beach, and the Atlantic Ocean. There are several versions of whom Newport News was named for, but the most widely accepted is that it was named for Captain Christopher Newport, who was in charge of the three ships that landed in Jamestown in 1607. The "news" part of the name came from the news that was sent back to England on the ships' safe arrival.

### Sights

#### THE MARINERS' MUSEUM

**The Mariners' Museum** (100 Museum Dr., 757/596-2222, www.marinersmuseum.org, Mon.-Sat. 9am-5pm, Sun. 11am-5pm, $13.95) is one of the largest maritime history museums in the United States. It has more than 60,000 square feet of gallery space showing maritime paintings, artifacts, figureheads,

# Northern Hampton Roads

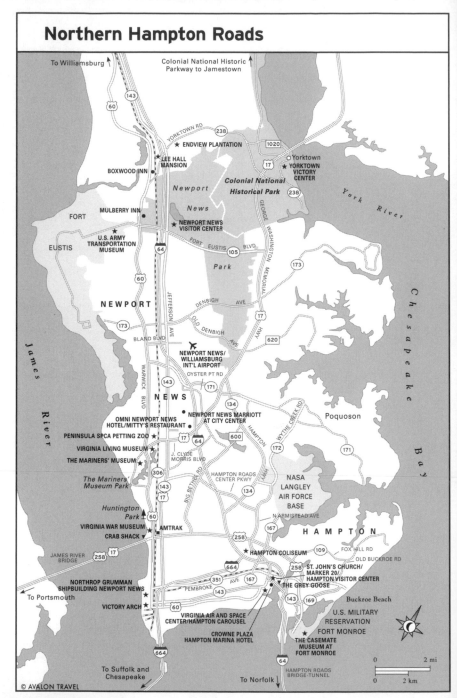

To Williamsburg

Colonial National Historic
Parkway to Jamestown

143
60

YORKTOWN RD    238

★ ENDVIEW PLANTATION    1020

○ Yorktown

★ LEE HALL
MANSION

BOXWOOD INN ●

17    ★ YORKTOWN
VICTORY
CENTER

*Newport*    Colonial National
*Historical Park*    238

*News*

*York River*

FORT    MULBERRY INN ●

★ NEWPORT NEWS
VISITOR CENTER

GEORGE

U.S. ARMY
TRANSPORTATION
MUSEUM

FORT    EUSTIS    BLVD    105

WASHINGTON    MEMORIAL

EUSTIS

*Park*    173

60

NEWPORT    DENBIGH    AVE

JEFFERSON    AVE    17

173    OLD    DENBIGH    AVE

BLAND BLVD    620

✈
NEWPORT NEWS/
WILLIAMSBURG
INT'L AIRPORT

OYSTER PT RD

WARWICK    BLVD    143    171

**NEWS**    134

OMNI NEWPORT NEWS
HOTEL/MITTY'S RESTAURANT ●    ● NEWPORT NEWS MARRIOTT
AT CITY CENTER

Poquoson

PENINSULA SPCA PETTING ZOO ★    17    64    600

HAMPTON

WYTHE CREEK RD

VIRGINIA LIVING MUSEUM ★    172    171

THE MARINERS' MUSEUM ★    J. CLYDE
MORRIS BLVD

*The Mariners'
Museum Park*    306    143
17

BIG BETHEL RD    HAMPTON ROADS
CENTER PKWY    134

NASA
LANGLEY
AIR FORCE
BASE

*Huntington
Park*    60    N ARMISTEAD AVE

VIRGINIA WAR MUSEUM ★    AMTRAK

CRAB SHACK ▼    258    167    **H A M P T O N**

JAMES RIVER
BRIDGE    258    17    ★ HAMPTON COLISEUM    109    FOX HILL RD

OLD BUCKROE RD

664    258    ST. JOHN'S CHURCH/
MARKER 20/
HAMPTON VISITOR CENTER

NORTHROP GRUMMAN
SHIPBUILDING NEWPORT NEWS ★    351    167
PEMBROKE    AVE    143    ● THE GREY GOOSE

To Portsmouth    *Buckroe Beach*

143    169

VICTORY ARCH ★    60

VIRGINIA AIR AND SPACE
CENTER/HAMPTON CAROUSEL

U.S. MILITARY
RESERVATION
FORT MONROE

CROWNE PLAZA
HAMPTON MARINA HOTEL    THE CASEMATE
MUSEUM AT
FORT MONROE

664    0    2 mi

To Suffolk and
Chesapeake

64    0    2 km

To Norfolk    HAMPTON ROADS
BRIDGE-TUNNEL

*James    River*

*Chesapeake    Bay*

© AVALON TRAVEL

# Shipbuilding in Newport News

Newport News is home to the largest privately owned shipyard in the country, **Northrop Grumman Shipbuilding Newport News,** on Washington Avenue along the James River. The facility was built in 1886 for a sum of $7 million and was called the Newport News Ship Building and Dry Dock Company. Its 4,000 employees repaired the many vessels that came to use the ever-growing transportation hub in the Hampton Roads area. The yard produced its first tugboat (named *Dorothy*) in 1891. By 1897, the company had produced three additional tugboats for the U.S. Navy.

Business took off with the onset of the Great Naval Race of the early 1900s. At the start of World War I, shipbuilding was in full swing and the company constructed 6 dreadnoughts and 25 destroyers for the U.S. Navy. The company has been going full force ever since, with its achievements including building the first nuclear-powered submarine and the famous ocean liner the SS *United States*.

Today, the company is the largest private employer in Hampton Roads. The 21,000 employees (many of whom are third- and fourth-generation shipbuilders) turn raw steel into some of the world's most complex ships. The shipyard is the country's sole designer and builder of nuclear-powered aircraft carriers and also one of only two companies that design and build nuclear submarines.

ship models, and small craft from around the world. Exhibits include vessels for warfare, exploration, pleasure, and fishing. A highlight of the museum is the **USS Monitor Center,** where a full-scale replica of the Civil War battleship USS *Monitor* is housed. In 1862 the *Monitor* battled the CSS *Virginia* in what went down in history as the first engagement of steam-powered iron warships (aka The Battle

of the Ironclads). Visitors can learn about the historic encounter in the Battle Theater. The center is also home to recovered parts of the original battleship, which sank off the coast of Cape Hatteras, North Carolina, in December 1862.

The museum offers countless other collections including the **Crabtree Collection of Miniature Ships.** The museum is very kid

The Mariners' Museum

friendly and offers numerous events, lectures, and even a concert series. Check the website for upcoming events.

## THE VIRGINIA LIVING MUSEUM

Endangered red wolves, loggerhead turtles, and moon jellyfish are just some of the amazing animals you can get close to at **The Virginia Living Museum** (524 J. Clyde Morris Blvd., 757/595-1900, www.thevlm. org, daily 9am-5pm, extended summer hours, $17). This is a wonderful place to learn about Virginia's natural heritage. Indoor exhibits, outdoor exhibits, four interactive discovery centers, and gardens showcase Virginia's geographical regions and the more than 250 species of plants and animals that live in the state. The 30,000-gallon aquarium is a focal point for kids of all ages. Many hands-on activities are also offered such as touch tanks and live feedings, and there is even a planetarium.

## VIRGINIA WAR MUSEUM

The **Virginia War Museum** (9285 Warwick Blvd., 757/247-8523, www.warmuseum.org, Mon.-Sat. 9am-5pm, Sun. noon-5pm, $8)

explains the development of the U.S. military from 1775 to modern times. Its many exhibits showcase war efforts throughout our country's history. Weapons, artifacts, and uniforms are displayed from the Revolutionary War through the Vietnam War and exhibits explain the evolution of weaponry, the role of women in the military, contributions made by African Americans to military history, and provide a tribute to prisoners of war.

## ENDVIEW PLANTATION

**Endview Plantation** (362 Yorktown Rd., 757/857-1862, www.endview.org, Apr.-Dec. Mon. and Thurs.-Fri. 10am-4pm, Sat. 10am-5pm, Sun. noon-5pm, Jan.-Mar. Thurs.-Sat. 10am-4pm, Sun. 1pm-5pm, $8) was a privately owned estate that was used briefly as a Confederate hospital during the 1862 Peninsula Campaign. The small, white, T-frame Georgian-style home was later occupied by Federal troops. The house sits on top of a knoll, and a spring flows at the base of the hill. This, coupled with the beautiful rolling farmland that surrounds the place has made it an attractive location for centuries. The city

the Virginia War Museum

of Newport News purchased the plantation in 1995 and restored it to its original configuration. School programs are held at the plantation, and guided tours of the house and grounds are offered periodically but not on a published schedule.

## LEE HALL MANSION

**Lee Hall Mansion** (163 Yorktown Rd., 757/888-3371, www.leehall.org, Apr.-Dec. Mon. and Thurs.-Fri. 10am-4pm, Sat. 10am-5pm, Sun. noon-5pm, Jan.-Mar. Thurs.-Sat. 10am-4pm, Sun. 1pm-5pm, $8) is the only remaining large antebellum plantation on the lower Virginia peninsula. The 6,600-square foot structure is a blend of several architectural styles, including Italianate, Georgian, and Greek revival. The primary style, however, is Italianate. The redbrick home was built on a rise in the 1850s and was home to wealthy planter Richard Decatur Lee. Due to the mansion's commanding view, the home served as headquarters for Confederate generals John Magruder and Joseph E. Johnston during the 1862 Peninsula Campaign. Visitors can take a step back in time to the mid-Victorian period and view hundreds of artifacts in the mansion's authentically furnished rooms. Combination admission tickets for Lee Hall Mansion, Endview Plantation, and the Virginia War Museum can be purchased for $21.

## PENINSULA SPCA PETTING ZOO

The **Peninsula SPCA Petting Zoo** (523 J. Clyde Morris Blvd., 757/595-1399, www.peninsulaspca.com, Mon.-Fri. 11am-6pm, Sat. 10am-5am, $2) is a fun place to bring the kids for a hands on experience with barnyard animals. The zoo is run by the nonprofit Peninsula Society for the Prevention of Cruelty to Animals (SPCA). Visitors can enjoy the company of sheep, goats, chickens, ducks, and other friendly animals.

## VICTORY ARCH

The **Victory Arch** (25th St. and West Ave., 757/247-8523, www.newport-news.org) was built in 1919. Troops returning from World War I marched through the arch in victory parades after disembarking from their ships. The arch was reconstructed in 1962, and an

the Victory Arch

# The Peninsula Campaign of 1862

The Peninsula Campaign of 1862 was an aggressive plan designed by Union forces during the Civil War to outsmart Confederate defenses in Northern Virginia by moving 121,000 troops by sea to the Virginia Peninsula between the York and James Rivers. This would place them to the east of Richmond, the Confederate capital. Having bypassed the Northern Virginia forces, the army, led by General George B. McClellan, would be able to advance on Richmond without meeting entrenched opposition.

The failure of this plan remains a highly debated episode in the war. Union troops moved slowly and never made a serious attack on Richmond, despite their strategic placement. Although they were met by small Confederate forces, McClellan blamed the failure on Washington for not providing men and support for the effort, even though his troops outnumbered the Confederates throughout the campaign.

From the Confederate standpoint, the Peninsula Campaign of 1862 resulted in the emergence of two great commanders, Stonewall Jackson and Robert E. Lee, who jointly kept the Union forces out of Richmond.

eternal flame was added to it on Memorial Day in 1969. Today the arch stands as a memorial to all men and women of the armed forces.

## Entertainment and Events
### FERGUSON CENTER
### FOR THE ARTS
The **Ferguson Center for the Arts** (1 Ave. of the Arts, 757/594-8752, www.fergusoncenter.org) at Christopher Newport University is a performance hall that also houses the university's theater, arts, and music departments. The center opened in 2005 and contains a 1,725-seat concert hall and a 200-seat studio theater. It offers a wide range of performances. Check the website for upcoming events.

### PENINSULA FINE ARTS CENTER
The **Peninsula Fine Arts Center** (101 Museum Dr., 757/596-8175, www.pfac-va.org, Tues.-Sat. 10am-5pm, Sun. 1pm-5pm) is dedicated to the promotion of the fine arts. It offers exhibits, a studio art school, an interactive gallery, educational programs, and hands-on activities for children.

## EVENTS
The **Newport News Fall Festival of Folklife** (www.nngov.com) is held on the first weekend in October and has been running for approximately four decades. The festival draws 70,000 visitors annually and has more than 230 exhibitors featuring trade demonstrations, crafts, and food.

The **Newport News Children's Festival of Friends** (www.nngov.com) is held at the beginning of May and offers a variety of themed areas for children. Activities, rides, entertainment, and food are all part of the fun of this popular festival that's been going on for more than a quarter century.

## Shopping
The **City Center at Oyster Point** (701 Town Center Dr., 757/873-2020, www.citycenteratoysterpoint.com, Mon.-Sat. 10am-9am, Sun. noon-6pm) is an outdoor town center with retail stores, gourmet eateries, spas, and salons.

The **Patrick Henry Mall** (12300 Jefferson Ave., 757/249-4305, www.shoppatrickhenrymall.com, Mon.-Sat. 10am-9am, Sun. noon-6pm) is the largest mall on the peninsula with more than 120 stores in a single-level, indoor configuration.

## Sports and Recreation

### PARKS

The **Newport News Park** (13560 Jefferson Ave., 757/886-7912, www.nnparks.com) is one of the largest municipal parks in the country, encompassing nearly 8,000 acres. Boat and bike rentals are available in the park as are hiking and biking trails, picnicking, canoeing, archery, disc golf, and fishing. The park's Discovery Center has many hands-on activities and historical artifacts.

**Huntington Park-Beach, Rose Garden & Tennis Center** (361 Hornet Cir., 757/886-7912) offers a public beach with lifeguards, a playground, baseball, boating, swimming, and tennis.

**King-Lincoln Park** (600 Jefferson Ave., 757/888-3333) overlooks the Hampton Roads Harbor and provides fishing, tennis, picnicking, playgrounds, and basketball.

**Riverview Farm Park** (100 City Farm Rd., 757/886-7912) has two miles of multiuse paved

trails, a 30,000-square-foot community playground, biking, hiking, and soccer fields.

**The Mariners' Museum Park** (100 Museum Dr., 757/596-2222, www.marinersmuseum.org) offers a five-mile trail along Lake Maury. There is also boating and hiking.

### GOLF

Golfers can get their fix at two local courses: **Kiln Creek Golf Club and Resort** (1003 Brick Kiln Blvd., 757/874-2600, www.kilncreekgolf.com, $32-42) and **Newport News Golf Club at Deer Run** (901 Clubhouse Way, 757/886-7922, www.nngolfclub.com, $34-38).

### FISHING

Fishing enthusiasts will enjoy the **James River Fishing Pier** (2019 James River Bridge, 757/274-0364, $9), which is made entirely of concrete and has LED lights. It is one of the longest fishing piers on the East Coast.

### BOATING

Boaters can make the **Leeward Marina** (7499 River Rd., 757/274-2359, www.nngov.

Huntington Park-Beach, Rose Garden & Tennis Center

COASTAL VIRGINIA<br>HAMPTON ROADS

com, May-Oct. daily 7am-7pm, Nov.-Apr. daily 8am-5pm) a base for exploration of the Hampton Roads Harbor and the Chesapeake Bay.

## Food

### AMERICAN

★ **Circa 1918 Kitchen & Bar** (10367 Warwick Blvd., 757/599-1918, Tues.-Sat. 5pm-10pm, $10-28) offers delicious food, a lovely wine list, friendly, professional service, seasonal selections, and wonderful specials. Sample menu items include duck meat loaf, Prince Edward Island mussels, and grilled lamb burgers. The restaurant is in the historic, two-block-long Hilton Village neighborhood. The atmosphere is relaxed and comfortable, and separate groups of patrons actually talk to each other. Don't shy away from interacting—you could get a great tip for what to order. This is a small restaurant with only about a dozen tables, so reservations are highly recommended.

**Fin Seafood** (3150 William Styron Sq., 757/599-5800, www.finseafood.com, daily 11am-10pm, $28-90) is a great choice for a romantic dinner or a large gathering. It is a local favorite for delicious seafood. They use mostly organic and sustainable produce and proteins, as well as seasonal ingredients.

**Second Street American Bistro** (115 Arthur Way, 757/234-4448, www.secondst.com, Mon.-Thurs. 11:30am-10pm, Fri.-Sat. 11:30am-12am, Sun. 11am-10pm, $8-27) is an upscale yet casual restaurant with a wide menu selection, including small plates, pizza, burgers, steak, chicken, ribs, fish, and pasta. They offer a three-course prix fixe dinner for $20.16 and a two-course prix fixe lunch for $10.16. There is also a wonderful wine selection, including a private-label petite sirah grown in Napa Valley.

**Brickhouse Tavern** (141 Herman Melville Ave., 757/223-9531, www.brickhouse-tavern.com, daily 11am-2am, $7-16) is a casual restaurant serving a variety of pub food, including burgers and pizza. **Chic N Fish** (954 J. Clyde Morris Blvd., 757/223-6517, Mon.-Sat. 11am-9pm, $5-26) serves up a little bit of everything including burgers, seafood and Korean fried chicken.

One of the best views in town is from the **Crab Shack** (7601 River Rd., 757/245-2722, www.crabshackonthejames.com, Sun.-Thurs. 11am-11:30pm, Fri.-Sat. 11am-12:30am, $9-21) on the James River waterfront. This casual seafood restaurant serves sandwiches and entrées in a window-lined dining room or on an outdoor deck.

### ITALIAN

For good mid-priced Italian food, try **Al Fresco** (11710 Jefferson Ave., 757/873-0644, www.alfrescoitalianrestaurant.com, lunch Mon.-Fri. 11am-3am, dinner daily 5pm-10pm, $12-24).

## Accommodations

### UNDER $100

The **Mulberry Inn & Plaza at Fort Eustis** (16890 Warwick Blvd., 757/887-3000, www.mulberryinnva.com, $65-115) is a 101-room hotel offering standard rooms, efficiencies, and studios that can hold up to four people. It is close to I-64 and has amenities such as an outdoor pool, a fitness center, and a business center. Hot breakfast is included.

The **Magnuson Hotel and Convention Center at Oyster Point** (1000 Omni Blvd., 757/873-6664, www.omnihotels.com, $55-99) is only a few blocks from the city center and has a heated indoor pool, a fitness room, free parking, and free Internet.

### $100-200

The **Newport News Marriott at City Center** (740 Town Center Dr., 757/873-9299, www.marriott.com, $159-259) is a 256-room hotel near shopping and many restaurants. It offers a pool and workout facility.

The **Comfort Suites Airport** (12570 Jefferson Ave., 757/947-1333, www.choicehotels.com, $134-154) is the hotel closest to the Newport News/Williamsburg International Airport. It offers all suite accommodations, a free airport shuttle, an indoor pool, and a spacious workout facility.

The **Hilton Garden Inn Newport News** (180 Regal Way, 757/947-1080, http://hilton-gardeninn3.hilton.com, $118-139) offers 122 guest rooms, an indoor heated pool and spa, an airport shuttle, and easy access to the city center and military bases.

For those seeking more privacy, **The Boxwood Inn** (10 Elmhurst St., 757/888-8854, www.boxwood-inn.com, $105-145) is a historic bed-and-breakfast built in 1897. It offers two rooms and two suites with genuine southern hospitality. Each room in the gracious white home has a theme: The Captain's Quarters is named for the area's rich maritime history; Miss Nana's Room is named for the former owner of the home; the Politician Suite is named for many political gatherings held at the home; and General Pershing's Suite is named for General John Pershing, who often stayed in the home while on hunting trips. Friday dinners are available by reservation.

## Camping

Year-round camping is available in the **Newport News Park** (13564 Jefferson Ave., 757/888-3333, www.nnva.gov and www.nnparks.com, $31.50-40). This is one of the biggest municipal parks on the East Coast, and it has 188 campsites with hot showers and restroom facilities. The 8,000-acre park is a combination of woods, meadows, and lakes (campsites are wooded).

## Information and Services

For additional information on Newport News, visit www.newport-news.org or stop by the **Newport News Visitor Center** (13560 Jefferson Ave., 757/886-7777, daily 9am-5pm), off I-64 at exit 250B.

## Getting There and Around

Newport News is located along I-64 and U.S. Route 60.

The **Newport News/Williamsburg International Airport** (PHF, 900 Bland Blvd., www.flyphf.com) is off I-64 at exit

255B. Downtown Newport News is a 15-minute drive from the airport.

**Amtrak** (9304 Warwick Blvd., 757/245-3589, www.amtrak.com) has a station in Newport News at Huntington Park. Consult the website for schedules and fares.

Newport News, Hampton, Norfolk, and Virginia Beach are connected by **Hampton Roads Transit** (757/222-6100. www.gohrt.com). Consult the website for schedules and fares.

# HAMPTON

Hampton is the oldest continuously inhabited English-speaking community in the United States, with a history dating back to 1607. It is also home to Langley Air Force Base. Hampton was partially destroyed during three major wars—the Revolutionary War, the War of 1812, and the Civil War—but was rebuilt each time and continues to undergo renovations even today. The city now offers an attractive waterfront filled with modern sailing and fishing boats and a variety of attractions for visitors and residents.

## Sights

### VIRGINIA AIR & SPACE CENTER

The **Virginia Air & Space Center** (600 Settlers Landing Rd., 757/727-0900, www.vasc.org, Sept.-Mar. Tues.-Sat. 10am-5pm, Sun. noon-5pm, extended summer hours, $18 includes IMAX) houses more than 100 interactive exhibits that detail the historic achievements of NASA. Topics include space travel, aircraft development, communications, and a hands-on space gallery. Hampton was the birthplace of the space program in the United States and has played an important role in the 100-plus-year history of flight. Displays include more than 30 historic airplanes, the Apollo 12 command module, a passenger jet, moon rocks, and many replicas.

### THE HAMPTON CAROUSEL

The **Hampton Carousel** (602 Settlers Landing Road, Carousel Park, 757/727-1610, www.visithampton.com, seasonally

the Virginia Air & Space Center

Tues.-Sun. 11am-8pm, $1) was originally built for an amusement park at Buckroe Beach, where it resided between 1921 and 1985. It is now on the waterfront in downtown Hampton, fully restored and protected from the elements. The merry-go-round's 48 horses and chariots were hand-carved out of hardwood, and it is adorned with original paintings and mirrors. It also still plays the original organ music. The carousel is open from the end of March through early September, but it is best to check the website because there are scheduled closures each month.

## THE CASEMATE MUSEUM AT FORT MONROE

**The Casemate Museum** (20 Bernard Rd., 757/788-3391, www.tradoc.army.mil, Tues.-Sun. 10:30am-4:30pm, free) on the grounds of Fort Monroe shares many exhibits about the fort, which was built in 1834 to protect the Chesapeake Bay, James River, and Hampton River. This is the largest stone fort in the country. The museum contains the prison cell where Confederate president Jefferson Davis was held and also the living quarters of Robert E. Lee while he was stationed there

from 1831 to 1834. Other displays include military uniforms and supplies. The grounds at Fort Monroe are open year-round for walking and other outdoor activities.

## ST. JOHN'S CHURCH

**St. John's Church** (100 W. Queens Way, 757/722-2567, www.stjohnshampton.org) is the oldest English-speaking parish in the United States. The church was founded in 1610, and the current structure was built in 1728. The church was designed in the shape of a Latin cross and boasts beautiful colonial-style brickwork, two-foot-thick walls, and stained glass windows. The church survived the Revolutionary War, the War of 1812, and the Civil War. The silver used for communion dates back to 1618 and is considered to be the most valuable relic in the American Anglican Church. Services are still held here; consult the website for details.

## Entertainment and Events

The **Hampton Coliseum** (1000 Coliseum Dr., 757/838-4203, www.hamptoncoliseum. org) is the premier venue in Hampton for concerts, performances, and sporting events. A list of upcoming events can be found on the website. The Coliseum is convenient to I-64 and offers free parking.

The annual **Hampton Jazz Festival** (www.hamptonjazzfestival.com) has been going on for almost 50 years. It is held for three days at the end of June in the Hampton Coliseum. Information on the lineup and tickets can be found on the website.

The **Hampton Cup Regatta** (www.hamptoncupregatta.com) is billed as the "oldest continually run motorsport event in the world." It is held for three days in mid-August in Mill Creek, between Fort Monroe and the East Mercury Boulevard Bridge. Another fun water festival is the **Blackbeard Pirate Festival** (www.blackbeardfestival.com) held at the beginning of June each year. The Hampton waterfront is overrun with pirate re-enactors as visitors are taken back to the 18th century. There is live music, children's activities, vendors, fireworks, and arts and crafts.

## Sports and Recreation

**Buckroe Beach** (100 1st St. South) is a wide, sandy, eight-acre beach on the Chesapeake Bay. There is a playground, picnic shelters, a bike path, and certified lifeguards on duty. Concerts are held in the summer months, as is an outdoor family movie series.

**Grandview Nature Preserve** (State Park Drive) is a local secret. This nature preserve and beach at the end of Beach Road in Grandview is great for families and allows dogs in the off-season.

Hampton is located at the entrance to the Chesapeake Bay and is a convenient stopping point for boaters. Those traveling by boat can stop at the **Blue Water Yachting Center** (15 Marina Rd., 757/723-6774, www.bluewateryachtsales.com), which offers daily dockage.

If you don't have your own boat but wish to take a relaxing sightseeing cruise, board the double-decker *Miss Hampton II* (757/722-9102, www.misshamptoncruises.com, $26 for 2.5-3 hours), a motorized vessel that offers cruising in Hampton Harbor and on the Chesapeake Bay.

Golf enthusiasts can play at the **Woodlands Golf Course** (9 Woodlands Rd., 757/727-1195, www.hampton.gov, $13-19) or the **Hamptons Golf Course** (320 Butler Farm Rd., 757/766-9148, www.hampton.gov, $14-21).

## Food
### AMERICAN

**Surf Rider Bluewater** (1 Marina Rd., 757/723-9366, www.surfriderrestaurant.com, $6-23) is a family-owned seafood restaurant in the Blue Water Yachting Center off Ivy Home Road. This is a great place for local seafood, which you can tell by the number of local residents eating here. Their crab cakes are famous as are the oysters, tuna, and hush puppies.

Another local favorite is **Marker 20** (21 E. Queens Way, 757/726-9410, www.marker20.com, Mon.-Fri. 11am-2am, Sat.-Sun. 10am-2am, $7-25). This downtown seafood restaurant has a large covered outdoor deck and inside seating. Enjoy a casual menu of soups, salads, sandwiches, and seafood specials, along with dozens of types of beer.

The cute **Grey Goose** (118 Old Hampton Way, 757/723-7978, www.greygooserestaurant.com, lunch Mon.-Sat. 11am-3pm, $6-10) serves homemade soups, salads, sandwiches, and bakery items made from fresh ingredients.

### SPANISH

The **Six Little Bar Bistro** (6 E. Mellen St., 757/722-1466, www.littlebarbistro.com, daily 5pm-2am, tapas $3-14) serves an eclectic assortment of tapas including herbed sausage, seaweed salad, pork, and chipotle crab cakes. There is also a large bar that is notorious for mixing potent cocktails. The food is delicious and the atmosphere is fun, but they do not split checks, so be prepared for this if you're with a group.

## Accommodations
### UNDER $100

The **Candlewood Suites Hampton** (401 Butler Farm Rd., 757/766-8976, www.

candlewoodsuites.com, $90-119) offers 98 reasonably priced, spacious rooms in a quiet location. The hotel is geared toward extended-stay guests and offers per diem rates for members of the armed services. The service is good, and the staff is caring and friendly. The rooms are well stocked, and the hotel is pet friendly. There are also free laundry facilities on-site.

### $100-200

The **Crowne Plaza Hampton Marina** (700 Settlers Landing, 757/727-9700, hwww.hamptonmarinahotel.com, $120-149) is a riverfront hotel in downtown Hampton. It is within walking distance to the Virginia Air & Space Center and a short drive to Langley Air Force Base, Fort Monroe, and Northrop Grumman.

### OVER $200

The **Embassy Suites by Hilton Hampton Hotel Convention Center & Spa** (1700 Coliseum Dr., 757/827-8200, www.embassysuites3.hilton.com, $219-475) offers 295 suites with kitchenettes. The hotel has a warm decor with an attractive atrium, and the staff provides good, reliable service. There's a restaurant and a nicely appointed fitness center. Spa service is also available.

## Information and Services

For additional information on Hampton, visit www.hampton.gov and www.visithampton.com or stop in at the **Hampton Visitor Center** (120 Old Hampton Ln., 757/727-1102, daily 9am-5pm).

## Getting There and Around

Hampton is approximately 10 miles southeast of Newport News.

The **Newport News/Williamsburg International Airport** (PHF, 900 Bland Blvd., Newport News, www.flyphf.com) is off I-64 at exit 255B. Hampton is a 20-minute drive from the airport.

**Greyhound** (2 W Pembroke Ave., 757/722-9861, www.greyhound.com) offers bus service to Hampton.

**Hampton Roads Transit** (www.gohrt.

com) is a public transit service that serves the Hampton Roads area including Hampton. It currently offers transportation by bus, light-rail, ferry, and Handi-ride (a service for people with disabilities).

# NORFOLK

Norfolk is the second-largest city in Virginia and home to the largest naval base in the world. A longtime navy town, the city has an appealing downtown area and a nice waterfront. The city has undergone a rebirth in recent history that is most evident in the delightful restaurants and shops in the trendy Ghent village, located just northwest of downtown, not far from the Elizabeth River. The city also boasts numerous universities, museums, and a host of other attractions including festivals and shopping.

## Sights
### CHRYSLER MUSEUM OF ART

The **Chrysler Museum of Art** (One Memorial Pl., 757/664-6200, www.chrysler.org, Tues.-Sat. 10am-5pm, Sun. noon-5pm, free) is one of Virginia's top art museums with 62 galleries and 30,000 pieces of artwork including paintings, textiles, ceramics, and bronzes. The art on display spans thousands of years and comes from around the world. A highlight is the glass museum (a museum within a museum) that is entirely devoted to glass art and features 10,000 glass pieces (spanning 3,000 years) and a glass art studio. Other collections include European painting and sculpture, American painting and sculpture, modern art, a gallery of ancient and non-Western art, contemporary art, photography, and decorative arts.

### NORFOLK BOTANICAL GARDEN

Something is always in bloom at the **Norfolk Botanical Garden** (6700 Azalea Garden Rd., 757/441-5830, www.norfolkbotanicalgarden.org, daily 9am-7pm, $11). This 155-acre garden contains more than forty different themed areas and thousands of plants. It is open to visitors year-round. Inside the garden is the

# Norfolk and Vicinity

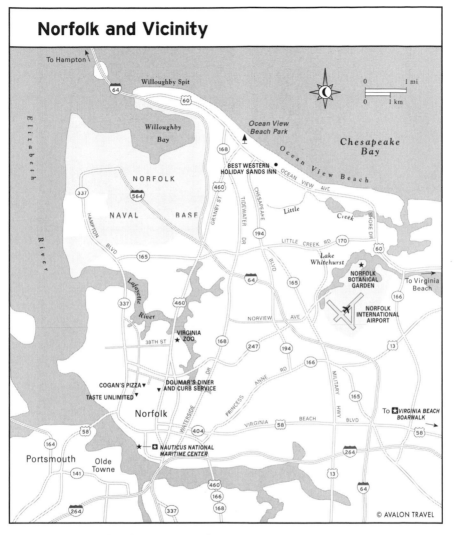

three-acre **World of Wonders Children's Garden,** which is geared toward children and families and houses several learning areas.

## ★ NAUTICUS NATIONAL MARITIME CENTER

The **NAUTICUS National Maritime Center** (1 Waterside Dr., 757/644-1000, www.nauticus.org, daily Memorial Day-Labor Day 10am-5pm, rest of the year Tues.-Sat. 10am-5pm, Sun. noon-5pm, $15.95) is an incredible

interactive science and technology center. They have a great floor plan with a lot of interesting permanent and rotating exhibits including hands-on activities for children (they will love the Morse code exhibit). Be sure to catch *The Living Sea* movie featured on a large panoramic screen that opens to a view of the water.

The ***Battleship Wisconsin*** is one of the prime on-site attractions, and the center features many exhibits related to the ship. It is

the Chrysler Museum of Art

one of the biggest and also one of the last battleships built by the U.S. Navy. The ship served in World War II, the Korean War, and Operation Desert Storm. Admission to the ship is included with admission to NAUTICUS, and visitors can take a self-guided tour of the deck. For $35.95 (which includes NAUTICUS admission), guided **Battleship Wisconsin Topside Tours** (11am, 1pm, and 3pm) are available. These tours include the administration area, radio room, main deck with enlisted berthing, the captain's cabin and sleeping quarters, the flag bridge, and the combat engagement center. Participants must be at least eight years old and have the ability to climb stairs to four decks and be comfortable in small spaces.

The **Hampton Roads Naval Museum** (free admission) is also located inside the NAUTICUS National Maritime Center on the second floor. The museum is run by the U.S. Navy and details the 237-year history of the Hampton Roads region fleet. Exhibits in the museum include an 18-pounder cannon from 1798, artifacts from the cruiser **CSS _Florida_** and the sloop-of-war **USS _Cumberland,_** a World War II Mark 7 undersea mine, and a torpedo warhead from a German submarine.

Allow at least 2-4 hours to explore the center and the ship. The facility includes a casual restaurant serving sandwiches, salads, beverages, and snacks.

## NAVAL STATION NORFOLK

Norfolk offers a unique opportunity to tour the largest naval base in the world. The **Naval Station Norfolk** sits on 4,300 acres on Sewells Point and is home to 75 ships and 134 aircraft. The 45-minute bus tour leaves from the **Naval Tour and Information Center** (9079 Hampton Blvd., 757/444-7955, www.norfolkvisitor.com) next to Gate 5. The tour rides past destroyers, aircraft carriers, frigates, amphibious assault ships, and the airfield. Tour times change frequently so call for a current schedule.

## VIRGINIA ZOO

The **Virginia Zoo** (3500 Granby St., 757/441-2374, www.virginiazoo.org, daily 10am-5pm, $14.95) occupies 53 acres adjacent to Lafayette Park. It opened in 1900 and houses more than 400 animals including elephants, giraffes, orangutans, otters, and birds. The zoo is operated by the City of Norfolk and the Virginia Zoological Society. It offers many educational and children's programs.

## ST. PAUL'S CHURCH

**St. Paul's Church** (201 St. Paul's Blvd., 757/627-4353, www.saintpaulsnorfolk.com) is the oldest building in Norfolk, dating back to 1739. A cannonball that was fired into the church on the night before the Revolutionary War began is still lodged in its southwestern wall. Tombstones in the church's historic cemetery date back to the 17th and 18th centuries. Episcopalian services are still held at St. Paul's.

## Entertainment and Events

**Chrysler Hall** (215 St. Paul's Blvd., 757/644-6464, www.sevenvenues.com) is the top performing arts venue in the Hampton Roads area. It hosts Broadway shows, concerts, theatrical performances, the **Virginia Symphony** (www.virginiasymphony.org), the **Virginia Arts Festival** (www.vafest.org), and the **Virginia Ballet.**

The **Virginia Opera** (www.vaopera.org, 866/673-7282) performs in three locations throughout Virginia (Norfolk, Richmond, and Fairfax). The Norfolk venue, the **Harrison Opera House** (160 E. Virginia Beach Blvd., 757/627-9545), is a beautifully renovated World War II USO theater that seats just over 1,600 people.

The **Scope Arena** (201 E. Brambleton Ave., 757/644-6464, www.sevenvenues.com) is a 12,000-seat complex that hosts concerts, family shows, and conventions. It is also the home of the **Norfolk Admirals** of the ECHL.

Norfolk also has a number of quality small venues featuring good nightlife and entertainment. The **NorVa** (317 Monticello Ave., 757/627-4547, www.thenorva.com) is a 1,500-person concert venue the hosts a variety of artists such as Ingrid Michaelson, Citizen Cope, and The Legwarmers. **The Banque** (1849 E. Little Creek Rd., 757/480-3600, www.thebanque.com) is a popular, award-winning country-and-western nightclub and restaurant offering a large dance floor and well-known artists.

**Norfolk Festevents** (757/441-2345, www.festevents.org) presents more than 65 days of events including concerts and festivals in

**Town Point Park** (on the Elizabeth River in the center of the business district in downtown Norfolk) and **Ocean View Beach Park** (at the end of Granby Street at Ocean View Avenue) from February through October. One of the most popular events, the **Norfolk Harborfest** is held annually for four days at the beginning of June and attracts more than 100,000 people. This large festival covers more than three miles on the Norfolk waterfront and offers visitors three sailboat parades, tall ships, the largest fireworks display on the East Coast, and seemingly endless entertainment. Another Festevent, the **Norfolk Jazz Festival** is a two-day festival held in mid-July. Tickets are $30-69. The **Town Point Virginia Fall Wine Festival** is held in Town Point Park for two days in October. More than 200 Virginia wines are featured. Tickets start at $20 and can be purchased online.

## Shopping

The **Macarthur Center** (300 Monticello Ave., 757/627-6000, www.shopmacarthur.com, Mon.-Sat. 10am-9pm, Sun. noon-6pm) is a large shopping mall with close to 150 retail stores and restaurants. There is also a movie complex.

A trendy little shopping area worth checking out is **The Palace Station & Shops of Ghent** (Llewellyn Ave. and 21st St., www.ghentnorfolk.org) in the historic Ghent neighborhood. Thirty-five unique shops and restaurants line this retail shopping complex near downtown Norfolk. Boutiques, antiques stores, gift stores, and craft stores are just some of the establishments found in this interesting area.

## Sports and Recreation

**Harbor Park** (150 Park Ave., www.milb.com) is home to the **Norfolk Tides,** the Class AAA affiliate of the Baltimore Orioles. The park is considered one of the best minor league baseball facilities in the country, boasting a practical design and a terrific view of downtown Norfolk. The park opened in 1993 on the Elizabeth River.

The **Norfolk Admirals** (www. norfolkadmirals.com) take to the ice seasonally at the **Scope Arena** to compete in the ECHL. Consult the website for schedules and tickets.

Those looking for a little local adventure can take in a **sand wrestling** (www. sandwrestling.com) competition. Sand wrestling, which is also known as beach wrestling, is a version of traditional wrestling. Established as an international style of amateur wrestling in 2005, it is quickly gaining popularity and offers competition for males and females of all ages.

Beachgoers can enjoy miles of public beach at **Ocean View Beach Park** (www.norfolk. gov). The park offers a boardwalk, bandstand, beach access ramp for people with disabilities, commercial fishing pier, and open recreation space. There is a bathhouse, and parking is free. Dogs are allowed on leashes in the off-season.

A trip with **American Rover Sailing Cruises** (333 Waterside Dr., 757/627-7245, www.americanrover.com, $20) is a relaxing way to tour the Hampton Roads Harbor and the Elizabeth River. The *American Rover*'s red sails are a distinctive sight in the Hampton Roads area. From April through October, they offer 1.5- and 2-hour narrated cruises. Guests can help out with sailing the ship or just sit back and relax.

## Food
### AMERICAN
★ **Freemason Abbey Restaurant** (209 W. Freemason St., 757/622-3966, www.freemasonabbey.com, Mon.-Thurs. 11am-9:30pm, Fri.-Sat. 11am-10:30pm, Sun. 9:30am-9:30pm, $9-30) is a local favorite in downtown Norfolk for fresh seafood, steak, and pasta. It is housed in a 140-year-old renovated church and has been a restaurant for more than two decades. The atmosphere is friendly, elegant, and casual with a beautiful decor that retains a church-like feel yet has cozy seating. Try the award-winning she-crab soup. Reservations are highly recommended on the weekends.

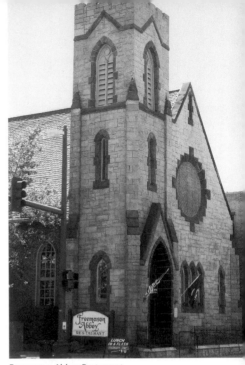

Freemason Abbey Restaurant

**Doumar's Barbeque & Curb Service** (1919 Monticello Ave., 757/627-4163, www. doumars.com, Mon.-Thurs. 8am-11pm, Fri.-Sat. 8am-midnight, $2-5) is a legendary diner that was featured on the show *Diners, Drive-Ins and Dives*. Its origin was an ice-cream stand that opened in 1907 in Ocean View Amusement Park. The business moved to its current location in 1934 and is still owned by the same family. Famous for barbecue and ice cream, they bake their own ice-cream cones in the original cone machine. Take a seat inside the diner, or dine from your car and enjoy their carhop service. This is a fun, genuine, old-school diner that is inexpensive and has a great history.

Seafood lovers can get their fix at **A. W. Schuck's** (2200 Colonial Ave., 757/664-9117, daily 11am-2am, $8-15). They seem to be firm believers that any meal can include seafood. Try their burger topped with lump crab, or a po'boy; both are well seasoned, huge, and delicious. Finding the place can be a bit tricky—look on 22nd Street in the plaza rather than along Colonial Avenue. The staff is friendly and attentive, and the atmosphere is social. This is a good choice for reasonably priced, yet tasty food.

## ITALIAN

**Razzo** (3248 E. Ocean View Ave., 757/962-3630, www.razzo-norfolk.com, daily 5pm-10pm, $8-19) is a big hot spot in a small package. This tiny Italian restaurant on Ocean View only has a handful of tables, but waiting for one is worth your time (and there's a well-stocked bar that can make that wait more enjoyable). The food is outstanding, with daily specials and homemade bread. When in doubt, order the chicken marsala.

## Accommodations

### $100-200

There are many chain hotels in Norfolk. A few stand out for above-average accommodations, good service, and proximity to downtown attractions and the airport, such as the **Courtyard Norfolk Downtown** (520 Plume St., 757/963-6000, www.marriott.com, $149-179), the **Holiday Inn Express Hotel & Suites Norfolk International Airport** (1157 N. Military Hwy., 757/455-5055, www.hiexpress.com, $149-162), and the **Residence Inn Norfolk** (227 W. Brambleton Ave., 757/842-6216, www.marriott.com, $149-239).

In addition to the selection of large chain hotels, there are some very nice bed-and-breakfasts and historic hotels in Norfolk. The **Page House Inn** (323 Fairfax Ave., 757/625-5033, www.pagehouseinn.com, $170-245) is a historic bed-and-breakfast (circa 1899) next to the Chrysler Museum of Art in the Ghent Historic District. This stately redbrick mansion has four guest rooms and three guest suites, decorated with 19th-century furniture, antiques, and art. A delicious full breakfast is served each morning, and refreshments are served each afternoon. The innkeepers are warm and welcoming.

The ★ **Freemason Inn Bed and**

**Breakfast** (411 W. York St., 757/963-7000, www.freemasoninn.com, $160-225) is known for its tasteful interior, spacious rooms, comfortable beds, and incredible food (they serve a three-course breakfast). Four elegant guest rooms and a friendly host make this a top choice in Norfolk. The inn is centrally located in a charming neighborhood near the harbor.

## Information and Services

For additional information on the Norfolk area, visit www.visitnorfolktoday.com.

## Getting There and Around

Norfolk is 16 miles south of Hampton.

The **Norfolk International Airport** (ORF, 2200 Norview Ave., www.norfolkairport.com) is convenient for those traveling by air to the Norfolk area. It is one mile east of I-64 (exit 279) and just minutes from downtown Norfolk.

The city is serviced by **Amtrak** (130 Park Ave., www.amtrak.com) rail service and by **Greyhound** (701 Monticello Ave., 757/625-7500, www.greyhound.com) bus service.

**Norfolk Electric Transit** (www.virginia.org) is part of Hampton Roads Transit and offers free bus service around town and stops at major attractions. It operates weekdays 6am-6:15pm at 15-minute intervals and 6:15pm-11pm at 30-minute intervals. Saturday service is 6am-12:15am at 30-minute intervals, and Sunday service is 7am-11:15pm at 30-minute intervals.

**Hampton Roads Transit** also offers additional bus routes around Norfolk (www.gohrt.com, $1.75) and **Paddlewheel Ferry** (www.gohrt.com, $1.75) service on three passenger paddle-wheel boats. Each boat holds 150 passengers and runs between downtown Norfolk (at the Waterside) and Portsmouth. The ferry operates every 30 minutes Monday-Thursday 7am-9:45pm, Friday 7am-11:45pm, Saturday 10am-11:45pm, and Sunday 10am-9:45pm. Extended service kicks in during peak summer weeks. Passengers are allowed to bring bicycles on board.

# Virginia Beach

Virginia Beach is the state's premier beach destination, with sand, surf, and ice cream. It is a thriving year-round city with more than 437,000 full-time residents as well as a bustling tourist destination, with nearly three million visitors annually. Everyone coming to town is greeted by **Neptune,** a 24-foot-tall statue by Paul DiPasquale. He stands on the boardwalk and invites children and adults alike to enjoy the wonders of the ocean responsibly. The resort area runs along more than 20 miles of beach, which is maintained and replenished on a regular basis. The area is booming with commercialism and has more than its share of touristy gift shops and oversize hotels, but also offers a variety of attractions, events, parks, and wildlife refuges. The farther north you travel, the quieter it gets, and the northern reaches are mostly residential.

The three-mile-long boardwalk is the center of activity, and the aquarium, water sports, fishing, and parks keep visitors coming back year after year. Accommodations are plentiful but also book quickly during the peak summer season, especially those right on the beach. The beach is busiest not only in the summer but also during March and April, when thousands of college students arrive for spring break. Keep this in mind when planning your trip since it may be best to avoid these windows unless you are joining in the fun.

Tourism in Virginia Beach began with the opening of the first hotel in 1884. The boardwalk was built just four years later. The strip has been growing ever since, and a few historic landmarks such as the Cavalier Hotel (circa 1927) still stand today.

A population boom in the 1980s resulted in some bad press for the beach area, which experienced some pains from the onslaught of visitors and the hard partying that came with them. Since then, the municipality has made a concerted effort and spent millions of dollars to revamp the beach's reputation as a family resort. They've succeeded on most levels by encouraging more high-end businesses to come to the beach and by making the main thoroughfares more visually pleasing to visitors with fresh lighting and landscaping. The area is now known for its excellence in environmental health, and as more and more sporting events are booked for the beach, it is becoming a destination for the fitness-minded. In a nutshell, Virginia Beach is a modern and affordable vacation destination that offers a little bit of everything.

## SIGHTS
### ★ Virginia Beach Boardwalk

No trip to Virginia Beach is complete without a stroll along the 28-foot-wide boardwalk running parallel to the ocean for three miles (between 1st Street and 42nd Street) on one of the longest recreational beach areas in the world. The boardwalk is perfect for getting some exercise with a view. There are lanes for walkers and bicycles, and many running events utilize

*Neptune* greets visitors to Virginia Beach.

# Virginia Beach

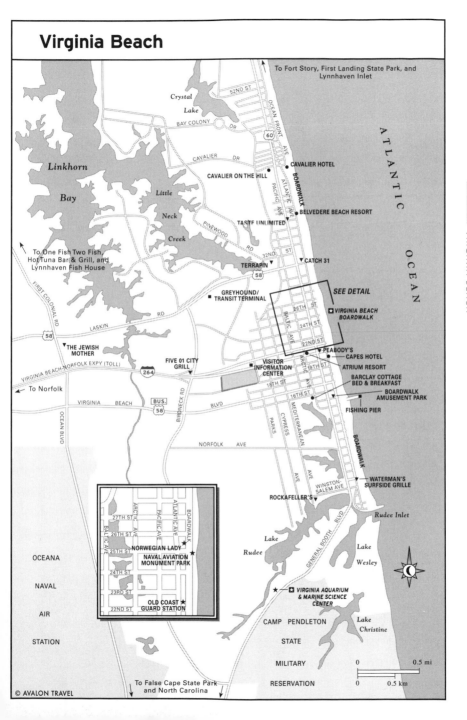

To Fort Story, First Landing State Park, and Lynnhaven Inlet

Crystal
Lake

Linkhorn

Bay

Little

Neck

Creek

To One Fish Two Fish,
Hot Tuna Bar & Grill, and
Lynnhaven Fish House

ATLANTIC

OCEAN

CAVALIER HOTEL
CAVALIER ON THE HILL
BELVEDERE BEACH RESORT
TASTE UNLIMITED
CATCH 31
TERRAPIN
GREYHOUND/TRANSIT TERMINAL
SEE DETAIL
VIRGINIA BEACH BOARDWALK
THE JEWISH MOTHER
FIVE 01 CITY GRILL
PEABODY'S
CAPES HOTEL
ATRIUM RESORT
VISITOR INFORMATION CENTER
BARCLAY COTTAGE BED & BREAKFAST
BOARDWALK AMUSEMENT PARK
FISHING PIER
To Norfolk
WATERMAN'S SURFSIDE GRILLE
ROCKAFELLER'S
Rudee Inlet

NORWEGIAN LADY
NAVAL AVIATION MONUMENT PARK
OLD COAST GUARD STATION

OCEANA
NAVAL
AIR
STATION

Lake
Rudee

Lake
Wesley

VIRGINIA AQUARIUM & MARINE SCIENCE CENTER

CAMP PENDLETON
STATE
MILITARY
RESERVATION

Lake
Christine

0        0.5 mi
0        0.5 km

To False Cape State Park and North Carolina

© AVALON TRAVEL

a portion of the boardwalk on their route, including the **Shamrock Marathon** (www.shamrockmarathon.com) and the **Rock 'n' Roll Marathon Series** (www.runrocknroll.competitor.com). The boardwalk is adorned with benches, grassy areas, play areas, amusement parks, arcades, hotels, restaurants, shops, and other entertainment. There is also a large fishing pier at 15th Street.

Some special features along the boardwalk include the **Naval Aviation Monument,** which stands at 25th Street and pays tribute to the navy, Marine Corps, and Coast Guard. Nearby is the **Norwegian Lady** statue that commemorates the lives lost during the shipwreck of a boat from Moss, Norway (a sister statue was erected in Moss). At 13th Street is the **Virginia Legends Walk,** a landscaped walkway that pays tribute to some of Virginia's most famous citizens, including Thomas Jefferson, Robert E. Lee, Captain John Smith, Ella Fitzgerald, and Arthur Ashe.

There are public restrooms at 17th, 24th, and 30th Streets.

## ★ Virginia Aquarium & Marine Science Center

The **Virginia Aquarium & Marine Science Center** (717 General Booth Blvd.,

757/385-3474, www.virginiaaquarium.com, daily 9am-5pm, $22) is a must-visit attraction in Virginia Beach. With its more than 800,000 gallons of aquariums, live animal habitats, numerous exhibits, and a National Geographic 3-D Theater ($8), you could spend several hours or an entire day here and not get bored. There are many hands-on experiences in the center, including a touch pool of friendly animals. A unique exhibit called *Stranded* enables visitors to learn about the Virginia Aquarium Response Team and the work they do to rescue and rehabilitate marine animals in need. Through this exhibit, visitors learn about recent patients the response team has helped, how they track rehabilitated animals, and human threats to marine mammals.

Another great attraction at the Virginia Aquarium & Marine Science Center is the **Adventure Park at Virginia Aquarium** (757/385-4947, $55). It offers adventure for children over five years of age and also for adults. The park is a trail of wooden platforms connected by zip lines and bridges. A play area is also available for younger children. This is a wonderful attraction when you need a break from the beach, and kids of all ages find it compelling.

the Virginia Aquarium & Marine Science Center

## Old Coast Guard Station

The **Old Coast Guard Station** (2401 Atlantic Ave., 757/422-1587, www.old-coastguardstation.com, May-Oct. Mon.-Sat. 10am-5pm, Sun. noon-5pm, Nov.-Apr. Tues.-Sat. 10am-5pm, Sun. noon-5pm, closed Mon., $4) houses more than 1,800 artifacts and 1,000 photographs that honor Virginia's maritime heritage. Two galleries relate the history of the U.S. Life-Saving and Coast Guard Services, along with shipwrecks off the Virginia coast. The building itself was constructed in 1903 and is the only one of five original life-saving stations built that year along the Virginia coast that remains standing. It now resides on the boardwalk at 24th Street, and the rooftop "Towercam" enables guests to look at ships in the Atlantic.

## The Old Cape Henry Lighthouse

**The Old Cape Henry Lighthouse** (583 Atlantic Ave., Fort Story, 757/422-9421, www.preservationvirginia.org, Nov. 1-Mar. 15 daily 10am-4pm, Mar. 16-Oct. 31 daily 10am-5pm, $8) is part of the Fort Story military base. It once protected the entryway to the Chesapeake Bay at the northern end of Virginia Beach. Construction of the lighthouse was authorized by George Washington as one of the first acts of the newly organized federal government, and it was the first federal construction project. Alexander Hamilton oversaw its construction. The lighthouse was completed in 1792. This octagonal sandstone edifice remains one of the oldest surviving lighthouses in the country and is a National Historic Landmark. Visitors can climb to the top of the lighthouse and enjoy commanding views of the Chesapeake Bay and the Atlantic Ocean. Guided tours of the grounds are also available, and there's a gift shop. To reach the lighthouse, you must drive through a security gate at Fort Story. Photo identification is required to enter, and car searches are frequently made.

# ENTERTAINMENT AND EVENTS

Endless entertainment can be found on the Virginia Beach boardwalk, including concerts, athletic events, and performances.

## Nightlife

Virginia Beach doesn't sleep when the sun goes down. In fact, in the summer it doesn't seem to sleep at all. Live music can be found at the **Hot Tuna Bar & Grill** (2817 Shore Dr., 757/481-2888, www.hottunavb.com, daily from 4pm). They offer Top 40 dance music starting at 10pm. Another dance bar is **Peabody's** (209 21st St., 757/422-6212, www.peabodysvirginiabeach.com). They've been around since 1967 and have one of the largest dance floors in the area.

If a game of pool is more your speed, try **Q-Master II Billiards** (5612 Princess Anne Rd., 757/499-8900, www.q-masters.com). They are the premier billiards room in the region and have 72 tables. They also host competitions.

For those wishing to kick back for some live folk, jazz, or blues, stop in **Jewish Mother & VB Tap House** (211 21st St., 757/222-1818, www.jewishmother.com). They offer live entertainment and a large menu that includes delicious deli sandwiches. If comedy is more up your alley, catch a show at the **Funny Bone Comedy Club & Restaurant** (217 Central Park Ave., 757/213-5555, www.vabeachfunnybone.com). They host well-known comics and offer tables with a full dinner and bar menu during the show. Shows are for ages 21 and older.

## Events

Some popular annual events include the **American Music Festival** (5th St. and Atlantic Ave., www.beachstreetusa.com, $40), the largest outdoor music event on the East Coast. It runs for three days over Labor Day weekend and features local and national artists. Sounds of rock, jazz, country, blues, and R&B flow out to the oceanfront from a huge stage on the beach at 5th Street and

# The Great Dismal Swamp

The **Great Dismal Swamp National Wildlife Refuge** (3100 Desert Rd., Suffolk, free) is a 112,000-acre refuge southwest of Virginia Beach. The refuge is primarily forested wetlands and is home to numerous birds and animals. It also encompasses 3,100-acre Lake Drummond, which is the largest natural lake in Virginia. One hundred miles of trails are open daily for hiking, walking, and biking (sunrise to sunset).

Although humans first occupied the swamp as much as 13,000 years ago, there was not much interest in the area until Lake Drummond was discovered by William Drummond (a governor of North Carolina) in 1665. The area was later surveyed, and the state line between Virginia and North Carolina was drawn through it in 1728. The name of the land was recorded as the Great Dismal (dismal was a common term at the time for a swamp). Shortly thereafter, George Washington visited the swamp and developed the Dismal Swamp Land Company, with designs on draining and logging parts of it. The name "great" was likely added to the swamp's name due to its large size. Logging continued in the swamp until 1976, with all parts of the swamp having been logged one or more times.

The dense forests in the swamp have traditionally been a refuge for animals, but have also been used by people for a similar reason. The swamp was at one time a haven to fleeing slaves, and as a result, the swamp was the first National Wildlife Refuge to be recognized officially as part of the Underground Railroad.

Today, more than 200 species of birds live in the refuge either permanently or seasonally. Perhaps an even more impressive fact is that 96 species of butterflies have also been recorded here. More than 47 mammals live in the refuge, including black bears, bobcats, white-tailed deer, river otters, and mink.

For more information, visit www.fws.gov/refuge or contact the park headquarters at 757/986-3705.

from stages in many parks along the water. Another favorite is the **Boardwalk Art Show and Festival** (http://virginiamoca.org) held annually for four days in mid-June. This event began in 1956 and is one of the oldest and best outdoor art shows on the East Coast. It is held on the boardwalk between 17th Street and 24th Street.

Runners won't want to miss the annual **Shamrock Marathon** (www.shamrock-marathon.com) weekend in mid-March. The Shamrock Marathon has been around since 1973 and is now a premier running event with numerous races that draw more than 24,000 participants.

## SPORTS AND RECREATION
### Parks and Wildlife
**First Landing State Park** (2500 Shore Dr., 757/412-2300, www.first-landing-state-park.org, daily 8am-dusk, $5) is the site where the first permanent English settlers landed in 1607. This 2,888-acre park offers 20 miles of hiking trails, biking, fishing, a boat ramp, and camping.

**Mount Trashmore Park** (310 Edwin Dr., 757/473-5237, www.vbgov.com, 7:30am-dusk, free) is a famous land-reuse park that was built on an old landfill. The 165-acre park was created by compressing multiple layers of waste and clean soil. The park includes playgrounds, picnic areas, volleyball courts, and a large skate park.

**Back Bay National Wildlife Refuge** (4005 Sandpiper Rd., 757/301-7329, www.fws.gov/backbay, daily during daylight hours, $5) includes approximately 9,000 acres of beach, marsh, and woods. It is a haven for many migratory birds. There is both fresh- and saltwater fishing, a canoe and kayak launch, biking, and hiking.

**False Cape State Park** (4001 Sandpiper Rd., 757/426-7128, www.virginiastateparks.

gov, 24 hours, $4) is an ocean-to-brackish water area that is only accessible by boat, bike, or on foot. The land trail leading in is five miles long. A tram from the Back Bay National Wildlife Refuge visitors center is also available (call for a schedule). Primitive camping is allowed.

## Boat Ramps

The **Owl Creek Boat Ramp** (701 General Booth Blvd.) is a free launch facility next to the Virginia Aquarium & Marine Science Center. Other boat ramps include **First Landing State Park** (2500 Shore Dr., www. virginiastatparks.gov), **Bubba's Marina** (3323 Shore Dr., www.bubbaseafoodrestaurant.com), and **Munden Point Park** (2001 Pefley Ln., www.vbgov.com/parks).

## Kayaking and Boat Tours

There are many local outfitters in the Virginia Beach area offering seasonal kayak tours, rentals, and eco-tours. **Chesapean Outdoors** (757/961-0447, www.chesapean. com) provides an exciting guided dolphin kayak tour ($60) where guests can paddle with bottlenose dolphins at the north end of Virginia Beach. They also offer guided sunset paddle tours ($55) and rentals (single kayak, one hour $20, two hours $30; tandem kayak, one hour $25, two hours $35). **Kayak Nature Tours** (757/480-1999, www.kayaknaturetours. net) also has guided dolphin kayak tours (2.5 hours, $60) and flat-water guided trips (2.5 hours, $50).

Explore the creeks near the **Virginia Aquarium & Marine Science Center** (www.virginiaaquarium.com) on a guided pontoon boat or ride along with aquarium staff on a 90-minute seasonal dolphin-watching excursion ($21). The aquarium also offers ocean collections boat trips, when a variety of sea creatures are brought on board, and winter wildlife boat trips (75 minutes, $19).

Kayaking tours are also available through **Back Bay Getaways** (757/721-4484, www.backbaygetaways.com, $35-45) and

**Ocean Eagle Kayak** (757/589-1766, www. oceaneaglekayak.com, $70).

## Fishing

The Virginia Beach coastline and inshore waterways are thoroughfares for many species of fish including tuna, bluefin, blue marlin, Atlantic mackerel, red drum, and flounder. Private fishing charters are available through a number of companies including **Dockside Seafood and Fishing Center** (3311 Shore Dr., 757/481-4545, www.fishingvabeach.com), **Rudee Inlet Charters** (200 Winston Salem Ave., 757/425-3400, www.rudeeinletcharters. com), **Virginia Beach Fishing Center** (200 Winston Salem Ave., 757/491-8000, www.virginiafishing.com), and **Fisherman's Wharf Marina** (524 Winston Salem Ave., 757/428-2111, www.fishermanswharfmarina.com).

There are also several fishing piers that are great for dropping a line, including the **Virginia Beach Fishing Pier** (15th Street), the **Little Island Fishing Pier** (3820 S. Sandpiper Rd., www.sandbridgepier.com), the **Lynnhaven Fishing Pier** (2350 Starfish Rd., www.lynnhavenpier.com), and the **Sea Gull Fishing Pier** at the Chesapeake Bay Bridge Tunnel (www.cbbt.com).

## Amusement Park

The **Atlantic Fun Park** (233 15th St., 757/422-0467, www.atlanticfunpark.com) has a yesteryear vibe that is nostalgic for parents and pure fun for the kiddies. The park offers thrill rides, family rides, and kiddie rides, including a 100-foot Ferris wheel. Single ride tickets ($3-5) or unlimited ride wristbands ($20-30) can be purchased.

## FOOD
### American

**Firebrew Bar & Grill** (1253 Nimmo Pkwy., Suite 117, 757/689-2800, www.fire-brew.com, Mon.-Thurs. 11am-10pm, Fri. and Sat. 11am-11pm, Sun. 11am-9pm) is a casual bar and grill with a few twists. Most menu items (flatbread, steak, tacos, etc.) are prepared on an open-flame fire deck, and the restaurant proudly states that they do not use microwaves or fryers. Their extensive bar includes local craft brews and a self-service wine station.

If you're looking for a good place to grab a sandwich, stop in **Taste Unlimited** (36th St. and Pacific Ave., 757/422-3399, www.tasteunlimited.com, Mon.-Sat. 10am-6pm, Sun. 11am-5pm, $6-11). This pleasant sandwich shop and specialty food store, a block from the beach, has ample seating, good variety, and a friendly atmosphere. They also sell wine, cheese, and other gourmet snacks, and at times there's even a little farmers market outside.

## Seafood

★ **One Fish Two Fish** (2109 W. Great Neck Rd., 757/496-4350, www.onefish-twofish.com, dinner daily from 5pm, $22-30) is an elegant but fun seafood and steak restaurant on Long Creek (in the Pier House building at the Long Bay Pointe Marina). It is comfortably away from the hubbub of the strip, and diners can enjoy a panoramic view of the water or be entertained by the activity in the exhibition kitchen. There's also an open patio. Seafood combinations are expertly and imaginatively prepared, and they offer an excellent selection of wine.

**Catch 31** (3001 Atlantic Ave., 757/213-3474, www.catch31.com, Mon.-Fri. 6am-2am, Sat.-Sun. 7am-2am, $25-43) is inside the Hilton Virginia Beach Oceanfront and is one of the finest restaurants along the main strip. They are known for offering at least 15 types of fresh fish, and their signature dish is the seafood towers that include crab legs, mussels, lobster, and shrimp. The restaurant's high ceilings, ocean-blue walls, and indoor/outdoor bar add to the ambience. If the weather is nice, dine outside on their beachfront terrace. They serve breakfast, lunch, and dinner.

A restaurant popular with Virginia Beach residents is **Rockafeller's** (308 Mediterranean Ave., 757/442-5654, www.rockafellers.com, Mon.-Sat. 11am-10pm, Sun. 10am-10pm, $16-33). This dependable local favorite offers seafood, steaks, pasta, and salads in a large three-story home on Rudee Inlet. Double-decker porches provide lovely seating, or you can dine inside. There's a bar and raw bar and nice views from indoors as well.

**Lynnhaven Fish House** (2350 Starfish Rd., 757/481-0003, www.lynnhavenfishhouse. net, Sun.-Thurs. 11:30am-9pm, Fri.-Sat. 11:30am-9:30pm, $11-33) serves up fresh surf dishes with a nice view of the oceanfront. They have a large fish selection on their dinner menu and creative lunch entrées such as seafood omelets and quiche.

**Waterman's Surfside Grille** (5th St. and Atlantic Ave., 757/428-3644, www.watermans.com, lunch daily 11am-4pm, dinner daily 4pm-10pm, $10-25) is one of the few freestanding restaurants left on the strip that isn't connected to a hotel. It offers a lively atmosphere, good seafood, and outstanding cocktails.

# ACCOMMODATIONS
## $100-200

The **Belvedere Beach Resort** (3603 Atlantic Ave., 800/425-0612, www.belvederebeachresort.com, $175-200) is a privately owned hotel on the oceanfront on the northern end of Virginia Beach. The light-filled, wood-paneled rooms offer private balconies with views of the beach. The hotel has adult-size bicycles for guest use and direct access to the boardwalk. Rooms are quiet, and the staff is very friendly and helpful. The **Wave Trolley** stops in front of the hotel for easy access to many places on the beachfront. This is not a luxurious resort, but a very pleasant, comfortable choice in a fantastic location. The hotel is open seasonally, normally April through the beginning of October. Minimum stays may be required. Coffeepots are available upon request.

## $200-300

The **Capes Hotel** (2001 Atlantic Ave., 757/428-5421, www.capeshotel.com, $192-277, closed Oct.-Mar.) is a pleasant oceanfront hotel on the boardwalk. It has an indoor pool with a view of the ocean and nicely kept grounds. The hotel is convenient to all the beach attractions. The 59 oceanfront rooms are cozy rather than large, but all are comfortable with an airy feel and good views. The service is also very dependable. There is a small café on-site with an oceanfront patio. This is not a luxurious resort, but it doesn't attempt to be; it's a good value in a great location, with a friendly staff.

The **Atrium Resort** (315 21st St., 757/491-1400, www.vsaresorts.com, $250-330) is a comfortable hotel a few blocks from the boardwalk. They offer 90 suites with well-appointed kitchenettes, an open-air lobby, and a small indoor pool. The rooms are well-kept, with updated televisions and comfortable beds. The hotel is owned by VSA Resorts, along with two others in Virginia Beach (Ocean Sands Resort and the Ocean Key Resort). They offer room rentals and vacation ownership (similar to a timeshare). Grocery delivery is available upon request. Orders can be placed online and delivered to your room upon arrival.

## Over $300

★ **The Cavalier Hotel** (4200 Atlantic Ave., www.cavalierhotel.com, $299 and up during off-season, $499 and up in peak season) is a historic hotel that opened in 1927. A Virginia Beach icon and a National Register of Historic Places property, the grand hotel was built on a hill overlooking the ocean and has welcomed seven U.S. presidents, celebrities such as Frank Sinatra, Judy Garland, and Bette Davis, and international dignitaries. It was also used as a naval training center during World War II. The hotel underwent a $70 million renovation from 2015 to 2017, at which point it became a member of Marriott International's Autograph Collection. Today the hotel portrays the bygone age of grand hotels as it sits majestically above the hubbub of activity on the oceanfront. The Cavalier Hotel offers 85 guest rooms and suites, three restaurants, a spa, a bourbon distillery and tasting room, a museum, ballroom, meeting space, poolside vistas and loggias, and a fitness center. At the time of publication, the hotel was closed for renovations, but is expected to reopen in April 2017.

The imposing 21-story **Hilton Virginia Beach Oceanfront** (3001 Atlantic Ave., 757/213-3000, www.hiltonvb.com, $329-599) offers oceanfront luxury with amenities such as a rooftop infinity pool, an indoor pool, the Sky Bar, a fully equipped fitness center, and

COASTAL VIRGINIA
VIRGINIA BEACH

The Cavalier Hotel

bicycle rentals. There are 289 modern rooms and suites, outfitted with a beach décor and offering a choice of city or ocean views. There are several on-site restaurants and convenient parking ($10 for self-park and $16 for valet per day).

## Bed-and-Breakfasts and Inns

The **Barclay Cottage Bed and Breakfast** (400 16th St., 757/422-1956, www.barclaycottage.com, $115-189) is a beautiful B&B offering five comfortable guest rooms. Three rooms have private bathrooms, and two others share bath facilities. Each room is individually decorated with its own colors and theme (such as nautical or floral). The white, two-story, porch-wrapped cottage (complete with rocking chairs) is within walking distance of many attractions and a few blocks from the beach.

The **Country Villa Bed and Breakfast** (2252 Indian River Rd., 757/721-3844, www.countryvillainn.com, $299-379) is a charming B&B on four acres in Virginia Beach. They offer two private guest rooms and personalized in-room spa services. Guests are served three-course gourmet breakfasts with outstanding personalized service. The inn is eight minutes driving from Sandbridge Beach and will provide beach chairs, towels, coolers, and umbrellas. There is also an outdoor hot tub and swimming pool.

## House and Condo Rentals

There are several local real estate offices in Virginia Beach that offer rentals for a week or longer. **Sandbridge Realty** (800/933-4800, www.sandbridge.com) is in southern Virginia Beach and offers a property search feature on its website, as does **Siebert Realty** (877/422-2200, www.siebert-realty.com), which is also in southern Virginia Beach.

## CAMPING

**First Landing State Park** (2500 Shore Dr., 757/412-2300, www.first-landing-state-park.

org, $24-32) on the north end of Virginia Beach offers 200-plus beach campsites near the Chesapeake Bay. There are also 20 cabins for rent ($94-139).

## INFORMATION AND SERVICES

For additional information on Virginia Beach, visit www.virginiabeach.com or stop by the **Visitor Information Center** (2100 Parks Ave., 757/437-4882, daily 9am-5pm). There are also two kiosks run by the Visitor Information Center that are available from May to September; they are on the Boardwalk at 17th Street and on Atlantic Avenue at 24th Street.

## GETTING THERE

Most people arrive in Virginia Beach by car. I-64 connects with the Virginia Beach-Norfolk Expressway (I-264) which leads to the oceanfront at Virginia Beach.

The **Norfolk International Airport** (ORF, 2200 Norview Ave., Norfolk, www.norfolkairport.com) is approximately 17 miles from Virginia Beach. Daily flights are available through multiple commercial carriers.

Rail service does not run to Virginia Beach, but **Amtrak** (800/872-7245, www.amtrak.com) serves Newport News with connecting bus service to 19th Street and Pacific Avenue in Virginia Beach. Reservations are required. Bus service is also available to Virginia Beach on **Greyhound** (971 Virginia Beach Blvd., 757/422-2998, www.greyhound.com).

## GETTING AROUND

There are plenty of paid parking lots in Virginia Beach. The cost per day ranges about $5-8. Municipal parking lots are located at 4th Street, 9th Street, 19th Street, 25th Street, and 31st Street. **Hampton Roads Transit** (www.gohrt.com, $1.75-3.50) operates about a dozen bus routes in Virginia Beach.

# Virginia's Eastern Shore

Visiting Virginia's Eastern Shore can be a bit like stepping back in time. The long, narrow, flat peninsula that separates the Chesapeake Bay from the Atlantic Ocean has a feel that's very different from the rest of the state. The pace is more relaxed, the people take time to chat, and much of the cuisine centers on extraordinary seafood fished right out the back door.

Traveling from the Virginia Beach area to the Eastern Shore requires passage over and through one of the great marvels of the East Coast. The **Chesapeake Bay Bridge-Tunnel** (www.cbbt.com) spanning the mouth of the Chesapeake Bay is an engineering masterpiece. The four-lane, 20-mile-long bridge-and-tunnel system is a toll route and part of Route 13. It takes vehicles over a series of bridges and through two-mile-long tunnels that travel under the shipping channels. Five-acre artificial islands are located at each end of the two tunnels, and a fishing pier and restaurant/gift shop were built on one.

Upon arrival on the Eastern Shore, you are greeted by endless acres of marsh, water, and wildlife refuge areas. Agriculture and fishing are the primary sources of revenue on the peninsula, and tourism in the towns provides a nice supplement.

There are a handful of charming towns that dot the coastline on both bodies of water, and most have roots prior to the Civil War. In fact, many beautiful 19th-century homes have been refurbished, as have the churches, schools, and public buildings.

The first town on the southern end of the Eastern Shore is Cape Charles, and the northernmost is Chincoteague Island. Bus transportation runs between the two on the **Star Transit** (www.vatransit.org, Mon.-Fri.).

## CAPE CHARLES

Cape Charles is the southernmost town on Virginia's Eastern Shore, 10 miles from the Chesapeake Bay Bridge-Tunnel. The town was founded in 1884 as the southern terminus of the New York, Philadelphia, & Norfolk Railroad. It was also a popular steamship port for vessels transporting freight and passengers across the Chesapeake Bay to Norfolk.

Today, Cape Charles is primarily a vacation town. It is not large, nor is it particularly well known, but this is part of the charm. It offers a quiet historic district, sandy beaches, golfing, boating, and other outdoor recreation.

## Sights

The **Historic District** (757/331-3259) in Cape Charles is approximately seven square blocks and boasts one of the largest groups of turn-of-the-20th-century buildings on the East Coast. The area offers a pleasant atmosphere of shops and eateries near the Chesapeake Bay waterfront. Route 184 runs right into the historic district and ends at the beach.

**Cape Charles Beach** (Bay Avenue, www.capecharles.org) has a pleasant, uncrowded atmosphere and wonderful sunsets over the Chesapeake Bay. The beach is clean, family oriented, and free to the public. The water is generally shallow with little to no waves.

The **Cape Charles Museum and Welcome Center** (814 Randolph Ave., 757/331-1008, www.smallmuseum.org, mid-Apr.-Nov. Mon.-Fri. 10am-2pm, Sat. 10am-5pm, Sun. 1pm-5pm, free, donations appreciated) is a nice place to begin your visit to Cape Charles. It is housed in an old powerhouse and has a large generator embedded in the floor. Visitors can view boat models, pictures, and decoys as they learn about the history of Cape Charles.

**Kiptopeke State Park** (3540 Kiptopeke Dr., 757/331-2267, www.dcr.virginia.gov, daily 6am-10pm, $5) is approximately 10 miles south of the Historic District in Cape Charles. It encompasses a half-mile of sandy beach open to the public during the summer. There are no lifeguards on duty, so swimming is at your own risk. There are also hiking trails, a fishing pier, a boat ramp, and a full-service campground. The park is known for its robust bird population. Many bird studies are conducted here by the U.S. Fish and Wildlife Service. Some of the birds encountered in the park include hawks, kestrels, and ospreys.

## Sports and Recreation

**SouthEast Expeditions** (239 Mason Ave., 757/331-2680, www.southeastexpeditions. com, starting at $45) offers kayaking tours in Cape Charles. Trips of different lengths are available, and paddlers of all experience levels are welcome.

Golfers will enjoy the beautiful atmosphere and two challenging courses designed by Arnold Palmer and Jack Nicklaus at the **Bay Creek Golf Club** (1 Clubhouse Way, 757/331-8620, www.baycreekgolfclub.com, $70-115).

A big annual event in the Cape Charles area is the **Eastern Shore Birding & Wildlife Festival** (www.esbirdingfestival.com). The area is one of the most important East Coast migration stops for millions of birds each year, and festivalgoers can observe the spectacle firsthand in early October.

## Food
### AMERICAN
★ **The Oyster Farm Seafood Eatery** (500 Marina Village Circle, 757/331-8660, www. kingscreekmarina.com, Sun. 11:30am-8pm, Mon.-Thurs. 11:30am-9pm, Fri.-Sat. 11:30am-10pm, $12-38) is the top choice for food and ambience in Cape Charles. The modern beachfront building offers a trendy "water-to-table" eating experience in a comfortable waterfront dining room. The food is delicious, with creative seafood items, entrees from the land, burgers, and tacos. The scene is semi-upscale with a lively clientele. This is a great place to bring the family or relax with friends for an unrushed and tasty meal. There is a beautiful waterfront patio and lawn games for entertainment.

The Bay Creek Resort's **Coach House**

**Tavern** (1 Clubhouse Way, 757/331-8631, www.baycreekresort.com, Sun.-Thurs. 7am-8pm, Fri.-Sat. 7am-9pm, winter hours Sun. 7:30am-8pm, Mon. 8am-8pm, Tues.-Thurs. 8am-5pm, Fri. 8am-9pm, Sat. 7:30am-9pm, $8-15) is at the golf clubhouse and overlooks the golf course. The rustic ambience of the beautifully appointed building is due in part to the use of reclaimed wood and bricks from a farmhouse that once stood on the property. The restaurant offers traditional pub fare with exquisite soups and sandwiches. There is patio seating, and the atmosphere is upscale and inviting.

For a quick and casual breakfast, burger, or seafood meal, stop in **Sting Ray's Restaurant** (26507 Lankford Hwy., 757/331-1541, www.cape-center.com, weekdays 6:30am-8pm, weekends 6:30am-8:30pm, $5-18). This restaurant shares a roof with a gas station and offers a full breakfast menu featuring homemade biscuits and omelets. The lunch menu includes hot dogs, burgers, and barbecue while the dinner menu offers a large variety of local seafood. Order at the counter, and the server will bring the food to your table.

## Accommodations
### $100-200
The **Fig Street Inn** (711 Tazewell Ave., 757/331-3133, www.figstreetinn.com, $160-200) is a year-round boutique bed-and-breakfast offering four comfortable guest rooms with private bathrooms. Each room has memory foam mattresses, lush towels, flat-screen televisions, wireless Internet, and a jetted tub or gas fireplace. The house has been renovated and is decorated with antiques. The beach and shops are within walking distance.

The **King's Creek Inn** (3018 Bowden Landing, 757/678-6355, www.kingscreekinn. com, $150-210) is a beautiful historic plantation home that has offered guest accommodations since 1746. The home has been fully renovated and has four guest rooms with private bathrooms. The inn sits on 2.5 acres and overlooks Kings Creek (with access to the

Chesapeake Bay). A private dock is available for guest use. The cozy salon offers a great ambience for breakfast, or guests can enjoy meals on their balconies. The home has a long and exciting history and some interesting legends that include stories of the Underground Railroad and a possible resident ghost.

## OVER $300
★ **Bay Creek Resort** (3335 Stone Rd., 757/331-8742, www.baycreek.net, $400-900) is the premier resort community in Cape Charles. The resort offers rentals of vacation homes, villas, and condos in a well-landscaped waterfront and golf community on more than 1,700 acres. Golf packages are available, and golf condos offer three-bedroom, two-bath units with garages and a balcony or patio. Single-family homes are also available overlooking the golf course. Those who prefer a water view will enjoy the Marina District. Rental options include single-family villas with views of the Chesapeake Bay or the Kings Creek Marina. One- and two-bedroom suites are also available. Nightly and longer-term stays can be accommodated. Visitors can stay in luxurious accommodations or dock their own boat in the large, modern marina. Two delicious restaurants are on the property, one at the marina and the other on the golf course. The staff is extremely helpful and friendly.

## Camping
Camping is available at **Kiptopeke State Park** (3540 Kiptopeke Dr., 757/331-2267, www.dcr.virginia.gov). The park has tent sites ($24), rental RVs ($120), a yurt ($120), and a six-bedroom lodge ($434). There is a two-night minimum stay required at the lodge during the peak summer season and a seven-night minimum at the yurt and rental RVs. There are sites for those driving their own RVs as well. All facilities except the yurt allow pets ($10 fee nightly). There is at $5 reservation fee.

## Information
For additional details on Cape Charles,

contact the **Northampton County Chamber of Commerce** (757/678-0010, www.northamptoncountychamber.com).

# ONANCOCK
Thirty-eight miles north of Cape Charles is the picturesque town of Onancock. The town sits on the shore of Onancock Creek and has a deepwater harbor. Cute 19th-century homes with gingerbread trim line the streets, and visitors can shop, visit art galleries, partake in water sports, or just relax and enjoy the tranquil atmosphere. The town was founded in 1680 by English explorers, but its name is derived from the Native American word *auwannaku,* which means "foggy place."

Onancock was one of the colonies' 12 original "Royal Ports." Its deepwater access to the Chesapeake Bay made it appealing for ships, and its port provided safety during storms. For more than 250 years, Onancock was the trade center on the Eastern Shore and was closely connected (in terms of commerce) to Norfolk and Baltimore.

The homes along Market Street belonged to sea captains who worked on the Chesapeake Bay. These homes harken back to a time during the steamboat era when Onancock was a stop on the way to bustling Baltimore.

Today, Onancock retains a small working harbor and offers a pretty port of call for recreational boaters. It has modern boats in its harbor, and outdoor enthusiasts paddle colorful kayaks around its waters. Its wharf is also the jumping-off point for a small ferry that goes to and from Tangier Island. The town is a pleasant place to spend a day or two, and about 1,500 people make it their permanent home. There are free parking areas located around town and by the wharf.

## Sights
The key sight in Onancock is **Ker Place** (69 Market St., 757/787-8012, www.shorehistory.org, Mar.-Dec. Tues.-Sat. 11am-3pm, admission by donation), one of the finest federal-style manors on the Eastern Shore. John Shepherd Ker was the owner

and a renaissance man of his time. He was a successful merchant, lawyer, banker, and farmer. His estate was built in 1799 and originally comprised 1,500 acres. The home is now restored to its original appearance and features period furniture, detailed plasterwork, and rich colors throughout. The headquarters for the **Eastern Shore of Virginia Historical Society** are in the house, and the second floor contains a museum, the society's library, and archives space. A smaller, newer section of the house serves as a welcome center with a museum shop. Visitors can view Eastern Shore artwork throughout the home and rotating exhibits are displayed regularly. Guided tours are given on the hour; reservations should be made by calling ahead.

## Sports and Recreation

A public boat ramp at the wharf has a launch for canoes and kayaks ($5 launch fee). **SouthEast Expeditions** (2 King St., 757/354-4386, www.southeastexpeditions. com) offers kayak rentals ($20-55) and tours ($45-125) from the wharf. Guided kayak trips are also offered by two local travel writers and kayak guides through **Burnham Guides** (www.burnhamink.com). Visitors arriving by boat can dock at the Town Marina but should call the **harbormaster** (757/787-7911) for reservations.

Free self-guided walking tours are a fun way to learn about the town. Pick up a tour brochure at the visitors center (located on the wharf) and learn about Onancock's historic homes and gardens.

## Food

**Mallards Restaurant** (2 Market St., 757/787-8558, www.mallardsllc.com, Sun.-Thurs. 11:30am-9pm, Fri.-Sat 11:30am-10pm, $8-25) is on the wharf. The menu includes fresh seafood, ribs, duck, pasta, and many more delicious entrées. Don't be surprised if chef Johnny Mo comes out of the kitchen with his guitar to play a few tunes. He's a local legend.

The **Blarney Stone Pub** (10 North St.,

the Yellow Duck Bakery

757/302-0300, www.blarneystonepubonancock.com, Tues.-Thurs. 11am-9pm, Fri.-Sat. 11am-10pm, Sun. 11am-7pm, closed Mon.$8-24) is an Irish pub three blocks from the wharf serving traditional pub fare. It has indoor and outdoor seating and frequent live entertainment.

If you're making the drive between Onancock and Cape Charles and need a sugary snack, drive through Exmore on Business Route 13 and stop at the **Yellow Duck Bakery** (3312 Main St., Exmore, 757/442-5909, www.yellowduckcafe.com, Mon.-Wed. 7am-3pm, Thurs.-Fri. 7am-5pm, Sat. 8am-3pm, under $10). They offer amazing sweet potato biscuits, shortbread "Yellow Duck" cookies, other types of cookies, and delicious muffins. You can drive through town and pick up Route 13 again on the other side.

## Accommodations

★ **The Charlotte Hotel and Restaurant** (7 North St., 757/787-7400, www.

The Charlotte Hotel and Restaurant

Eastern Shore in Virginia. A delicious full breakfast is served daily.

**The Inn & Garden Café** (145 Market St., 757/787-8850, www.theinnandgardencafe. com, $110-130) has four guest rooms and was built in 1880. The on-site restaurant serves American food and guests can choose to eat in the cozy dining room (with a fireplace) or in an all-season gazebo with broad garden views.

## Information and Services

Additional information on Onancock can be found at www.onancock.org. There is also a small, seasonal visitors center at the wharf.

## ★ TANGIER ISLAND

Tangier Island is a small 3.5-mile-long island, 12 miles off the coast of Virginia in the middle of the Chesapeake Bay. It was first named as part of a group of small islands called the Russell Isles in 1608 by Captain John Smith when he sailed upon it during an exploration of the Chesapeake Bay. At the time the island was the fishing and hunting area of the Pocomoke Indians, but it was allegedly purchased from them in 1666 for the sum of two overcoats. Settlers were drawn to the island for the abundant oysters and crabs.

The unofficial history of the island states that John Crockett first settled here with his eight sons in 1686. This appears to be accurate since most of the 600 people who live on Tangier Island today are descendants of the Crockett family and the majority of the tombstones on the island bear the Crockett name. The island was occupied by British troops during the Revolutionary War, and it has also survived four major epidemics, with the most devastating being the Asian cholera epidemic of 1866. So many people died in such a short period of time that family members buried their dead in their front yards. Cement crypts can still be seen in many yards on the island.

There is a tiny airstrip, used primarily for the transport of supplies, but most visitors come by ferry (without their cars). There are

thecharlottehotel.com, $130-180) is a boutique hotel with eight guest rooms. The owners take great pride in this lovely hotel and even made some of the furnishings by hand. There is an award-winning restaurant on-site that can seat more than 30 people, and the American cuisine served is made from products supplied by local watermen and farmers.

**The Inn at Onancock** (30 North St., 757/787-7711, www.innatonancock.com, $185-205) is a luxurious bed-and-breakfast with five guest rooms, each offering stylish modern bathrooms and feather top beds. Full-service breakfasts are served in their dining room, or guests can choose to eat on the porch in nice weather. A wine hour is also hosted every evening. Soda and water are available to guests all day.

The **Colonial Manor Inn** (84 Market St., 757/787-2564, www.colonialmanorinn.com, $109-139) offers six spacious rooms decorated with period furnishings. The home was built in 1882 and is the oldest operating inn on the no true roads on the island and golf carts and bicycles are used to get around.

Tangier Island is only five feet above sea level, and it is known as the "soft-shell crab capital" for its delectable local crabs. It is also known for the unique dialect the people on Tangier Island speak. They converse in an old form of English and have many euphemisms that are unfamiliar to visitors. It is thought that the island's isolation played a role in preserving the language that was spoken throughout the Tidewater area generations ago.

Tangier Island can be toured in a couple of hours. The ferry schedules are such that they allow enough time to cover the sights on the island, grab lunch, and head back the same day. If you enjoy the slow pace of the island, limited overnight accommodations are available, but be aware there is not much, if any, nightlife and the island is "dry." Addresses aren't frequently used when describing how to get to a place on Tangier Island. Basically, you can see the whole island from any given point. The ferry dock drops visitors off in the heart of the small commercial area, and if you can't see the establishment you are looking for immediately, take a short walk or ride down the main path and you'll find it. The island residents are also very friendly, so if in doubt, just ask someone walking by.

There are very limited services on Tangier Island. The island hasn't changed much in the last century, and it looks much as it did 30 or 40 years ago. There is a post office and one school that all local children attend (most go on to college elsewhere in the state). There is spotty cell service on the island, but some establishments do offer wireless Internet. More important, there are no emergency medical facilities on the island; however, there is a 24-hour clinic, **The Tangier Island Health Foundation** (www.tangierclinic. org), where a physician's assistant is available.

Many establishments do not accept credit cards, so it's best to bring cash and checks. There are no banks or ATMs on the island.

## Sights

### TANGIER HISTORY MUSEUM AND INTERPRETIVE CENTER

The **Tangier History Museum and Interpretive Center** (16215 Main Ridge, 757/891-2374, www.tangierisland-va.com/water_trail_brochure, mid-May-mid-Oct. daily 10am-5pm, other times by appointment, $3) is a small museum down the street from the ferry dock. It is worth a visit and the small fee to learn about life on Tangier Island and its interesting heritage. View island artifacts and a rare five-layered painting of the island that illustrates the erosion it has experienced since 1866. Visitors can also learn about the many sayings that are common on the island but completely foreign to those on the mainland, such as "He's adrift," which means, "He's a hunk," and the term "snapjack" which means "firecracker." A handful of kayaks are available behind the museum for visitors to borrow (for free) for exploring the surrounding waterways.

### TANGIER BEACH

At the south end of Tangier Island is the nice, sandy public **Tangier Beach.** Rent a golf cart from **Four Brothers** and head out of the village on the winding paved path and over the canal bridge. The beach is at the very end of the path on the left side of the island. There's a small parking area for carts and a sandy path to the beach. There is no lifeguard on duty so swimming is at your own risk. Bring plenty of water with you since there are also no services at the beach. Water machines and soda machines can be found along the golf cart paths on the island if you need to pick up beverages on your way. There is also a very small grocery store near the ferry dock with a few bare essentials, but it's best to bring provisions with you.

## Shopping

There are two small gift shops on Tangier Island: **Wanda's Gifts** (757/891-2230) and **Sandy's Gifts** (757/891-2367). Both are on the main path not far from the ferry dock. They sell souvenir T-shirts and trinkets.

## Sports and Recreation

Kayaking the waterways of Tangier Island is a wonderful way to explore the marshes. Kayaks can be borrowed from the Tangier History Museum, and a listing of water trail routes can be found at www.tangierisland-va.com. The marshes also offer a terrific opportunity for bird-watching. Black skimmers, great blue herons, common terns, double-crested cormorants, Forster's terns, clapper rails, and ospreys are just some of the birds living on the island.

Since there are no roads on Tangier—only paved paths—the place is very conducive to casual biking. Bikes can be brought over on the ferry on weekdays only (call ahead to schedule) and a fleet of older-model cruising bikes can be rented from **Four Brothers** (www.fourbrotherscrabhouse.com) on the island. Since the island is only 3.5 miles long, it is easy to cover the entire length by bicycle in a short time.

For a unique local experience, take a **Crab Shanty Tour** (757/891-2269, ask for Ookire). This 30- to 45-minute tour is led by a Chesapeake Bay waterman. Other island tours are available outside the ferry dock. Tour guides wait in golf carts for guests when the ferries arrive and offer guided tours in their vehicles.

## Food

Visitors arriving by ferry will likely see the **Waterfront** (757/891-2248, mid-May-Nov. 1 Mon.-Sat. 10am-4pm, Sun. 1pm-4pm, under $15) as they depart the ferry. This small, seasonal restaurant is right by the dock and offers a variety of casual food including burgers, fried seafood baskets, and crab cakes.

**Four Brothers Crab House & Ice Cream Deck** (757/891-2999, www. fourbrotherscrabhouse.com, lunch and dinner daily) will likely be the next establishment you see when you take the short path from the dock to the main path in the small commercial area. While this is the place to rent golf carts, crabbing equipment, and bicycles, they also serve a casual menu of seafood and sandwiches on their deck, along with 60 soft-serve ice-cream flavors. Four Brothers also offers free wireless Internet; however, they do not accept credit cards. Another fun place for ice cream is **Spanky's Place** just down the path.

A short walk from the ferry terminal is **Lorraine's Restaurant** (757/891-2225, lunch Mon.-Sat. 10am-2pm, dinner Mon.-Fri. 5pm-10pm, Sat. 5pm-11pm, Sun. noon-5pm, under $15). Take a right on Main Street, and the restaurant is on the right. They serve snacks, lunch, and dinner. Like all the restaurants on the island, local, fresh seafood is the specialty, and this place is known for its soft-shell crabs. Lorraine's also delivers to any of the inns on the island.

Across from Lorraine's, **Fisherman's Corner Restaurant** (757/891-2900, www. fishermanscornerrestaurant.com, daily 11am-7pm, $15-26) has a wide menu with steaks and seafood. Sandwiches and a kid's menu are also available. It's no surprise that fresh crab is a highlight, and their crab cakes contain large, succulent blue crab meat with little filler.

The best-known and oldest restaurant on the island is ★ **Hilda Crockett's Chesapeake House** (757/891-2331, breakfast daily 7am-9am, lunch/dinner daily 11:30am-5pm, breakfast $10, lunch/dinner $22). They offer an all-you-can-eat breakfast with selections such as scrambled eggs, fried bread, and potatoes. They are most famous, however, for the family-style lunch and dinner. For $22, guests can enjoy unlimited homemade crab cakes, clam fritters, ham, potato salad, coleslaw, pickled beets, applesauce, green beans, corn pudding, and rolls. The family-style setting means you may share a table with other guests.

## Accommodations

It is difficult to find more friendly innkeepers than those at the **Bay View Inn** (757/891-2396, www.tangierisland.net, $125-150). This family-run bed-and-breakfast offers seven motel-style rooms, two cottages, and two guest rooms in the main house. A scrumptious homemade breakfast is included with your stay. The inn is on the west side of the island and has lovely views of the Chesapeake Bay and decks to watch the sunset from. The inn is open year-round. They do not take credit cards.

**Hilda Crockett's Chesapeake House** (757/891-2331, www.tangierisland-va.com, $100-155) is the oldest operating bed-and-breakfast on the island and was established in 1939 as a boardinghouse. It is in the small commercial area not far from the ferry dock. There are eight guest rooms in two separate buildings.

Those arriving by private boat can rent a slip at the **James Parks Marina** (16070 Parks Marina Ln., 757/891-2581). They offer 25 slips and showers, but no pump-outs. Docking fees start at $25.

## Information and Services

For additional information, visit www.tangier-island.com.

## Getting There

Getting to Tangier Island is half the fun.

There are three seasonal ferries that travel to and from the island May-October. The first is the **Chesapeake Breeze** (804/453-2628, www.tangiercruise.com, $27 round-trip for same-day service, $40 for overnight), a 150-person passenger boat that leaves at 10am daily from Reedville for the 1.5-hour trip. The ship heads back to Reedville at 2:15pm. The second is the **Steven Thomas** (410/968-2338, www.tangierislandcruises.com, $27 round-trip for same-day service, $35 for overnight), a 90-foot, 300-passenger boat that leaves from Crisfield, Maryland, daily (May 15-Oct. 15) at 12:30pm and arrives on Tangier at 1:45pm. The return voyage departs Tangier at 4pm. The third ferry is the **Joyce Marie II** (757/891-2505, www.tangierferry.com, Tues.-Sun., $25 round-trip for same-day service, $30 for overnight), a small fiberglass lobster boat that holds 25 people and runs from Onancock, Virginia, to Tangier Island. The trip takes 65 minutes. Ferry service is offered twice a day with departures from Tangier Island at 7:30am and 3:30pm and departures from Onancock at 10am and 5pm.

## Getting Around

There are no cars on Tangier Island. The best way to get around is by renting a golf cart from

Hop on a ferry to Tangier Island at the Reedville ferry terminal.

**Four Brothers Crab House & Ice Cream Deck** ($50 for 24 hours, $25 for a half day) or a bicycle ($10 a day). The owners will make you feel welcome immediately, and Tommy is sure to put you in a good mood for your ride around town.

# CHINCOTEAGUE ISLAND

Chincoteague Island is 7 miles long and just 1.5 miles wide. It is nestled between the Eastern Shore and Assateague Island. Chincoteague is famous for its herd of wild ponies, and many children and adults first became familiar with the island through the popular book *Misty of Chincoteague*, which was published in 1947. Many local residents made appearances in the movie that followed.

The island is in the far northeastern region of the Eastern Shore in Virginia and has a full-time population of 4,300 residents. It attracts more than one million visitors each year to enjoy the pretty town and to visit the Chincoteague National Wildlife Refuge and the beautiful beach on nearby Assateague Island.

Chincoteague is a working fishing village with world-famous oyster beds and clam shoals. It is also a popular destination for bird-watching. During the summer, the town is bustling with tourists, but in the off-season things slow down considerably and many establishments close.

The town of Chincoteague is accessed via Route 175. A scenic causeway spans the water and marsh and ends on Main Street, which runs along the western shore of the island. Maddox Boulevard meets Main Street and runs east to the visitors center and Chincoteague National Wildlife Refuge.

## Sights
### ★ CHINCOTEAGUE NATIONAL WILDLIFE REFUGE

The **Chincoteague National Wildlife Refuge** (8231 Beach Rd., 757/336-6122, www.fws.gov, May-Sept. daily 5am-10pm, Mar.-Apr. and Oct. daily 6am-8pm, Nov.-Feb. daily 6am-6pm, $8) is a 14,000-acre refuge consisting of beach, dunes, marsh, and maritime forest on the Virginia end of Assateague Island and was established in 1943. The area is a thriving habitat for many species of waterfowl, shorebirds, songbirds, and wading birds. The popular herd of wild ponies that Chincoteague is known for also lives in the refuge.

Assateague Island itself extends south from Ocean City, Maryland, to just south

the beach at Chincoteague National Wildlife Refuge

of Chincoteague Island. It is a thin strip of beautiful sand beach, approximately 37 miles long. The entire beach is a National Seashore, and the Virginia side is where the Chincoteague National Wildlife Refuge is located. The refuge entrance is at the end of Maddox Boulevard. A visitors center is situated near the beach, and is where information and trail brochures can be obtained. One of the main attractions is the **Assateague Island Lighthouse,** which visitors can hike to. The lighthouse is painted with red and white stripes and is 142 feet tall. It was completed in 1867 and is still operational. There are also 15 miles of woodland trails for hiking and biking (the wild ponies can often be seen from the trails).

The road ends at the Atlantic Ocean where there's a large parking area for beachgoers. Parts of the beach are open to swimming, surfing, clamming, and crabbing.

To get to the refuge, travel east on Route 175 onto Chincoteague Island and continue straight at the traffic light onto Maddox Boulevard. Follow the signs to the refuge.

## OYSTER AND MARITIME MUSEUM

The only oyster museum in the country is in Chincoteague. The **Oyster and Maritime Museum** (7125 Maddox Blvd., 757/336-6117, Tues.-Sun. 11am-5pm, $3) is on Maddox Boulevard just prior to the entrance to the National Wildlife Refuge. The museum is dedicated to sharing the history of the island and details of the oyster trade and the local seafood industry. One of the most noteworthy exhibits in the museum is the Fresnel lens that was part of the Assateague Island Lighthouse. This lens helped guide ships as far out to sea as 23 miles for nearly 96 years.

## CHINCOTEAGUE PONY CENTRE

For those wishing to see the local ponies up-close, the **Chincoteague Pony Centre** (6417 Carriage Dr., 757/336-2776, www.chincoteague.com/ponycentre, Mon.-Sat. during summer) has a herd of ponies from the island in their stable and a field facility

a foal at the Chincoteague Pony Centre

for visitors to enjoy. The center offers pony rides, riding lessons, shows, day camps, and a large gift shop.

## Entertainment and Events

The premier event on Chincoteague Island is the annual **Wild Pony Swim** (www.chincoteaguechamber.com) that takes place each year in late July. At "slack tide," usually in the morning, the herd of wild ponies is made to swim across the Assateague Channel on the east side of Chincoteague Island (those ponies that are not strong enough or are too small to make the swim are ferried across on barges). The first foal to complete the swim is named "King" or "Queen" Neptune and is given away in a raffle later that day. After the swim, the ponies are given a short rest and are then paraded to the carnival grounds on Main Street. The annual Pony Penning and Auction is then held, in which some foals and yearlings are auctioned off. Benefits from the auction go to support the local fire and ambulance services. The remaining herd then swims back across the channel.

Another big event in town is the **Chincoteague Island Oyster Festival** (8128 Beebe Rd., www.chincoteagueoysterfestival.com, $45). This well-known event has been happening for more than 40 years and offers all you can eat oysters prepared every which way imaginable. It is held in early October, and tickets are available online.

## Sports and Recreation

Kayaks can be launched on the beach on Assateague Island, but not in areas patrolled by lifeguards. Kayak tours are available through **Assateague Explorer** (757/336-5956, www.assateagueexplorer. com, $49-$59). **Snug Harbor Resort** (7536 East Side Rd., 757/336-6176, www. chincoteagueaccommodations.com) also offers tours ($49) and rents kayaks (single kayak half day $38, full day $48, tandem kayak half day $48, full day $58).

**Jus' Bikes** (6527 Maddox Blvd., 757/336-6700, www.jus-bikes.com) rents bicycles ($4 per hour or $12 per day), scooters ($15 per hour or $45 per day), surreys ($20 per hour or $75 per day), tandems ($5 per hour or $25 per day), three-wheelers ($3 per hour or $18 per day), and low-speed vehicles ($45-$199).

Fishing enthusiasts can have all their needs met at several fishing and tackle establishments including **Capt Bob's Marina** (2477 Main St., 757/336-6654, www. captbobsmarina.net) and **Capt Steves Bait & Tackle** (6527 Maddox Blvd., 757/336-0569, www.stevesbaitandtackle.com).

For an interactive cruise, contact **Captain Barry's Back Bay Cruises** (6262 Main St., 757/336-6508, www.captainbarry.net). They offer hands-on, interactive "Sea Life Expeditions" ($40) and "Champagne Sunset Cruises" ($40) leaving from the Chincoteague Inn Restaurant at 6262 Main Street.

## Food
### AMERICAN
If you like a casual beach environment, eating outside, and lounging in hammocks, then **Woody's Beach Barbeque and Eatery**

(6700 Maddox Blvd, Mon.-Sat. 11am-8pm, Sun. 1pm-8pm, $6-20) is worth checking out. They offer delightful barbecue and crab sandwiches, yummy sweet potato fries, and peach tea. The restaurant is dog friendly and there are outdoor games for the kids.

For a quick bite to go, stop at the ★ **Sea Star Café** (6429 Maddox Blvd., 757/336-5442, http://www.seastarcafeci.com, Thurs.-Mon. 11am-6pm, daily July and Aug., $5-10). They have yummy sandwiches and wraps to go (order at the window; be sure to know what you're ordering before going up when there's a crowd). Everything is fresh and made to order, and they have a large vegetarian menu. The café sits back off the road a little and offers a few picnic tables but no restrooms. The menu is handwritten on a chalkboard and items contain whatever is fresh that day.

### SEAFOOD
Seafood is the mainstay on Chincoteague Island, and the local oysters and crabs are especially delicious. Many restaurants are only open seasonally; so visiting in the off-season can pose a bit of a challenge in finding open eateries.

**AJ's on the Creek** (6585 Maddox Blvd., 757/336-5888, www.ajsonthecreek.com, Mar.-Dec. Mon.-Thurs. 11:30am-8:30pm, Fri.-Sat. 11:30am-9:30pm, $14-30) is the longest-operating restaurant on the island under one management. They are one of a few upscale restaurants on the island, and they serve delicious seafood menu items such as crab imperial, shellfish bouillabaisse, crab cakes, and grilled scallops. The restaurant is owned by two spunky sisters originally from Pittsburgh.

Don't let the plain exterior of **Bill's Seafood Restaurant** (4040 Main St., 757/336-5831, www.billsseafoodrestaurant. com, daily from 6am for breakfast, lunch, and dinner, $12-27) fool you. They offer delightful seafood entrées such as lobster tail, scallops, oysters, and crab cakes, as well as pasta selections. This is one of the few restaurants in town that is open all year.

## TREATS

The **Island Creamery** (6243 Maddox Blvd., 757/336-6236, www.islandcreamery.net, year-round Sun.-Thurs. 11am-9pm, Fri.-Sat. 11am-10pm) is "the" place to go for ice cream. The place is large for an ice-cream joint and offers friendly smiles, samples, and dozens of flavors. It's a popular stop, so the line can be long and parking difficult, but it's worth it.

## Accommodations

### $100-200

If you're looking for a charming bed-and-breakfast, spend a night at ★ **Miss Molly's Inn** (4141 Main St., 757/336-6686, www.missmollys-inn.com, $110-200) on Main Street. This beautiful Victorian B&B offers seven delightful guest rooms and five porches with rocking chairs. The home overlooks the bay and has a pretty English garden. Marguerite Henry stayed at the bed-and-breakfast when she wrote the famous book *Misty of Chincoteague,* and the room she stayed in has since been named after her. A full breakfast is included. The sister inn to Miss Molly's is the **Island Manor House Bed and Breakfast** (4160 Main St., 757/336-5436, www.islandmanor.com, $165-210), which offers eight guest rooms and plenty of common areas. This house was built in the popular Maryland-T style, which borrows from both federal and Georgian architecture. Refreshments are available 24 hours a day. They provide a gourmet breakfast each day and easy are within access to Main Street attractions.

The **Dove Winds** (7023 Maddox Blvd., 757/336-5667, www.dovewinds.com, $89-160) is a nice, clean hotel offering mini townhouses for rent with two-bedroom guest accommodations. The units aren't fancy, but they are comfortable and offer more privacy than a typical hotel. Each includes a kitchen, living room, and two bathrooms. The Dove Winds also offers two- and three-bedroom cottages. An indoor pool and hot tub are on-site.

### $200-300

The ★ **Hampton Inn & Suites Chincoteague Waterfront** (4179 Main St., 757/336-1616, www.hamptoninnchincoteague.com, $239-312) is known as one of the premier Hampton Inns in the country. Its bayfront location offers beautiful views, and it is close to many shops and restaurants in town. The rooms are well appointed with light wood furniture, and everything is oriented toward

Island Creamery

the water. The landscaping is appealing, the breakfasts are better than standard chain fare, and there is a boat dock next to the hotel. Amenities include a large indoor heated pool, a fitness center, laundry facilities, a waterfront veranda, and wireless Internet. The staff and owner are also very friendly. Ask for a room on the third floor with a balcony looking over the water and don't be surprised if you spot dolphins swimming by.

## Camping

Camping is available on Chincoteague Island at several campgrounds. The **Maddox Family Campground** (6742 Maddox Blvd., 757/336-3111, www.chincoteague.com, $40-$50) has 550 campsites and 361 utility hookups March-November. **Tom's Cove Campground** (8128 Beebe Rd., 757/336-6498, www.tomscovepark. com, $33-53) has waterfront campsites near the pony swim, three fishing piers, and a pool. They are open March-November. **Pine Grove Campground** (5283 Deep Hole Rd., 757/336-5200, www.pinegrovecampground. com, $33-43) offers campsites on 37 acres April-November. There are six ponds on the property.

## Information and Services

For additional information on Chincoteague Island, visit www.chincoteaguechamber. com or stop by the **Chincoteague Island Visitor's Center** (6733 Maddox Blvd., 757/336-6161, Mon.-Sat. 9am-4:30pm).

## Getting There

Visitors should arrive on Chincoteague Island by car; the surrounding waters are shallow and difficult to navigate by boat. The closest airport is **Wicomico Regional Airport** (410/548-4827), which is 52 miles away in Salisbury, Maryland.

# Background

# The Landscape

## GEOGRAPHY

The Chesapeake Bay is within the Atlantic coastal plain (also called the Tidewater), the easternmost portion of Virginia and Maryland, bounded on the west by Washington DC and Richmond. It includes salt marshes, coastal areas, the Eastern Shore, and the Atlantic beaches.

## CLIMATE

The climate of the Chesapeake Bay is considered subtropical, which is defined by hot, humid summers and mild, cool winters. The abundance of water in this area, which includes the Atlantic Ocean, the Chesapeake Bay, and many large rivers and their tributaries, fuels the humidity. Spring and fall bring comfortable temperatures and beautiful seasonal changes.

## ENVIRONMENTAL ISSUES

The Chesapeake Bay faces many problems including nutrient and sediment pollution from agriculture, storm water runoff, wastewater treatment plants, and air pollution; contamination from chemicals; overharvesting; invasive species; and the effects of development on its shores and tributaries. All of these threats impact the health of the bay and its ability to maintain a viable aquatic ecosystem.

Excess nutrients are the primary pollutant in the Chesapeake Bay. They increase algae bloom growth, which blocks vital sunlight to aquatic grasses. These grasses are crucial to the bay's ecosystem since they provide food and habitat to aquatic animals, reduce erosion, and produce oxygen. In addition, when the algae die and decompose, it depletes the water of the oxygen that all aquatic animals need.

The issues facing the bay are not localized problems. The Chesapeake Bay's watershed covers 64,000 square miles through six states and DC. There are 17 million residents living in this area.

Mass media attention in recent years has led to a greater awareness of the issues facing the bay and its tributaries, but there is still a very long way to go before the problems are solved.

The **Chesapeake Bay Foundation** (www.cbf.org), headquartered in Annapolis, Maryland, is the largest conservation organization dedicated to the well-being of the Chesapeake Bay watershed. Its famous "Save the Bay" slogan defines the continued quest to protect and restore the bay's natural resources.

Another environmental issue that is common to both Virginia and Maryland is the need for healthy farming. Unsustainable farming practices have contributed to water and air pollution throughout both states and have also resulted in soil erosion, animal abuse, and poor human health. Organizations such as **Environment Virginia** (www.environmentvirginia.org) and **Environment Maryland** (www.environmentmaryland.org) are looking for ways to expand opportunities for sustainable farmers that grow food in ways that don't pollute the environment.

## PLANTS

The Chesapeake Bay's central location on the East Coast allows it to boast both southern and northern flora, including cypress swamps in the coastal regions.

---

**Previous:** midshipmen in formation at the US Naval Academy in Annapolis; a skipjack at the Chesapeake Bay Maritime Museum in St. Michaels.

## Trees

There are forested areas in the Chesapeake Bay. Common trees include the loblolly pine, which is the most important commercial timber tree in Virginia, the eastern red cedar, black willow, black walnut, bitternut hickory (swamp hickory), American beech, American elm, yellow poplar, sycamore, northern red oak, and white oak (which is the Maryland state tree).

Many ornamental trees are also native to the region such as holly, red maple, magnolia, and the flowering dogwood (which is both the state tree and the state flower of Virginia).

## Plants, Shrubs, and Flowers

Because of the mild climate, there are many flowering shrubs and ferns in the region. Nothing announces the arrival of spring like the bright yellow blooms of the forsythia. This sprawling bush is a favorite of homeowners since it provides pretty blooms in the spring and a good screen in the summer. Several varieties of azaleas are native to the region, and in May residential neighborhoods are painted in their vibrant red, pink, purple, and white blooms. Rhododendrons are also native to the region, as are the butterfly bush (sometimes referred to as summer lilac) and the stunning hydrangea.

Spring and summer yield thousands of wildflowers. Species include hepatica, violets, trillium, wild geraniums, mountain

a great blue heron at Chincoteague

laurel, columbine, and wild sunflowers. In the coastal areas, wildflowers grow among marsh grasses and over sand dunes.

Many native flowers grow quite well, such as the woodland sunflower, hibiscus, lupine, lobelia, and phlox. The coastal region has plant species that exclusively call the area home such as the New York aster and seaside goldenrod.

## Tree Trivia

- Black walnuts give off a toxic chemical that inhibits other tree species from growing near them.
- The popular weeping willow is related to the black willow, but is native to Asia.
- Early settlers extracted the oil found in bitternut hickory nuts and used it as fuel for their oil lamps.
- Vessels in white oak wood are plugged with a substance that makes the wood watertight. This is why whiskey and wine barrels are made from the wood.
- The northern red oak is one of the most popular timber trees in the Atlantic region.

# More Than Tasty Bivalves

Oyster lovers flock to the Chesapeake Bay region to feast on the famous eastern oyster. For more than 100 years, this delectable yet peculiar-looking creature flourished in the bay and was one of the most valuable commercial fishing commodities. However, in recent decades, overharvesting, disease, and pollution have severely reduced its numbers. This is more than just a bummer for oyster eaters; oysters are a vital piece of the Chesapeake Bay's ecosystem.

Oysters provide habitat for many aquatic animals. Their hard shells with many nooks and crannies act as much-needed reefs and are relied on by hundreds of underwater animals such as sponges, crabs, and fish. Oysters and their larvae are also an important food source for many aquatic residents and some shorebirds. In addition, oysters are filter feeders, which means they pump large amounts of water through their gills when they eat. This filters the water, removing chemical contaminants, nutrients, and sediments, which helps keep the water clean. One oyster can filter more than 50 gallons of water in a single day.

## ANIMALS

The coastal regions' wetlands, marshes, and rivers entice populations of lizards, muskrats, butterflies, and snakes. White-tailed deer, red foxes, raccoons, opossums, squirrels, chipmunks, beaver, and more recently, coyotes, can also be found in coastal areas, but less forest means fewer places to hide from predators and the harsh summer sunshine.

There is only one venomous snake found in the coastal regions, the northern copperhead, which has dark-colored cross bands shaped like an hourglass.

## Birds

The Chesapeake Bay is prime for bird-watching. More than 40 types of ducks, geese, and swans alone have been documented in water-rich areas. This area is also home to osprey, oystercatchers, plovers, peregrine falcons, black skimmers, great blue herons, and dozens of other shorebirds.

Many hawks live throughout the region and the red-tailed variety can frequently be spotted (although they will surely see you before you see them). Another impressive and often seen bird is the turkey vulture, also known as a buzzard. They are huge and can have a wingspan up to six feet. Wild turkeys are also prevalent and look like they walked out of a children's Thanksgiving story. Game birds such as the grouse are residents of the area and sometimes startle hikers by launching themselves in the air when they see someone approach.

# History

## IN THE BEGINNING

It is believed that the first humans arrived in the Virginia and Maryland region approximately 18,000 years ago. They were hunter-gatherers most likely organized into seminomadic bands. As time went on, hunting tools became more efficient, and delicacies from the Chesapeake Bay such as oysters became an important food source. With new developments came the first Native American villages and the formation of social structures. Successive Native American cultures continued for thousands of years prior to the arrival of Europeans.

## THE COLONIAL PERIOD

After many failed attempts at establishing a permanent settlement, in 1607 the first

English settlers arrived at the mouth of the Chesapeake Bay in three ships and traveled 30 miles up the James River under the guidance of Captain John Smith. The settlers disembarked and promptly began to build a settlement at what later became Jamestown.

They found the coastal area inhabited by Algonquian natives (called the Powhatan Confederacy) who controlled land stretching from what is now North Carolina to the Potomac River. These native settlements included approximately 10,000 people who relied on hunting, fishing, and farming for survival. Another native group controlled what is now Maryland and the mountain regions of both states stretching west into the Allegheny Mountains.

The settlers were met with rich lands, many game animals, and initially friendly natives. Even so, they were not prepared for the physical labor and inevitable problems that came with starting a new settlement, and the colony nearly failed in the first few years. Around 1612, a colonist named John Rolfe brought in the first tobacco seeds, which he had gathered from an earlier voyage to Trinidad. The first tobacco crops were planted and were soon in high demand back in England. This provided an instant boost to the New World's economy.

Put mildly, life was very difficult for the early settlers. Disease, famine, and attacks from Native Americans wiped out much of the early population. Although the Native Americans were initially friendly, it didn't take long for their feelings to change when they realized the settlers intended to stay permanently. In just a couple of years, most of the Native American settlements had been seized, and it became unsafe for the settlers to venture past their settlement fences. A temporary truce resulted in 1614 from the marriage of the 13-year-old daughter of Chief Powhatan, named Pocahontas (who had earlier saved Captain John Smith's life when her father tried to kill him), to John Rolfe. The truce ended quickly with a surprise Powhatan attack that killed 400 settlers.

Meanwhile, in 1609, an Englishman named Henry Hudson arrived in the Delaware Bay. Working on behalf of the Dutch West India Company, Hudson was pleased with the wonderful conditions he found in the region. As a result, in 1631, a group of Dutch West India traders established a small whaling port and tobacco-growing center in what is now Lewes, Delaware. At the same time, Maryland's first European settler, William Claiborne, came to that region and established a fur-trading post on Kent Island.

In 1632, Charles I of England granted approximately 12 million acres north of the Potomac River and Virginia to Cecilius Calvert, second Baron Baltimore. The area was substantially larger than today's Maryland, and Maryland later lost some of the land to Pennsylvania. The first full settlement was established in 1634 on St. Clement's Island.

Maryland was established as a refuge for religious freedom for Catholics, although many Protestants moved there also. This caused religious feuds for years in the colony. At the same time, its economy relied on tobacco fueled by African slave labor and indentured servants. Farming, tobacco, and the abundance of land slowly brought prosperity to the early colonies.

As land along the coast filled up, pioneers began to move farther inland toward the mountains. New immigrants continued to arrive, including people from places such as Germany and Scotland.

In 1649 a settlement called Providence was founded on the north shore of the Severn River and was later moved to a more protected harbor on the south shore. It was then called Town at Proctor's, which changed to Town at the Severn, and later Anne Arundel's Towne. The city became very wealthy as a slave trade center. In 1694, the town became the capital of the royal colony and was renamed Annapolis for the future queen of Great Britain, Princess Anne of Denmark and Norway. Annapolis was incorporated in 1708 and flourished until the Revolutionary War.

By the early 1700s, many colonists in

Colonial Williamsburg

money as possible out of the colonists through taxes while extending them far fewer rights than held by those living in the home country. One of the final straws came in 1763 with the passing of a law prohibiting westward expansion of the colonies, which angered many colonists. A passionate and heated speech delivered by Patrick Henry in Williamsburg in 1765 implied publicly that the colonies might be better off without King George III. Tension between England and the colonies continued to grow, and rebellious outbreaks such as the Boston Tea Party in 1773 began to grow more frequent. Maryland had its own tea party in Chestertown in 1774, when colonists burned the tea-carrying ship *Geddes* in the town's harbor.

In 1775 Henry delivered his famous speech at St. John's Church in Richmond where he was quoted as saying, "I know not what course others may take; but as for me, give me liberty or give me death."

Virginia were enjoying generous fortunes earned through growing tobacco. The Church of England was the official church in Virginia, which differentiated it from Maryland and the New England colonies. But the church became a secondary interest since there was a short supply of clergy and houses of worship. In 1705, Virginia's capital was moved from Jamestown to nearby Williamsburg.

Virginia and Maryland were regions of large plantations and minimal urban development. Since much of the plantation labor was supplied by indentured servants, few women came to the area. This, combined with a high rate of disease, made for the slow growth of the local population.

By 1700, most Native Americans had been driven out of Virginia and Maryland. At the same time, the number of African slaves had grown rapidly in the region as the number of indentured servants declined. Throughout the first half of the century, tensions between the colonies and their European motherland grew as England tried to squeeze as much

## THE REVOLUTIONARY WAR

Although no major Revolutionary War battles were fought in Maryland, it was the first colony to adopt a state constitution. Virginia became a primary center of war activity since it was the largest and most populated colony. Virginia experienced fighting from the earliest days of the war, although it managed to escape much of the destruction for the first three years. Virginia's capital was moved to a safer location at Richmond in 1780 after British ships sailed into the Hampton Roads area, and the capital has remained there ever since.

Major Virginia confrontations included the Battle of Great Bridge, where British authorities were removed from the colony, and the Yorktown Campaign. The Yorktown Campaign moved through Petersburg when British forces landed along the James River in 1781 in order to support Lord Cornwallis's army based in North Carolina. Twenty-five hundred British troops moved against Petersburg, and a clash with 1,200 militia occurred in what is now the neighborhood of Blanford.

The most well-known battle took place in Yorktown where 18,000 members of the Continental and French armies defeated British forces, causing their surrender in 1781. This battle was the final victory that secured America's independence.

# EXPANSION

In 1788, Virginia became the 10th state in the new nation. One year later, Virginia-born George Washington became the first U.S. president. Many of the country's founding fathers came from Virginia, including Thomas Jefferson, James Madison, and George Mason. At the time, the state was home to 20 percent of the country's population and more than 30 percent of its commerce. A new law that enabled owners to free their slaves was also passed, and by 1790, there were more than 12,000 free African Americans in Virginia.

The city of Baltimore incorporated in 1797 and experienced rapid growth as a shipbuilding and industrial center. By 1800, its population outnumbered that of Boston, and the development of Maryland's resources became a priority. Virginia fell behind in this aspect of development, and the port in Hampton Roads paled in comparison to that in Baltimore.

Baltimore was spared seizure during the War of 1812, but suffered a 25-hour attack at Fort McHenry (during which Francis Scott Key wrote "The Star-Spangled Banner"). British troops went on to burn the young capital city of Washington DC.

After the war, steam locomotives and clipper ships were developed, greatly expanding trade possibilities. A series of canals was built, including the Chesapeake & Ohio Canal along the Potomac River, and railroads such as the Baltimore & Ohio Railroad were constructed. This greatly increased access between East Coast ports and land west of the Appalachians. By the mid-1800s, railroad lines ran through both Virginia and Maryland, bringing wealth and prosperity to many agricultural-based businesses, although it was not until after the Civil War that railroads connected all primary population centers in Virginia.

# THE AMERICAN CIVIL WAR

Thomas Jefferson predicted a conflict regarding the issue of slavery. He felt that "God is just: that his justice cannot sleep forever" and a change in the current situation was very possible. Soon, calls for emancipation spread through the North, and scattered revolts against slavery gained momentum. In 1859, a raid on the federal arsenal in Harpers Ferry led by an American abolitionist named John Brown resulted in the death of 21 people—both free African Americans and whites—and the realization by the country that slavery opponents were willing to kill and die themselves for their cause.

In 1860, Abraham Lincoln was elected president and pledged to keep slavery out of the territories. In December that same year, South Carolina seceded from the Union and was followed shortly thereafter by Mississippi, Alabama, Georgia, Florida, Louisiana, and Texas.

Although technically still a slave state in 1860, Maryland was one of the border states that stayed with the Union during the Civil War, but Maryland soldiers fought on both sides. Virginia, however, joined its southern neighbors and seceded from the nation in 1861, after which it became a prominent Confederate state.

Four years of bloody fighting took place on soil passionately defended less than a century before in the Revolutionary War. More than 600,000 Americans lost their lives in the war, more than those lost in both World Wars combined. Virginia suffered more casualties and witnessed more major battles than any other state. In just four years, the state was left in ruins. Some of the major battles fought in Virginia include the First

Antietam National Battlefield

and Second Battles of Bull Run (Manassas), Battle of the Ironclads, Seven Days' Battles, Battle of Fredericksburg, and Battle of Chancellorsville. Maryland also hosted several well-known battles, including the famous Battle of Antietam, the Battle of South Mountain, and the Battle of the Monocacy.

Richmond was burned on April 3, 1865. Six days later, General Robert E. Lee asked General Ulysses S. Grant for a meeting. Terms of the surrender were drafted and signed at Appomattox Court House, and the Confederate army turned over arms in a formal ceremony on April 12.

## MODERN TIMES

The 1900s brought a diversification of industry to both Virginia and Maryland. Baltimore suffered a devastating fire in 1904, but recovered quickly. World War I gave a boost to Maryland by increasing the demand for

industrial products, while Virginia benefited from enormous expansion to the Newport News shipyard. The Great Depression slowed growth in some markets, but overall, both Virginia and Maryland fared well through that difficult time.

By the middle of the 20th century, Virginia had evolved from a rural state into an urban one. World War II had again given a boost to the Hampton Roads area in support of the Norfolk Naval Base and shipyard. In contrast, as American industry diminished, Maryland turned to agriculture and U.S. government-related research and services.

In the late 20th century, the Washington DC area experienced an economic and technological boom, resulting in an increase in population, housing, and jobs in both Virginia and Maryland. By the early 1990s, Virginia had a population of more than 6 million while Maryland had 4.7 million.

# Government and Economy

## VIRGINIA GOVERNMENT

Virginia is traditionally a conservative state. It is governed by the Constitution of Virginia, which was adopted in 1971 and is the seventh constitution. There are three branches of government in Virginia: the legislative, executive, and judicial branches. The executive branch has three elected officials: the governor, lieutenant governor, and attorney general, which are elected individually statewide to four-year terms.

Virginia's governor is the chief executive officer of the Commonwealth and the commander in chief of the state militia. Governors can serve multiple terms, but they must be nonconsecutive. The lieutenant governor is the president of the Senate of Virginia and first in the line of succession to the governor. A lieutenant governor can run for reelection. The attorney general is second in line of succession to the governor and the chief legal advisor to both the governor and the General Assembly. He or she is also the chief lawyer of the state and heads the Department of Law.

The legislative branch in Virginia is the General Assembly made up of 40 senators (serving four-year terms) and 100 delegates (serving two-year terms). The General Assembly claims to be the "oldest continuous law-making body in the New World" and traces its roots back to the House of Burgesses in Jamestown.

The Virginia judiciary is made up of the Supreme Court of Virginia and subordinate courts such as the Court of Appeals, the Circuit Courts, and the General District Courts. The judiciary is led by the chief justice of the Supreme Court, the Judicial Council, the Committee on District Courts, and Judicial Conferences.

Thomas Jefferson designed the State Capitol Building in Richmond, and Governor Patrick Henry laid the cornerstone in 1785.

## MARYLAND GOVERNMENT

Maryland is traditionally a liberal state. Like Virginia, Maryland has a state constitution and three branches of government. Maryland is unique in the sense that it allows each of its counties to have significant autonomy.

There are five principal executive branch officers in Maryland: the governor, lieutenant governor, attorney general, comptroller, and treasurer. With the exception of the treasurer, all are elected statewide, with the governor and lieutenant governor running on one ticket. The treasurer is elected by both houses of the General Assembly on a joint ballot.

The legislative branch is a General Assembly made up of two houses with 47 senators and 141 delegates. Members of both houses are elected to four-year terms. Each house establishes its own rules of conduct and elects its own officers.

Maryland's judiciary branch consists of four courts. Two are trial courts (the District Court and Circuit Courts), and two are Appellate Courts (the Court of Special Appeals and the Court of Appeals). The Court of Appeals is the highest court.

## VIRGINIA'S ECONOMY

Virginia is traditionally a wealthy state and typically has the most counties and independent cities in the top 100 wealthiest jurisdictions in the country. Perhaps the wealthiest southern state prior to the Civil War, Virginia recovered quickly from its Civil War scars and also weathered the Great Depression much better than the rest of the South. Much of the wealth is concentrated in the northern part of the state near Washington DC, where housing prices are sky-high. Loudoun and Fairfax Counties have two of the highest median household incomes out of all the counties in the nation. Virginia is one of 24 right-to-work states where union security agreements are prohibited.

Virginia's economy includes a balance of income from federal government-supported jobs, technology industries, military installations, and agriculture. The military plays a prominent role in the state's financial picture with facilities such as the Pentagon in Arlington, Marine Corps Base Quantico, and the privately owned Northrop Grumman shipyard in Newport News.

High-tech firms and government contractors have replaced dairy farms and now dominate Northern Virginia, which is home to seven Fortune 500 companies. Richmond has an additional nine, which puts it in the top six metro areas for bragging rights to the most Fortune 500 companies.

Although modern farming techniques have put many small farmers out of business and sent them to metropolitan areas in search of new careers, agriculture still plays a role in much of the state with crops such as tobacco, sweet potatoes, peanuts, tomatoes, apples, grains, hay, and soy. True to its roots, Virginia is still the fifth-largest tobacco producer in the country. Livestock is also a thriving commodity, and cattle fields can be seen along much of

I-81 in the western part of the state. Despite the natural resources of the Chesapeake Bay, Virginia makes only a small portion of its revenue from the fishing industry.

## MARYLAND'S ECONOMY

Maryland is a small but wealthy state whose economy has traditionally been heavily weighted toward manufacturing. Two Maryland counties, Howard and Montgomery, are consistently listed in the nation's top 10 richest counties.

In recent years, Maryland's economic activity has included a strong focus on the tertiary service sector, which is largely influenced by its proximity to Washington DC. Technical administration for the defense and aerospace industry and bioresearch laboratories is also key in its economy. In addition, many government agencies have satellite headquarters in Maryland for which they need staffing.

Transportation is another major revenue maker for Maryland, thanks to the Port of Baltimore. The port is the second-largest automobile port in the country, but also accommodates a large variety of other goods including bulk commodities such as petroleum, sugar,

Many cow pastures dot the Virginia landscape.

iron ore, and fertilizers. These goods are distributed on land in trucks and by rail, further adding to the transportation influence.

A third major contributor to the state's economy is educational and medical research. Several key institutions are located in the state, the largest being Johns Hopkins University. Johns Hopkins is currently the largest single employer in the Baltimore area.

Maryland is also known for its food production thanks mostly to commercial fishing in the Chesapeake Bay and offshore in the Atlantic Ocean. Prime catches include blue crab, striped bass, menhaden, and oysters. Dairy farming in the Piedmont region also contributes to the economy.

# People and Culture

## PEOPLE AND CULTURE IN VIRGINIA

Traditionally, the people in Virginia were hardworking farmers, political pioneers, and sailors. The early colonists came mostly from rural England but were soon joined by French, Irish, German, and Scots-Irish who immigrated from abroad. African Americans were a large part of early culture in Virginia; many initially arrived as indentured servants, followed by larger numbers through the African slave trade. Native American populations were devastated by European disease to the point that just a very small population survived to see modern times.

Today Virginia is largely diversified with 85 percent of its residents living in metropolitan areas. Race relations are generally better in Virginia than in most southern states, although this is not apparent in every area.

African Americans make up the largest minority in Virginia, totaling nearly 20 percent. The African American population is heavily concentrated in the eastern portion of the state with the largest populations being in Richmond and Norfolk. Second is the Hispanic population, which comprises approximately 8 percent of the population (located primarily in Northern Virginia), followed by an Asian population of approximately 6 percent (also primarily in Northern Virginia).

Many parts of southern and western Virginia embrace the culture of the southern United States. It is there you can find authentic southern cuisine and Virginia-specific food such as Virginia ham (country ham produced in Virginia), Virginia barbecue (pork with a vinegar-based sauce, similar to North Carolina barbecue), marble cake, shoofly pie, Brunswick stew, and peanut soup.

The first colonists who came to Virginia were motivated primarily by material wealth and not religious freedom. This is not to say that the colonists weren't religious; they just assumed religion and government went together and that the Anglican Church would be the designated church. There was some rivalry between Virginia and Catholic-established Maryland, although to attract settlers, the Anglicans of Virginia were flexible to newcomers. As such, they encouraged groups such as the Pennsylvania Dutch to move south into the Shenandoah Valley in part so they could alert eastern settlements of attacks by the French or Native Americans coming from bases in the Ohio River Valley. To this day, the German Mennonite heritage is still evident west of the Blue Ridge.

Thomas Jefferson and James Madison led first Virginia and then the nation to end government involvement in religion. This spread tolerance of religious freedom throughout the state and resulted in a permanent acceptance throughout the Commonwealth of various forms of religion and the option to follow no religion at all.

It's almost impossible to summarize the attitudes of Virginians across the board because the state is so diverse. But in the smaller towns and rural areas, everyone waves, people ask strangers for directions, and you might get slipped a free piece of apple pie at a local diner for no apparent reason. Many areas in Virginia still offer a secure sense of community, although in some cities crime is unfortunately an issue.

## PEOPLE AND CULTURE IN MARYLAND

Historically, Marylanders were fishers and farmers. The state is now primarily urban with dense populations, especially in Baltimore and near Washington DC.

Unlike Virginia, Maryland was founded as a place for Roman Catholics to escape religious persecution since the Catholic religion was repressed in England following the founding of the Anglican Church. The Catholic faith is still the most prevalent in Maryland, although it only makes up approximately 15 percent of the population.

During colonial times, groups of Quakers moved into Maryland from Pennsylvania, and in the mid-17th century a group of conservative Protestants called Puritans settled south of Baltimore. Although Puritans are not defined as such today, another conservative Protestant group, the Old Order Amish, is still strong in some areas of southern Maryland and the Eastern Shore. Their horse-drawn wagons can be seen on many roads throughout those areas.

Other religions quickly made their way into Maryland with the first Lutheran church being built around 1729 and the first Baptist church in 1742. Methodists came to the state as well, and a large Jewish population settled in Baltimore in the early part of the 1800s.

Today Maryland is widely accepting of religious diversity, and people from all faiths (and of no faith) can be found within its borders.

Maryland has always had a large African American population. During the time of slavery, Maryland had the largest population of free African Americans of the northeastern slave states. Today, African Americans make up 30 percent of Maryland's population.

Unfortunately, race relations have traditionally been strained in Maryland, and many neighborhoods are strictly delineated by race. Baltimore is the most diverse area of the state.

## THE ARTS

Virginia and Maryland offer numerous opportunities for residents and visitors to not only enjoy the arts but to become part of them. In fact, the arts are an important part of many people's lives in this region, whether they realize it or not. Access to top-rated performances, historic architecture, quality handicrafts, and literature is often taken for granted by the people who live here. A recent survey in Maryland, for instance, showed that 90 percent of the state's residents engaged in art in some form or another over the past year, whether by attending a musical performance, taking part in a festival, or visiting a museum or gallery. A stunning 84 percent said they create art in some form or another themselves. Another example is the **Virginians for the Arts** organization, which lists more than 4,500 state organizations and individual advocates for the arts in Virginia alone.

These states' long histories, diversified populations, proximity to the nation's capital, and relative tolerance for religious and social beliefs open the region to many traditional and forward-thinking expressions of art, which in turn, has created a thriving artistic community open to everyone who passes through the area.

# Essentials

# Transportation

Due in part to its proximity to large cities like Baltimore and Washington DC, the Chesapeake Bay is easily accessible from many parts of the United States and from other countries. There are also major airports near Richmond, Norfolk, and Newport News/Williamsburg in Virginia.

## AIR

The major airport in the area is the **Baltimore Washington International Thurgood Marshall Airport (BWI)** (410/859-7040, www.bwiairport.com), near Baltimore, Maryland. It is approximately 15 minutes to downtown Baltimore by car. BWI is serviced on weekdays by MARC commuter trains at the BWI Marshall Rail Station. Free shuttles are available from the station to the airport terminal. Shuttle stops can be found on the lower-level terminal road. Metrobus service is available between BWI and the Greenbelt Metrorail station (Green Line) on the **BWI Express Metro.** Bus service is available seven days a week with buses running every 40 minutes.

Washington DC, about an hour away by car from Baltimore and Annapolis, also has two major airports. The first is **Ronald Reagan Washington National Airport (DCA)** (703/417-8000, www.metwashairports.com), just outside Washington DC in Arlington, Virginia. Taxi service is available at the arrivals curb outside the baggage claim area of each terminal. Rental cars are available on the first floor in parking garage A. A shuttle to the rental car counter is available outside each baggage claim area. The second is **Washington Dulles International Airport (IAD)** (703/572-2700, www.metwashairports.com), 27 miles west of Washington DC in Dulles, Virginia. Most major airlines serve these airports.

The **Washington Dulles Taxi and Sedan** (703/554-3509, www.washingtondullestaxisedan.com) provides taxi and sedan service for passengers at all three airports. Shuttle service is also available from all three airports through **SuperShuttle** (800/258-3826, www.supershuttle.com).

The **BayRunner Shuttle** (www.bayrunnershuttle.com) provides daily, scheduled shuttle service between the Eastern Shore of Maryland and BWI. Areas serviced on the Eastern Shore include Kent Island, Cambridge, Easton, and Ocean City.

## CAR

The Chesapeake Bay is easiest to explore by car. A large network of interstate highways provides access throughout the entire area.

I-95 is the main north-south travel route along the East Coast and connects Baltimore, Washington DC, and Richmond. This highway is a toll road in Maryland.

U.S. 50 is the major route through the Eastern Shore in Maryland. It starts in Ocean City, runs west to Salisbury, then turns north to Cambridge, across the Bay Bridge (where there is a toll), past Annapolis, and continues west into Washington DC. It then continues into Virginia as a minor route.

Speed limits are posted throughout Virginia and Maryland. The maximum allowable speed limit in Virginia is 70 miles per hour, while in Maryland it is 65 miles per hour, although most roads in both states have speed limits posted much below their maximums. Keep in mind that state-maintained roads can have both a name and a route number.

In Virginia, all drivers are banned by law from text messaging, and drivers under the age of 18 are prohibited from using cell phones and text messaging. In Maryland, text messaging and handheld cell phone usage are banned for all drivers. Drivers under 18 are prohibited from all cell phone use. Seatbelt laws are enforced throughout both states.

Both states' departments of transportation are good resources for maps, toll rates, webcams, road conditions, and details on HOV restrictions. Visit www.virginiadot.org and www.mdot.maryland.gov.

## TRAIN

**Amtrak** (800/872-7245, www.amtrak.com) has locations in Baltimore, Williamsburg, Newport News, and Norfolk. Although a train ticket can rival the cost of airfare, it can also be more convenient and more comfortable to travel by train.

Amtrak also connects to the **Maryland Area Rail Commuter (MARC)** (410/539-5000, www.mta.maryland.gov) train in Maryland. MARC operates on weekdays only and provides service to Baltimore.

## BUS

**Greyhound** (800/231-2222, www.greyhound. com) has locations in Baltimore, Hampton, Newport News, Norfolk, Ocean City, and Virginia Beach. Tickets are less expensive when purchased in advance and often discounts are available to students, seniors, and military personnel.

Local bus service is available in many cities. A tourist-friendly bus system exists in Baltimore with the **Charm City Circulator** (www.charmcitycirculator.com, free). **DART First State and the Delaware Transit Corporation** (www.dartfirststate.com) offers public bus transportation between Ocean City and the Delaware beaches. A parking lot ($8) is north of Rehoboth Avenue on Shuttle Road. With the price of parking, you receive four free unlimited-ride daily bus passes. Stops are located throughout the resort areas. **Hampton Roads Transit** (www.gohrt. com) is a public transit service that serves the Hampton Roads area including Hampton. It currently offers transportation by bus, light-rail, ferry, and Handi-ride (a service for people with disabilities).

## WATER

If you're lucky enough to cruise into the Chesapeake Bay on a private boat, you'll have options for docking in marinas along the bay itself, the Intracoastal Waterway, and the Potomac River. Most towns on the water offer marina slips, but making plans ahead of time is advised, especially during the prime summer months and in popular areas such as Annapolis.

# Recreation

## BOATING AND SAILING

The Chesapeake Bay has 11,684 miles of shoreline, which is more than the West Coast of the United States. Every town on the bay has a marina and access can also be gained from public boat ramps in many locations. Many visitors even arrive from other regions by water. Take a look at the boats in Annapolis Harbor and where they're from; there's a good reason Annapolis is called the "Sailing Capital of the World." It's a sailor's dream.

Commercial and recreational powerboats must be registered in Virginia or Maryland if that is where they are primarily used.

## CANOEING AND KAYAKING

Dozens of outfitters and liveries rent canoes and many offer guided trips in the region. Kayaking has become extremely popular over the last decade and tours and instruction are now available on many eastern rivers, lakes, the Chesapeake Bay, and at the beaches.

White-water kayaking is a much more specialized sport enjoyed throughout the region on rivers such as the Potomac and James. A training center for racing is located on the Potomac River. Additional information can be obtained from the **Potomac Whitewater Racing Center** (www.potomacwhitewater. org).

# FISHING

Favorite spots include on the Chesapeake Bay (bluefish, flounder, and drum), off the shore of Virginia Beach (marlin, sea bass, and sailfish), Sandy Point State Park (striper, white perch, and rockfish), Point Lookout State Park (rockfish, bluefish, and hardhead), and Assateague Island (surf fishing for stripers).

Licenses are required in both Virginia and Maryland. Virginia fishing licenses can be purchased online from the **Virginia Department of Game and Inland Fisheries** (www.dgif.virginia.gov/fishing/regulations/licenses.asp). Both "freshwater" licenses (resident $23, nonresident $47) and "freshwater and saltwater" licenses (resident $40, nonresident $71) are available. Licenses are good for one year from the date of purchase.

Maryland fishing licenses can be purchased online from the **Department of Natural Resources** (www.dnr.state.md.us/service/license.asp) or by calling 855/855-3906. Nontidal licenses are $20.50 for residents and $30.50 for nonresidents. Chesapeake Bay and coastal sport-fishing licenses are $15 for residents and $22.50 for nonresidents. Licenses are valid from January 1 to December 31 of the same year.

# CRABBING AND CLAMMING

Getting dirty in the mud and risking losing a finger are free if you are doing so to crab or clam for personal use only. Public access to beaches and marsh areas is prevalent in the area, but keep in mind that limits and regulations apply. Current Virginia regulations can be found at http://mrc.virginia.gov/regulations/recfish&crabrules.shtm and those for Maryland at http://dnr.maryland.gov/service/fishing_license.asp.

# BIKING
## Road Cycling

Wide, flat roads with little traffic make the Eastern Shore a favorite place to bike almost any time of the year. The terrain is nearly pancake flat, although there is often a headwind. The famous **Seagull Century** (www.seagullcentury.org) is held each October on the Eastern Shore of Maryland. **Bike Virginia** (www.bikevirginia.org) is a six-day bike tour that goes through a different part of Virginia each year in June. Riders can choose from a variety of distances to pedal each day.

Not all roads are conducive to road cycling, given the extreme traffic conditions in many urban areas. Be wise about choosing a biking route; accidents do happen, and usually the bike is on the worse end of it.

# GOLF

There are many public golf courses in the bay. A listing of courses in Virginia can be found at www.virginiagolf.com, and a listing of Maryland courses can be found at www.golfmaryland.com.

# Travel Tips

## FOREIGN TRAVELERS

Visitors from other countries must present a valid passport and visa issued by a U.S. consular official unless they are a citizen of a country eligible for the Visa Waiver Program (such as Canada) in order to enter the United States. A foreign national entering the country by air that is a citizen of a country eligible for the Visa Waiver Program must present an approved Electronic System for Travel Authorization and a valid passport. A list of exceptions can be found on the Department of Homeland Security website at www.cbp.gov.

## ACCESS FOR TRAVELERS WITH DISABILITIES

Accessibility is in the eye of the beholder. Despite the Americans with Disabilities Act, it is unfortunate that universal access in public places is still not a reality in most parts of the country. The bay is no exception. Although many restaurants, theaters, hotels, and museums offer ramps or elevators, some smaller, privately owned establishments (such as bed-and-breakfasts) do not always provide these necessities. Many historic properties are also not up to ADA standards because they are prevented from updating by law or by architecture. It is best to call ahead and verify the type of access that is available.

**Accessible Virginia** (www.accessible-virginia.org) is a great resource for information on access throughout Virginia. A list of state and public lands in Maryland that offer accessible amenities can be found on **Maryland's Department of Natural Resources** website at www.dnr.state.md.us/publiclands/accessforall.asp.

## SENIOR TRAVELERS

Numerous hotels, venues, and attractions offer discounts to seniors; all you have to do is ask when making your reservations or purchasing your tickets. The **American Association of Retired Persons (AARP)** (www.aarp.org) is the largest organization in the nation for seniors. They offer discounts to their members on hotels, tours, rental cars, airfare, and many other services. Membership in AARP is just $16 a year, so it's worth joining.

## GAY AND LESBIAN TRAVELERS

Densely populated areas such as Norfolk, and Virginia Beach have LGBT-friendly communities and businesses, but these are rarer in rural areas. Baltimore and Rehoboth Beach have large LGBT populations and readily accept same-sex couples and families. Most establishments welcome business from everyone, so unless you need specialized accommodations, travel shouldn't be a concern. The **Gay and Lesbian Travel Center** (www.gayjourney.com) is a great resource for travel.

## TRAVELING WITH CHILDREN

Although most places don't make specific accommodations for children, in general, most tourist attractions throughout the area are family friendly (except for obvious exceptions where noted). Baltimore offers museums devoted specifically to children, but many other sights have a children's component to them. For a list of kid-oriented attractions in Virginia, visit the "Cool Places for Kids" section of the Virginia is for Lovers website at www.virginia.org/coolplacesforkids.

The Chesapeake Bay area has been getting more pet-friendly in recent years.

## TRAVELING WITH PETS

In recent years more and more pet-friendly establishments have been popping up in the Chesapeake Bay. Many higher-end hotels (such as the Kimpton hotel chain) allow four-legged family members, and some establishments even host doggie happy hours. It's not uncommon for attractions, stores, historical sites, campgrounds, outdoor shopping malls, parks, beaches, and even the patios at some restaurants to welcome dogs with open arms. It is always best to call ahead before assuming an establishment is pet friendly. Service and guide dogs are welcome nearly everywhere with their human companions.

## TIPPING

A 15-20 percent tip is standard throughout Virginia and Maryland on restaurant bills. Other service providers, such as taxi drivers and hairstylists, typically receive 10-15 percent. Bellhops and airport personnel normally receive $1-2 per bag.

# Information and Services

## TOURIST INFORMATION

For information on tourism specifically in the Chesapeake Bay, visit the **Find Your Chesapeake site** (www.findyourchesapeake.com). For information on tourism in Virginia, visit the **Virginia is for Lovers site** (www.virginia.org) or the official **Virginia state site** (www.virginia.gov/visit). For information on tourism in Maryland, visit the **Maryland Office of** **Tourism site** (www.visitmaryland.org). For information on tourism in Washington DC, visit the official **DC tourism site** (www.washington.org).

## COMMUNICATIONS AND MEDIA

### Cell Phone Coverage

Cell phone coverage is generally available in most parts of the Chesapeake Bay. There are scattered pockets of spotty coverage even near large cities, but overall, coverage is reliable. Any time you head into a more rural area or offshore, be sure to bring supplies in case of an emergency instead of relying on your cell phone.

## Internet Access

Internet access is readily available in hotels throughout the Chesapeake Bay and is very commonly included with the price of a room, or else as an add-on. A list of free Wi-Fi hotspots in the area can be found at www.openwifispots.com.

# Health and Safety

For emergencies anywhere in the Chesapeake Bay, dial 911 from any telephone at no charge. From a cell phone, the state police can be reached by pressing #77. Generally speaking, hospitals in the area are very good, and excellent in the larger cities. Emergency room treatment is always costlier than a scheduled appointment, but emergency care facilities can also be found in most areas to treat minor conditions.

## LYME DISEASE

**Lyme disease,** which is transmitted through the bites of deer ticks, is a risk. Use insect repellent, and check yourself thoroughly after spending time in the woods or walking through tall grass. If you are bitten, or find a red circular rash (similar to a bull's-eye), consult a physician. Lyme disease can be life-threatening if it goes untreated.

## INSECTS

Mosquitoes are common in the area and aside from being annoying can carry diseases. Damp, low areas can harbor large populations of these little vampires, so use insect repellent and steer clear of stagnant water. **Bees, wasps, yellow jackets,** and **hornets** are all permanent residents of the region and are particularly active (and aggressive) in the fall.

Female **black widow spiders** are also found in the region and can be identified by a small red hourglass shape on their black abdomens. They live in dark places such as rotting logs and under patio furniture. Symptoms of their bite include severe abdominal pain and should be treated. The males are harmless. The **brown recluse spider,** contrary to common belief, is not native to this region. They can on occasion be found here, but only as a transplant.

## ANIMALS

Swimming in the Atlantic Ocean or the Chesapeake Bay could put you in contact with stinging **jellyfish** or **sea nettles** (especially in the Chesapeake Bay). **Sharks** are also found occasionally in both bodies of water and have even been spotted in the Potomac River near Point Lookout.

There is only one type of **venomous snake** in the region, the northern copperhead. This snake can be found everywhere and has dark-colored cross bands shaped like an hourglass.

## PLANTS

**Poison ivy, poison oak,** and **poison sumac** are all native to the region and should be avoided even if you have never had a prior allergic reaction (you can develop one anytime). As the saying goes, "Leaves of three, let it be." Local mushrooms and berries can also be poisonous, so don't eat them unless you are 100 percent sure of their identification.

## WEATHER

In addition to the obvious presence or prediction of a tornado, tropical storm, hurricane, or snowstorm (all of which are possible but rare in the region), be aware that **lightning** is a greater danger on exposed ridges, in fields, on golf courses, on the beach, or anywhere near water. Thunderstorms can pop up quickly, especially during the summer months, so check the weather before venturing out and be prepared with a plan B. Hypothermia can also be an issue. Being wet, tired, and cold is a dangerous combination. Symptoms include slurred speech, uncontrollable shivering, and loss of coordination.

## CRIME

Downtown areas of larger cities such as Baltimore and Norfolk can be unsafe, especially at night. Ask hotel staff about the safety of the area you're staying in, lock your doors, take a cab instead of walking, and don't leave valuables in your car.

# Resources

## Suggested Reading

### HISTORY
#### General History

Barbour, Philip, and Thad Tate, eds. *The Complete Works of Captain John Smith, 1580-1631.* Chapel Hill: University of North Carolina Press, 1986. Three volumes of Captain John Smith's work.

Doak, Robin. *Voices from Colonial America: Maryland 1634-1776.* Washington DC: National Geographic, 2007. First-person accounts, historical maps, and illustrations tell Maryland's history.

Jefferson, Thomas. *Notes on the State of Virginia.* Chapel Hill: University of North Carolina Press, 1996. This classic shows Jefferson's personality and discusses life in the 18th century.

Kelly, C. Brian. *Best Little Stories from Virginia.* Nashville, TN: Cumberland House Publishing, 2003. A collection of more than 100 stories since Jamestown's founding.

McWilliams, Jane W. *Annapolis, City on the Severn.* Baltimore: The Johns Hopkins University Press, 2011. The story of Annapolis.

#### Civil War History

Catton, Bruce. *America Goes to War: The Civil War and Its Meaning in American Culture.* Middletown, CT: Wesleyan University Press, 1992. An interesting study on the Civil War.

McPherson, James. *Battle Cry of Freedom: The Civil War Era.* New York: Ballantine Books, 1988. Perhaps the best single-volume history of the war.

### SCIENCE AND NATURE

Duda, Mark Damian. *Virginia Wildlife Viewing Guide.* Helena, MT: Falcon Press, 1994. Provides information on 80 of Virginia's best wildlife-viewing areas.

Fergus, Charles. *Wildlife of Virginia and Maryland and Washington, D.C.* Mechanicsburg, PA: Stackpole Books, 2003. Provides details on the animals in the diverse habitats throughout Virginia and Maryland.

Frye, Keith. *Roadside Geology of Virginia.* Missoula, MT: Mountain Press, 2003. Provides general information on the state's geology.

### RECREATION
#### General Outdoor

Carrol, Steven, and Mark Miller. *Wild Virginia.* Helena, MT: Falcon Press, 2002. A guide to wilderness and special-management areas throughout Virginia with a focus on the western and southern areas.

#### Bicycling

Adams, Scott, and Martin Fernandez. *Mountain Biking the Washington, D.C./ Baltimore Area.* 4th Edition. Guilford, CT: Falcon Guides, 2003. A great guide to mountain biking around Washington DC and Baltimore.

Homerosky, Jim. *Road Biking Virginia.* Guilford, CT: Falcon Guides, 2002. Wonderful resource for road bikers in Virginia.

## Fishing
Beasley, Beau. *Fly Fishing Virginia: A No Nonsense Guide to Top Waters.* Tucson, AZ: No Nonsense Fly Fishing Guidebooks, 2007. An award-winning guide to fly-fishing spots in Virginia.

Gooch, Bob. *Virginia Fishing Guide.* 2nd Edition. Charlottesville: University Press of Virginia, 2011. A wonderful guide to fishing in Virginia.

## Kayaking
Gaaserud, Michaela Riva. *AMC's Best Sea Kayaking in the Mid-Atlantic.* Boston: Appalachian Mountain Club Books, 2016. A great resource for coastal kayaking in Virginia and Maryland.

# Internet Resources

## STATE RESOURCES
**www.virginia.com**
General travel information within Virginia.

**www.virginia.gov**
The official Commonwealth of Virginia website.

**www.virginia.org**
The official visitors website for the Commonwealth of Virginia.

**www.maryland.gov**
The official Maryland website.

**www.visitmaryland.org**
The official tourism website for Maryland.

## HISTORY
**www.vahistorical.org**
The Virginia Historical Society's comprehensive website.

**www.mdhs.org**
Information on historical Maryland.

## RECREATION
**www.nps.gov**
The National Park Service website, a comprehensive guide to national parks throughout the country.

**www.dcr.virginia.gov**
Information on the Virginia Department of Conservation and Recreation.

**www.dnr.maryland.gov**
Information on the Maryland Department of Natural Resources.

**www.baydreaming.com**
Offers an excellent list of marinas and boating facilities in the Chesapeake Bay area.

**www.thebayguide.com**
A guide to boating in the Chesapeake Bay area.

**www.findyourchesapeake.com**
The Chesapeake Bay Gateways Network website provides information on public access parks around the bay.

## LOCAL RESOURCES
**www.hometownfreepress.com**
A guide to local newspapers.

**www.chesapeakeboating.net**
*Chesapeake Bay Magazine* is full of interesting articles on the bay area.

**www.baydreaming.com**
A guide to Chesapeake Bay events.

# Index

# List of Maps

# Photo Credits

Title Page: the Power Plant and *Chesapeake* lightship in Baltimore's Inner Harbor © Jon Bilous | Dreamstime.com; page 4 Virginia Beach © Ritu Jethani | Dreamstime.com; page 5 (top) lobster buoys in Reedville © Michaela Riva Gaaserud, (bottom) the Drum Point Lighthouse on the Chesapeake Bay in Maryland © Patrick Davis/123rf.com; page 6 (top left) © Americanspirit | Dreamstime.com, (top right) *Neptune* sculpture by Paul DiPasquale © Paul DiPasquale | Dreamstime.com, (bottom) © Joshua Mcdonough | Dreamstime.com; page 7 (inset) © Paul Haagenson | Dreamstime.com, (bottom left) © Michaela Riva Gaaserud, (bottom right) © Izanbar | Dreamstime.com; page 8 © Jon Bilous | Dreamstime. com; page 9 © Flownaksala | Dreamstime.com; page 10 © Michaela Riva Gaaserud; page 12 © Ted Levitt/ courtesy of Chick & Ruth's Delly; pages 13-60 © Michaela Riva Gaaserud; page 63 © La Wanda Wilson | Dreamstime.com; pages 68 (top) © Michaela Riva Gaaserud, (bottom) © Dave Newman | Dreamstime. com; page 69 © Vladimir Ivanov | Dreamstime.com; pages 74-75 © Michaela Riva Gaaserud; page 79 © Ted Levitt/courtesy of Chick & Ruth's Delly; pages 80-91 © Michaela Riva Gaaserud; page 93 © Michaela Riva Gaaserud; page 95 © Robert Crow | Dreamstime.com; pages 97-118 © Michaela Riva Gaaserud; page 120 © Zrfphoto | Dreamstime.com; pages 122-141 © Michaela Riva Gaaserud; page 143 © Michaela Riva Gaaserud; page 145 © Adam Parent | Dreamstime.com; pages 149-157 © Michaela Riva Gaaserud; page 166 © Kclarksphotography | Dreamstime.com; pages 167-188 © Michaela Riva Gaaserud; page 190 *Neptune* sculpture by Paul DiPasquale © 2005, photo © M.P. Prucha; page 192 © Michaela Riva Gaaserud; page 197 courtesy of the Cavalier Hotel; pages 202-210 © Michaela Riva Gaaserud; page 212 (top) © Americanspirit | Dreamstime.com, (bottom) © Richard Gunion | Dreamstime.com; page 214 © Howard Nevitt, Jr. | Dreamstime.com; pages 217-221 © Michaela Riva Gaaserud; page 224 (top) © Poobear88 | Dreamstime.com, (bottom) © Sherryvsmith | Dreamstime.com; page 229 © Michaela Riva Gaaserud

# Also Available

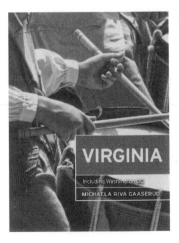